BOOKING PERFORMANCE TOURS

MARKETING AND ACQUIRING LIVE ARTS AND ENTERTAINMENT

TONY MICOCCI

ALLWORTH PRESS
NEW YORK

12   11   10   09   08   5   4   3   2   1

Published by Allworth Press
An imprint of Allworth Communications, Inc.
10 East 23rd Street, New York, NY 10010

Cover design by Derek Bacchus

Cover photos:
Top: *Tomáš Kubínek: Certified Lunatic and Master of the Impossible*—Photo by D.A. Hill
Lower left: André De Shields and Christina Sajous in William Shakespear's *King Lear*, directed by Alfred Preisser, produced by the Classical Theatre of Harlem—Photo by Ruth Sovoronsky
Lower right: Maude Mitchell in *Mabou Mines DollHouse*, adapted from Henrik Ibsen's *A Doll's House* and directed by Lee Breuer, produced by Mabou Mines—Photo by Richard Termine

Interior design by The Roberts Group
Page composition/typography by Integra Software Services, Pvt., Ltd., Pondicherry, India

ISBN-13: 978-1-58115-500-6
ISBN-10: 1-58115-500-X

Library of Congress Cataloging-in-Publication Data

Micocci, Tony.
Booking performance tours : marketing and acquiring live arts and entertainment/ by Tony Micocci.
p. cm.
Includes bibliographical references.
ISBN-13: 978-1-58115-500-6 (pbk.)
ISBN-10: 1-58115-500-X (pbk.)
1. Performing arts–Marketing.   2. Performing arts–Management.   I. Title.

PN1590.M27M53 2008
791.069'8—dc22
                                    2007040714

Printed in the United States of America

Contents

Dedicated to
Marcel Marceau
A friend, consummate entertainer, and true citizen of the world.

Introduction

This book is really two books.

The first is a *how-to* book, to the degree possible, given that it attempts to cover the booking process for an enormous range of live productions that are all very different in their processes and relationships. But there are dos and don'ts, definitions of terms and procedures, and advice on subjects such as negotiating, deal structures, and contracts, which I hope will be helpful both to newcomers in the field and perhaps to professional colleagues interested in hearing someone else's approaches to these things.

The second book waxes more philosophical. I feel it is extremely important for us all to ponder the broader context of what we do, both in terms of today's society and values and from a historical perspective. Unfortunately for those looking for a clear and precise guide to doing this work, the worrisome lesson from this book is that our field is caught—as is so much of our society—in a state of cataclysmic change. A lot of what carried the field through the last fifty years is falling apart, and new ideas and relationships are just beginning to emerge. It is either an exciting or a threatening time depending on one's point of view. Either way, the changes and uncertainties present great challenges to all who enter.

Having begun with that warning, there are two important elements that pervade our work in arranging touring of live performing arts and entertainment, no matter what job we have or function we serve.

First, this is a *people business* because the entire process—communication, sales, negotiation, and public relations—is influenced by human relationships and the building of trust between individuals.

Second, at the core of what we do all the time is the *communication and transmission of information*. In the booking process we don't make anything, we don't deliver anything to the public, and we don't put shows on stages. But we expose that which has already been made, support the creation of that which will be made, and undertake the planning and agreements that will deliver live, touring performances to the public. And we do it entirely through an endless process of communication and transmittal of information.

People Business

It is often said that those in the nonperforming aspects of the arts and entertainment field don't leave this business, they just change chairs. The longer I work in the business the more that appears true as people I worked with in one capacity ten, twenty, and thirty years ago show up again in entirely other capacities, perhaps in other parts of the world, tied in some manner to the production or presentation of the performing arts. And with all systems and bureaucracies aside, no amount of contracting or paperwork can supplant being able to speak in person to someone on the opposite side with whom a rapport has been established.

Probably the biggest divide is between the performers and creators on the one side—those with the gift and inclination to get out on the stage and perform and to conceive and creatively contribute to the productions we enjoy—and everyone "backstage." But even these lines get blurred. I think of program directors of significant music-presenting organizations who are also themselves conductors (and, in one case, a superb singer). I think of two major New York City arts organizations whose present chief executive officers were former performers. Ultimately they are all working toward much the same ends.

My own journey started as a lighting designer, led to production/stage management in modern dance, segued to managing and programming performing arts centers, and has arrived at managing artists and productions, consulting, and running a booking agency that operates worldwide. I believe that exposure to all facets of producing and delivering shows can enhance one's understanding of and success in the field. Personally, I tend to trust administrators who are former production and stage managers as they are experienced in delivering on time and (often) within budget, and in working up close and personally with artists in the tricky balance between what the artist wants and what the artist can have—themes that continue to play through our business in myriad ways. While I live in awe of that spark in artists that allows them to create and perform, I strongly believe that those interested in any nonperformance careers in this field should complete any internal tug-of-war they may have with their performing drives before jumping into administration.

For our purposes in this book, we will speak of shows ready to tour—be they solo shows or full productions—not individual actors, dancers, directors, or choreographers seeking to be hired to work in productions.

Communication

Regarding the centrality of *communication* to our business, this extends far beyond the communication between the artist and the audience when the show is in the theater. It is communication in the form of the booking agent understanding what the show is about and the producers' and creators' visions, and communicating that understanding to the presenter who will bring the show into her theater. Once that decision is made, it is communication through the contracting process so that the final document communicates in concrete, written terms that to which the parties have agreed. And it is communication of the show's selling points to the presenter's designers, copywriters, and media as they work toward selling tickets through further communicating outward to the prospective audience members. And beyond the immediate booking, it is the continued communication between agent and presenter about how the presentation went and what the presenter will bring next!

Disclaimers

Several disclaimers are worth mentioning before we proceed.

- As I will repeat at relevant points in the book, I am neither an attorney nor a CPA. So while I hope there is some value to be had from my experience shared in legal and accounting matters, please do not take precipitous legal or financial action on my advice alone.

- I use "he" and "she" somewhat at random throughout in reference to positions that are ably held in various institutions by people of both genders.

- I have assumed the immodest task of overviewing the tour booking of live art/entertainment performances crossing genres and across the nonprofit/for-profit (or "cultural" and "commercial") divide, believing, as I do, that ultimately both sides align in their interests to put quality live performances in front of audiences. To keep this book readable it is necessary to skim some subjects that could easily warrant entire books on their own.

- Much of the book is based on the United States of America, which is my home and to which I refer as the US and occasionally America. I am well aware that the term America refers to two continents involving a number of countries and acknowledge the distinction. As much of my work over the years has involved moving artists between the US and other countries, and occasionally between countries not including the US, I share observations on international activity throughout. I believe in the global interconnectedness of the spirit and of people involved in and who enjoy theater, and am pleased to work with many who adopt Marcel Marceau's lifelong credo to be first and foremost "citizens of the world." *Foreign* is a term entirely relative to where one considers home.

The subjects of our first section are the players, the relationships, the negotiations, the deals, and the confirming documents related to the process of booking touring engagements. There is great temptation to look earlier in the cycle at the process of creating the productions that ultimately tour and to look later at the process of presenting the shows to the public after they have been booked. And while I don't deny a peek now and then, I will attempt to be true to the title of the book and focus only on the arcane but vital booking part of the cycle.

The subject of our second section is the sociohistoric context and trends in which we are operating in the early twenty-first century, at a time when nonprofit structures are being severely challenged, market driven entertainment is on the rise, and revolutions are afoot both in technological delivery systems of entertainment and in the demographics of who is here to (hopefully) appreciate the results of our efforts.

New leadership and ideas are urgently needed. Welcome!

Booking Performance Tours—The Web Site

Recognizing that the field of performance tour booking is in a constant state of flux, and this book, by necessity, is not, we are creating a Web site at *www.bookingperformancetours.com* intended over time to become both a resource and meeting place for students, educators, agents, artists, presenters, promoters, and all involved or interested in performance tour booking. Taking advantage of the more fluid technology of the Internet, the site will allow us to pick up where this book leaves off in updating best practices, sharing experiences, asking questions, connecting with colleagues, entering debate, and participating in the global dialogue the field urgently requires in our twenty-first century—the "communication age." Please visit the site, make yourself known, and comment, criticize, praise, and ask as may be helpful to you wherever you are niched—or hoping to join—our global enterprise!

Thanks

Proper thank yous for information and inspiration for this book would have to include the many artists, presenters, agents, and friends I have worked with and learned from over the years, and the list would be long. I must start with my good friend Maria Shustina at the US Embassy in Moscow who arranged for me to come and talk to very promising arts administration students in Russia, the notes from which formed the backbone of the book. For giving time and sharing extra wisdom during the writing, an incomplete list of those warranting special thanks includes Bobby Rossi, Paul Organisak, Alice Prine, Jim Freydberg, Elizabeth Williams, Peter Grilli, Michael Pappone, Dan Sher, Ken Golden, John Starr, John Luckacovic, Simon Shaw, Justin d'Appolito, Rhys Williams, the Streb Company, and David Anderson. To two people who actually read the rough work and provided valuable feedback, *ochen spacibo*: Elaine Lipcan and Jonathan Secor, as well as to Jonathan's arts management students at the Massachusetts College of Liberal Arts for testing the rough chapters in class. On the office and home fronts, my patient and ever supportive associate through most of the writing, Erica Laird, has helped keep me sane through the process, and without my amazing daughter, Alair, my loving partner, Martha, encouragement from my writer sister Rhoda, and inspiration from my published author mother, this book simply wouldn't be.

Tony Micocci
New York City
March, 2007

SECTION I

THE NUTS AND BOLTS

CHAPTER 1

Roles and Relationships

In our examination of the tour booking process we will focus on five players: the Producer (including Tour Producer), the Manager, the Booking (Sales) Agency or Agent, and the show itself—often somewhat unaesthetically referred to as the *product*—all on the *selling* side of the table, and the Presenter on the *buying* side. These are not the only players in the process, but they are the primary ones: the people or organizations that created and control the production, the person or agency who acts as salesperson, and the person or organization that brings it into a performance venue on tour.

Our examination will focus on *The Road*[1] or touring, as distinct from the initial creation process and the first home engagements of shows, though of course all are, to a degree, interconnected.

On the Selling Side

We'll look at the players on the offering side of the imaginary bargaining table.

Producer

Every show has a producer who creates the show. This role can range from a young solo dancer who works up the show in his living room or a friend's loft or studio to the producer of a unique rock-and-roll production/tour or the Walt Disney Company, *Cirque du Soleil*, or other large-scale institutional producer spending millions to create live entertainment. As in the film industry, the producer is the person or entity who owns or obtains the concept and underlying rights for the show, secures the funding and artistic and support resources, and brings the show to life. He, she, or they will engage the *agent* or *agency* and contract to deliver the show to the *presenters* either directly or through a secondary *tour producer* or *promoter*.

Occasionally one will see the sort of distinctions in the live arts one also sees in the film industry, such as *executive producer* (normally the lead producer who is primarily responsible for the business aspects) and *line producer* (the person on the front lines who sees the ideas into reality), but this is generally limited to the largest productions only, and for our purposes we will address the role of producer as the single person or, more typically, corporate entity responsible for putting the show together.

Tour Producer

Unlike the producer, who creates a new production and might or might not become involved in touring, a tour producer is a producer who re-creates or otherwise obtains an existing production specifically to tour. In the primary definition of the term, the tour producer is the same as the producer in that this person or organization obtains the rights, hires the cast and creative team, and assembles the production, a large distinction being that such shows are normally revivals of existing shows and are rarely created completely new solely for touring. Beyond actually producing revived or restaged shows, tour producers might secure product from other sources, such as productions of resident theaters, London's West End, Irish dance companies, or Australian stompers, and repackage the shows for touring. Some tour producers have in-house booking agents to book the tours; others use out-of-house agencies.

Alternate Definitions of Tour Producer

In addition to this primary definition, there are two other applications of the concept of tour producer, each with a slightly different emphasis:

- In the case of popular music, as we will examine in more depth in a separate chapter, a tour producer is generally referred to as a *promoter*, but with more emphasis on producing the tour of the show than on producing the show itself. In this case, the promoter is acting as a middleperson, contracting for the services of the artist or show for X number of performances over Y period of time, usually in a defined geographic region, who then either herself rents the theaters and presents the shows, thereby taking all the financial risk, or who seeks to copresent with, or sell off performances to, local presenters to mitigate risk.

- In the case of international touring, where the cost and effort to cross oceans for a tour plus lack of expertise about the territories being visited mean that the artist needs a local organizer and prefers a basic income guaranteed from a tour, an agency may often end up in the position of a tour producer in guaranteeing to meet the needs of the show and selling dates to presenters.

What is common to all tour producers is that they take on proactive roles in generating or supporting shows to tour, and often assume some measure of financial risk, whether the shows are purchased from others for resale or produced themselves. Their relationships with booking agents vary. In the case of popular music they will typically buy the acts *from* or *through* booking agents. In the case of tour producers of theatrical properties, they will often engage the service of booking agents to make the engagement sales.

As noted above, and discussed further in chapter 2, it is not uncommon for agents to assume the role of tour producer in certain circumstances.

Manager

Most artists and productions have managers before they have booking agents. It is often the manager who decides or guides the artist or show producers in decisions about the role of touring in the productions' overall business plans and with what agencies the artists or shows should be working.

In the case of an individual performing artist such as a concert pianist guest performing all over the world, the manager might play a very strong role in that person's life. This might extend beyond making sure she gets bookings to overseeing the overall career strategy of the artist, handling press inquiries, booking flights and hotel rooms, and even managing the artist's money. Many managers represent multiple clients, though highly successful artists can afford private and exclusive managers.

There are management companies as well as individual managers. Some agencies include both management and booking within the services they provide. This is the case with the giant William Morris Agency, and some, such as Columbia Artists Management Inc. (CAMI) and International Management Group (IMG Artists), actually have the word "Management" in their titles.

At the opposite extreme in scale are small management firms. Most are for-profit companies, but there are also nonprofit service organizations that provide basic management services to artist clients in addition to offering representation at booking conventions.

In the case of an institutional producing entity—in the US often a non-profit organization such as a dance or theater company—the manager might be a staff person carrying the title of *executive director*, reporting to a board of directors. This person generally has total responsibility for the administration of the company and often leadership in the strategic planning process for the organization. There may also be a *managing director*, often the number two person in the organization, reporting to the executive director and responsible for the internal operations of the organization and the nuts and bolts of getting shows out on the Road.

In the case of a stand-alone for-profit production, often operating under a limited liability company or stock company established just for that production, the manager will be a professional *general manager* (GM), usually experienced in Broadway or Off-Broadway productions, who receives a retainer from the corporate entity and often also owns *points* in the show (usually a percentage of the producer's share of the profits after the investors have been *made whole* or recouped their investment). Depending on the experience and interest of the investors in the show, the GM is looked to for both professional management of the show's operation and leadership in strategizing the life of the production.

Opera companies often like the term *general director*, which can either be equal to the *artistic director*, both reporting directly to the board, or, in some cases, can be the sole senior executive holding the reins of both the artistic and administrative departments. This latter is rare, not only because the workload to handle both the administrative and artistic direction roles can be enormous and because the skill sets needed for each aren't often embodied in one person but also because the dialectical money–art tension between these two roles, within reasonable limits, is vital to the health of most organizations. In what is often discussed as the *three-legs-of-the-stool* business model for artistic nonprofits involving a chief administrator, artistic director, and board of directors, the dynamic between the first two is at the core of the resource–goals balance with which every organization constantly wrestles.

The word *manager* also shows up in production areas such as *company manager*, *production manager*, and *stage manager*. These roles can be critical to the delivery of the production, but they are not deeply involved in the booking process except in the development of tour budgets, and the production manager is often consulted on the suitability of a venue for prospective presentation of the show.

Sales Agency or Agent

For every touring production there is a person or organization acting in the capacity of *booking agent* or *agency*. For a small start-up artist, this is often the artist him/herself. At the opposite extreme, the agency might be part of the enormous CAMI, IMG Artists, the William Morris Agency, or Opus 3 Artists (formerly ICM Artists, LTD, a subsidiary of International Creative Management).[2] In between these extremes, the booking process may be undertaken by the artist's manager or by one of several hundred smaller agencies that often specialize in particular art forms such as classical music, dance, or folk arts. As noted above, the agent may actually be operating in the same office as the producer or manager. But if the artist or producer of a show wants the show to tour, someone has to be the salesperson.

For our purposes in this book we will address ourselves to circumstances in which the shows are represented by independent professional agents or agencies on the assumption that other than those few artists who actually like to book themselves, the majority don't. There are several hundred agencies in the US with most but by no means all located in New York City. Some have agents based in multiple locations serving their respective regions or *territories*. The larger agencies serving the US tend to break the country into territories, with a West Coast agent, Midwest, etc. Some, with multiple disciplines, tend to sort instead by art form, so there will be a dance agent or department, theater, etc. And some group their more contemporary work under one agent, separating it from the more classical.

However, all agencies share the same basic limits on resources; namely, the time agents have available on the phone, e-mailing, and traveling to communicate with as many buyers as possible about their artists and productions—the *roster*. Agencies will allocate their resources on some cross-matrix of number of productions and territory, so a single agent may be representing many productions in a relatively small geographic area, or vice versa.

Note that there is another type of agency that represents actors, musicians, composers, etc., for the purpose of engaging those individuals in a production. But for our purposes, our reference to agents will be strictly as booking agencies representing productions ready to perform and, occasionally, projects seeking commissioners to help them into existence.

Legal Registry Requirements for Agencies

Some states, including California, New York, and New Jersey, have laws requiring anyone seeking employment for others—including theatrical agencies—to be licensed by the State.

Article 11, Section 172, of the New York State General Business Law[3] addresses the licensing of employment agencies in that State as follows:

> *No person shall open, keep, maintain, own, operate or carry on any employment agency unless such person shall have first produced a license therefore as provided in this article. Such license shall be issued by the commissioner of labor, except that if the employment agency is to be conducted in the city of New York such license shall be issued by the commissioner of consumer affairs of such city.*

The statute defines the term "employment agency" to include a "theatrical employment agency," which is defined in Article 11, Section 171, as follows:

> *"Theatrical employment agency" means any person who procures or attempts to procure employment or engagements for circus, vaudeville, the variety field, the legitimate theater, motion pictures, radio, television, phonograph recordings, transcriptions, opera, concert, ballet, modeling or other entertainments or exhibitions or performances, but such term does not include the business of managing such entertainments, exhibitions, or performances, or the artists or attractions constituting the same, where such business only incidentally involves the seeking of employment therefore.*

Note the distinction being made between the roles of *agent* and *manager*.

Types and Styles of Agencies

Given the importance played by agents in the process of tour booking, we will dig deeper in understanding the different types and styles of agencies, and their functions as effective curators and, to some degree, gatekeepers of artistic product.

In addition to the obvious issue of size and scale of agencies, characterized by the number of artists on their rosters and the number of agents on the phones, there are various other important points of distinction producers will have in mind in considering agencies to represent their shows:

- *Artistic disciplines of attractions represented.* Rather than offering a smorgasbord of productions, most agencies will define one or more artistic niches in which they operate as areas of specialty: dance, classical music, "new" or "world" music, Broadway, dramatic productions, etc. While genre-focus is especially true of smaller boutique agencies, even CAMI, IMG, and Opus 3 have classical music at their core despite having opened up over the years to a broad artistic range. Especially among smaller agencies, the discipline on which an agency focuses often stems from the background, tastes, and areas of expertise of the individual or group of individuals who started the agency, often musicians, actors, or dancers themselves.

- *Target audience.* Related to the artistic genres or disciplines are the target ticket-buying audiences for the rosters of particular agencies. The most obvious are those agencies representing children's entertainment or family programs that are geared to audiences that include children, or nostalgia shows targeted at audiences of a certain age, and presenters who program for these demographics. Additional focused audience segments include classical music aficionados, corporate event producers, casino patrons, or youthful, large-scale pop music audiences.

- *Performance fee range.* Artist fees, which relate directly to venue size, the ticket price an audience will pay, and the size of the community in which the presenters operate, can often be a sorting factor among agencies, though most try to cover a broad enough range to not be too narrowly pigeonholed.

- *Artist turnover.* Turnover in artists and productions on an agency's roster is normal, but repeated high turnover should be viewed with suspicion as it may mean that the relations are consistently not work-ing. Some annual turnover is not a bad thing as it keeps presenters returning to that agency to see what is being offered for the new sea-son. Agencies without any turnover, which represent the same artists year after year, sometimes with no new productions being offered by those artists, risk being perceived as stale by presenters.

- *Sales style.* Different agencies have different styles, ranging from the hard-hitting, completely bottom-line oriented, to the more nuanced and educational. This to some degree relates to the style of artist represented. Selling Tony Bennett or Nora Jones requires a distinct style in which the agency and buyer know what they are getting and the emphasis in negotiations is less on convincing a presenter to take the show and more on finding a deal formula that both sides can live with. This differs greatly from selling a new, experimental performance art company from Zimbabwe, where a lot of buyer (and audience) education about the show is likely to be needed.

- *Reputation.* From the perspectives of both producers considering signing with an agency and buyers considering engaging through an agency, the agency's overall reputation in the field for effectiveness, honest dealing, and delivering on time and according to terms agreed upon, are significant factors. Whether the contract is ultimately signed by the agency or the producer, buyers will look to the agency to help insure the show's delivery. Likewise, producers will trust their agencies to not send their shows on tours that are logistically impos-sible or into inappropriate venues.

Agency as Curator

The function of agency reputation goes beyond bridging reliable artists and trustworthy presenters and involves a curatorial role as well. A good agent gets to know his/her significant buyers, their venues, programmatic goals, and audiences' tastes as intimately as possible, is choosy in the productions he will represent, and selects appropriate artists for his markets. As much as possible, and certainly with repeat buyers, an agent recommends artists on a selective basis with knowledge of the buyers' venues and audiences. Agency representatives are expected not only to know all about the particular productions on the agency's roster but to be able to report on how those shows fit into the broad context of their artistic fields. Over time, done effectively, this earns the agency an informal role as curatorial advisor to the presenter (see more on the definition and importance of *curation* in chapter 10). Obviously, with thousands of presenters out there, such a personal approach by agents with all buyers is near impossible, but well worth the effort to the degree possible. As we will explore in the chapter on *technology*, contact management software helps this process a great deal.

The Show Itself or *Product*

For the purposes of this discussion, we will use the terms *artist*, *show*, *act*, and *production* to reflect either an individual performing artist or a production, and occasionally the term *company* to reflect an ongoing institutional performing company such as a dance, theater, or opera company.

Show Categories

- *Solo artists or small ensembles.* This can be anything from a solo mime to comedian or classical pianist, and might include a chamber music ensemble, dance duo, etc. The artist might travel with a backup band or alone. Depending on the art form and what is most important, the support personnel traveling may include a music director (for a popular musician using a local orchestra), sound engineer (for a musician), and a lighting director and stage manager. Such artists often do not have corporations, either nonprofit or profit making, and sign contracts as private individuals or as *sole proprietors*[4] if their contracts are not signed on their behalf by their agents or managers. The *producer* is often the artist him/herself.

- *Stand-alone productions.* This is an independently established production not involving an ongoing dance or theater company, often a commercial production operating under what in the US is a limited liability company or limited partnership established just for this production. This encompasses many Broadway productions. The defining aspect of such productions compared to the solo artist or small ensemble is often the need to raise investment capital to mount the show, which is where the sale of either membership in an LLC or stock in a corporation comes into play. These shows are legally produced by the company set up for this purpose, but in practical terms, decision making is often lead by the general manager. The GM is an employee of the production company but also usually has a stake in the outcome of the show in the form of a percentage of ownership (*points*). Functioning in many ways as a freelance parallel to the salaried executive director of a nonprofit reporting to a board of directors, a wise GM will lead the producers in decision making but rarely make unilateral decisions related to the show without consultation and approval of the investor group. For our purposes in examining touring, these decisions will include whether to tour the show, when, and with what booking agency for representation.

- *Institutionally produced productions.* This group is characterized by what in the US are generally nonprofit institutions. In our case, the focus is on institutions that view touring as a core activity in their business models (such as many US dance companies, jazz ensembles, and some orchestras and theater companies), rather than those (such as resident theaters and opera companies) that don't. Orchestras, opera companies, and large ballet companies, by sheer number of personnel and institutional orientation, tend to be expensive to tour and do so only on a limited basis. Theater companies can be ensemble companies that exist almost entirely for touring or producing companies resident in a home base—most members of the League of Resident Theaters (LORT)—which may from time to time send a show out on the Road but don't consider touring to be central to their mission. The exception to the latter are some LORT's that do make efforts to move their shows to Broadway—renowned institutions such as Arena Stage in Washington, DC, and the La Jolla Playhouse in Southern California have a long history of this. And, of course, if successful on Broadway, the shows might subsequently tour. But sending shows directly out on tour is not a common practice of LORT's.

- *Popular musicians.* With a business model often built around the sale of recordings and the building up of fan bases, and enormously influenced by hit charts and awards such as the Grammys, these artists tend to tour either on an ongoing or seasonal basis, or, in the case of major names playing large arenas, to offer concerts on a periodic basis timed with the release of new recordings. In the case of artists who tend to tour either constantly or seasonally, the production of the show functions almost as with the solo artists and small ensembles above, where the producer of the show is in effect the artist. In the case of the major names, such as Madonna or The Rolling Stones, where the production elements are often considerably larger and the deal making more complex, the tours will have commercial producers often known to and trusted by the artists to protect their interests in this often cut-throat field. We will address this area in greater depth in chapter 15.

The Artists and Shows—the Product

The core and driving force of the industry is, of course, artistic direction. Without it, there is no industry—only managers, technicians, and empty theaters. While we are generally using *artist* to refer to performers and creators, in this case we are speaking of two modes of artistic direction: individual creators (*creative*) and artistic directors (*curatorial*). These are the individuals who are the originators of the artistic ideas that end on up on the stages and who in some institutions control the artistic choices of productions to go on the stage.

Creative artists can be *original creators*, those whose unique images, scripts, or movement concepts expand our views of the world and can have lasting effect on our daily lives. At its best, this originality conjures the term *genius*. Such individuals are often remembered as having initiated entirely new streams of creative thought, which influence following generations of artists and audiences as well as their contemporaries.

They can alternately be *derivative* or *adaptive creators*, who take the work of others and find new meaning, new interpretations, or new approaches to extend the life of earlier work or make it relevant to a different demographic. These creators might bridge artistic forms, creating a ballet from a novel or an opera from a play.

Creative artists may be found at the center of institutions, an excellent example being most US modern dance companies, which were founded around the visions of singular creative artists. Or they may be jobbed in as a director might be hired for a Broadway production or an opera. Many are both. The artistic directors of resident theaters often freelance on outside productions, too.

For those institutions that produce the work of others, including some orchestras, resident theater companies, and even dance companies, the creative artistic director also plays a *curatorial* role[5] in choosing what other productions will be produced by the institution and who will direct them. In this regard, the artistic directors are acting in the role of curators of the work of others as well as directing or conducting their own—a role that not all directors are well suited for in a field that by its nature attracts individuals with large egos associated with their own work. It is akin to a museum engaging a great painter to also evaluate and choose from the work of other painters, a surprisingly complex challenge for many artists!

From our touring perspective it is important to reflect on those producing institutions that also occasionally present touring productions. The artistic directors of these institutions often have a significant hand in, or at least final approval of, the selection of shows to be presented. But experience shows that, for most such institutions, other staff members are more directly involved in choosing and negotiating for outside shows to come in, while the attention of the artistic director is more focused on choosing shows for new productions, and on her own directing and work with guest directors.

Two areas of note in artists' relationships to institutions:

Performer Continuity

Using American modern dance as our model, many artistic directors/ choreographers not only choreograph work but develop an entire movement style or vocabulary that underpins their work. As such, they are not only teaching moves to blank-slate dancers but training dancers in their unique style prior to or as part of the creation of the performable work, a process that can take months or even years. As much as possible, therefore, a choreographer will seek to keep available and reuse a core set of dancers who have been trained in his/her style. Since the significant downsizing of the dance industry in the US in the past decade, this has become increasingly difficult as artistic directors who could previously retain a group of dancers on year round salary can no longer afford to do so and must work with *pick up* companies when creating a new work or when performance opportunities arise.

This issue of performance style or technique unique to the creator can also be found in certain ensemble theater companies such as Anne Bogart's superb SITI Company with its highly developed and sophisticated training and creating methodology, which depends on the continuity of a core set of actors trained in this style. This issue also arises in less mainstream art forms such as puppetry, pantomime, and new music involving highly idiosyncratic performance techniques. Marcel Marceau's development of his codified *Conventions of Character* is a good example.

Ownership Rights

As we have seen recently with several highly publicized cases of creators (or their heirs) doing battle with the institutions formed around them, the issue of who owns the rights to the creative works is often complex, increasingly so as new forms of media transmission come into common usage. As with any estate planning, the key is to come to agreement on this early in the relationship to avoid fights later. If an artistic director is retained by a theater/dance/opera company, who owns the performing rights to the productions created by that person while in the employ of the company? Is the creator simply an employee with all output the property of the company, or does the creator own the work and the institution have use of it? And who will own those rights when the individual is either no longer employed by the company or dies, with the company wishing to continue to perform the works and perhaps to license them to other companies to perform?

This question is exploding an area of law relating to intellectual property rights, which goes far beyond our scope except as it pertains to the rights being available for public performances on tour. The legal battles over performance rights following the death of the great dance creator Martha Graham forced a major tour to be cancelled and for the company itself to shut down for a period of time that affected its visibility in the touring world. Identity battles in the international circus and ballet worlds following the collapse of the Soviet Union have lingering repercussions, with imitations continuing to trade on the previously highly regarded names of the Moscow Circus and various Russian ballet companies.

Who's on the Buyer Side of the Table?

With the producers, managers, agents, and *product* on one side of the table, let's look across at who is on the other side of the tour booking process. While it seems somewhat unaesthetic to refer to this side as *buyers*, for our purposes it is a good word because it encompasses not only performing arts centers, festivals, universities, churches, and community-based organizations, but also commercial presenters, regional promoters, and corporate events producers. Collectively we can also refer to this group as *presenters* as they present the productions to the ticket buying public.

Institutional Nonprofits

- Government-owned arts centers, ranging from Parks Department facilities to municipal auditoria[6]

- Independent nonprofit arts centers, from the Flynn Center in Burlington, Vermont, to the Pittsburgh Cultural Trust and the Center Theatre Group in Los Angeles

- Academic institutions, notably college and university performing arts centers

- Churches, mosques, temples, and synagogues

- Community organizations, ranging from entertainment programs in gated residential communities to rest homes, YM/WCAs, and JCCs

- LORT members

- Festival organizations such as jazz festivals and First Nights

- Symphony orchestras as presenters

- Associations (e.g., the National Music Educators Association)

For-Profit Organizations

- Venue operators that either own, operate, or have exclusive programming control over performance facilities. This can mean local ownership or management but is more often national chains that seek synergies though the operation and/or programming of multiple venues. Note that one venue might have multiple presenters: A municipally owned theater might have a local nonprofit organization manage it and program the more *cultural* events requiring contributed subsidy and have an exclusive contract with a nationally or regionally operating for-profit company to secure and bring in the expensive pop music and Broadway productions. Large university facilities may be programmed by an in-house university office but also have an exclusive contract with a regional or national purveyor of the large-scale, high-risk productions.

- Regional and national tour producers, promoters, resellers, and packagers of shows, who buy shows or acts for a window of time in a region and then set up tours in which they either resell the shows to local presenters or present themselves. In most cases these producers do not own venues, but may have a first option or proprietary use rights to venues for presentation. This is most common in the popular music and Broadway touring fields, though occasionally involves other types of acts with which the promoters believe they can make a profit.

    Often a promoter will contract with a venue to use X number of dates in the year and guarantee $Y rent in exchange for having exclusive use of the venue for popular music and other commercial acts, thereby controlling competitive access. The venue itself may be owned and/or operated by a nonprofit that appreciates the guarantee of revenue and venue use by such producers as well as the derivative revenue from ticket sales fees, the sale of merchandize and concessions, parking fees, and access to artists unattainable on their own. To add to the confusion, some of these promoting organizations—especially those involved with Broadway productions—may actually invest in the original productions of shows with touring rights to their region acquired as a condition of their investment.

Endnotes

1   In her interesting dissertation *The Syndicate and the Shuberts* (December 2000), Abby Manzella, a student of American Studies at the University of Virginia, asserts that the term "The Road" in reference to theatrical touring derived from the fact that tour routing at the dawn of large-scale theatrical touring in the US in the late nineteenth century was often established based on the schedules and routes of railroad trains. The document is available online at *http://xroads.virginia.edu/~hyper/INCORP/theatre/syndicate.html.*

2   Note that the operating structures of these large companies vary. In some, the booking agencies function as semiautonomous units from the management side, broken out by artistic genre and/or territories. In others, the agents and managers work in more of a team style with groups of artists or productions that they represent *and* book.

3   *www.labor.state.ny.us/formsdocs/wp/ls390.pdf*

4   The simplest form of legal business designation in the US, filing a sole proprietorship with one's home state provides a first level of legal protection for the individual and affirms one's serious intention to conduct business. Surprisingly large enterprises are often run as sole proprietorships. The move from this level to a limited liability company or some form of stock company is often motivated by either a) a desire for increased legal protection for the individuals involved or b) to provide a structure that will allow investment by outsiders. Sole proprietorships are often referred to informally as "d.b.a."s, referring to the opportunity for the applicant to identify a business name by which the individual is "doing business as (filed name)."

5   See more on the definition and process of *curation* in chapter 10.

6   Government-owned facilities tend to be operated on some arrangement by independent organizations as governments don't like to be in the theater business. This can involve nonprofit operators such as Wolf Trap Foundation for the Performing Arts in Vienna, Virginia, operating a facility owned by the National Parks Department, or various New York City venues that are members of the Cultural Institutions Group, such as Carnegie Hall, City Center, and the New York State Theater at Lincoln Center. These venues are owned by the City of New York and operated by nonprofit organizations established for that purpose. This can also involve for-profit companies such as SMG, Live Nation, Comcast, or TheatreDreams, which operate venues of various sizes, often owned by municipalities. The functions of these organizations as presenters is not affected by this relationship except that the governmental contracts often come with mandates to offer prime dates at "favored nation" rental rates to local performing companies such as the orchestra, ballet, and opera companies, which limits the venue's availability for presentation of touring artists. For-profit facility managers also tend to be far less artistically adventurous in their program selection than their nonprofit counterparts, and less risk taking in the degree of presenting versus renting.

CHAPTER 2

Producer/Agency Relationship

The relationship between an artist or producer and the booking agency is a form of marriage. At its best, it is dynamic and exciting and results in a high level of touring and revenue for both parties. At its worst, it is an irritating, blame-producing relationship that should be ended at the earliest opportunity. The most important factors to successful relationships are thorough due diligence at the outset in choosing one's "partner,"[1] and good communications.Like a successful marriage, a productive agency relationship needs active, ongoing attention on both sides.

As a producer brings a show to the marketplace, the first questions he will consider are how attractively his show is viewed in the field, how desirable it is to an agent, and how much choice and negotiating clout he has. He might cast a fairly broad net at first in his search for an agency, pitching to a large number to get a feel of his show's position.

As the mating process narrows the list of agencies to those with serious desires to represent the show and that the producer feels are right, each side is effectively selling itself to the other. An agent pursuing a show will seek to impress the producer with his clout and reach, and may promise the moon and the stars if the producer will place his show on the agency's roster. If it is the producer doing the pursuing, he will seek to convince the prospective agency that he has the most spectacular, in-demand production on the planet, sought after by every major agency, and easily bookable by any novice agent with a telephone and a Rolodex. It is often through such veils of posturing and, in some cases, self-delusion that players must attempt to look as they consider this most important relationship.

Producers Choosing Agencies

The first issue a producer will often consider is whether she wants an agent who will work exclusively for her or to be with an agency with a roster of other shows.

In-House versus *Out-of-House*

For some established dance and theater companies, for artists just starting up, and for a few highly successful and well-paid solo artists, the role of booking agent is handled *in house*, that is, a staff member engaged directly by the producer, company, or artist exclusively represents the production. In some cases, especially among newer artists and companies, the in-house manager and booking agent can be the same person. But whether the same person or not, the functions of each are different, and for our purposes we will assume they are separate people or entities.

The *in-house* agent relationship is financially viable if the business model for the established company or producer and the volume of its touring justify the financial commitment to an annual salary, or that percentage of the annual salary corresponding to the person's time allocated to booking, plus booking expenses. For institutions such as this, if the salary for which an effective agent can be hired, together with costs of conferences, brochures, telephone, etc., is approximately equivalent to a 10–20 percent agency commission on engagement fees received, institutional artists and producers often find it more appealing to have a directly accountable in-house person responsible for this task. The arguments go that this person will really understand the company or production, the agent will devote more time to selling the company or production, and the company or producer can directly monitor the booking efforts being made. The obvious financial concerns with this model are a) the cash flow challenge of paying the salary of the in-house agent long before the tour revenue is received and b) the risk that the touring generated will not be sufficient to allow the commission portion to cover the guaranteed salary of the agent plus expenses. (Some producers address this latter issue by guaranteeing a lower salary plus a percentage of booking income, which lowers the company's financial risk, eases its cash flow, and provides an added financial incentive to the agent.)

Artists themselves often prefer having in-house agents in the belief that their work will be better understood and receive more sales attention. There is often some validity to this, especially for an artist or company whose work is complicated to describe. But what appeals to the artist's ego and what is in the artist's best business interests are often not the same, and there are downsides to this as well.

From a business perspective, for many artists there is a constant—even career-long—debate over whether their interests are better served by having their own staff members booking the tours for their companies or signing with outside agencies.

Pros for In-House Booking

- The agent or individual is exclusive to this producer, and the producer knows the person is completely dedicated to the artistic enterprise. Time spent talking with prospective presenters at conferences or on the phone will be about this production or company only.

- The person will really get to know the nuances of the company and vision of the artistic director, along with their special needs when on tour, and won't send the company to inappropriate venues or overwork the performers.

- The person will have a more intimate knowledge of the production's financial realities that will better inform her choices of target presenters and subsequent negotiations.

Pros for Out-of-House Booking

- The producer's work is part of a bigger agency representing a variety of productions, perhaps with multiple sales agents. This translates to more clout and reach to the presenting field, and presumably more resources dedicated to the booking process than an in-house person will have.

- Having multiple productions provides opportunities for the agents to pitch this producer's work to presenters for whom the show or producer is new as they may piggyback on discussions of other productions on the roster.

- There is cost efficiency in sharing the expenses of brochure production and distribution and of conference attendance among multiple productions.

- The agent is only paid on commission and only when the fee payments are received; the producer is not committed to paying a full salary or to shelling out in advance of funds coming in.

MY OBSERVATIONS . . .

. . . on the plus side of in-house representation:

- Artistic directors often have a higher comfort level feeling that they can have direct access to the person doing their company's booking. They also appreciate having someone who will really understand their inner creative vision and be able to speak with greater authority about the artistic product, and knowing that their comfort level is not going to be ignored.

- The in-house agent often does know the work more intimately than outside agents can hope to—some dance companies are even represented by former company dancers—and can speak about it with passion, which counts for much in this people/communication business.

. . . on the drawbacks to in-house representation:

- Presenters may judge the show before the agent ever gets to talk with them. They are uncomfortable talking to people so dedicated to one show because if they don't book you they'll feel bad, and they often prefer talking with agents representing multiple artists/productions for that reason. Presenters often feel they can have a much more candid conversation about likes, dislikes, and "will it sell?" worries with an independent agent than with someone directly representing a single show or artist. So if a presenter saw a bad production from a company or heard a bad report some time ago and thinks she doesn't like the work, the in-house representative will have less opportunity to tell her about the new dancers, new choreography, etc., and get her to take another look.

- With in-house representation, the production will not benefit from collateral association with other shows on a roster. Remember this is a people business, and often a presenter, once having had good experiences with an agent, will tend to go back to that agent again and ask, "what else do you have for me?" This provides an opportunity to introduce a production to this presenter with which she might not otherwise be familiar, a moment that the exclusive in-house agent will never have.

Combining Both

Some producers quite effectively pursue a combination of both: they sign with an agency and also take booths at conferences, or at least have staff representatives attend, to add to the sales clout. The person the producer sends to the conferences is not a dedicated booking person, since that role is being taken by the out-of-house agent. Rather it will be the manager, executive director, or other producer rep whose salary is paid on the basis of other functions with the producer. If the company can afford this, it is an excellent combination as it a) expands the visibility of the company at the conferences and increases the number of presenter contacts and b) makes a company member available if a presenter wants to discuss aspects of the company's work that go beyond the knowledge of the agent. It gives the presenter, who is wary of offending the artist or direct artist's manager, a choice: if he knows he wants the show he can talk directly with the show's rep for detailed information, but if he is new to the show and not sure of his interest, talking with the agent provides an opportunity for a more comfortable initial arms=length introduction to the artist.

Everyone hates giving bad news to artists about bookings that did not materialize or performances that did not sell well. It is often easier for a less personally involved agent than for someone whose sole income is dependent on that one artist.

Out-of-House: Choosing the Right Agency

For most productions, the tour agent function is handled by an *out-of-house* agency (or agencies if the globe is broken up into international territories). There are over two hundred such agencies in the US, most but not all in New York City, ranging from the powerhouses of CAMI, IMG Artists, Opus 3 Artists, and the William Morris Agency, representing hundreds of artists/productions, to midsize and small agencies. Some operate internationally. The worldwide headquarters for IMG Artists is actually in London, not New York, and is part of a larger organization, one of whose primary income activities is representation of sports stars. Some, such as the William Morris Agency and, until recently, the agency formerly known as ICM Artists,[2] are part of larger California-based entertainment agencies for which even what seems like a large agency from the perspective of the performing arts is in fact quite small when viewed against rosters of highly paid film and sports stars.

Big Agency versus Small

Assuming election of *out-of-house* booking representation, a key next decision is the size of agency by which the artist would like to be represented. There is tremendous allure to the idea of being repped by a CAMI or the like, notably the presumption of a huge national sales force hard at work securing bookings, and the anticipated cachet and clout associated with being on the roster of the same agency as *Stomp*, *Cats*, the American Ballet Theatre, and the Warsaw Philharmonic (at the time of this writing). And it is true that almost every presenter feels compelled to have conversations with the area representatives of the big agencies in planning each season, whereas they don't have the same compulsion about smaller agencies.

The downsides, as producers will quickly discover, center on the fact that while there may be a larger sales force, there is sometimes a *much* larger artist list. And with so many artists and shows to represent in their given territory, it is unlikely that the average agent will have the time to get more than a cursory understanding of each, and the agents have a lot of artists to discuss with each presenter. So the amount of time and emphasis any one agent will spend on any one show in conversations with presenters may be surprisingly small.

The virtues of and drawbacks to small agencies, as one might expect, mirror those of the large: more understanding of and attention to the shows, less competition among productions to discuss with presenters, but less over-all reach and clout with presenters.

 MY EXPERIENCE OF LARGE VERSUS SMALL AGENCIES

Almost invariably as an agent, when I am approached by a producer coming from another agency, and I ask why he is leaving the other agency, his response is that the agents "don't understand the work nor take the time and effort to learn about it," "don't attend rehearsals and performances," and are "not available to talk." It also means that the show is not getting booked to the producer's satisfaction or most of these complaints would undoubtedly disappear.

Significant Issues within the Agency Agreement

There are several issues that should be part of the discussion and agreement from early on to avoid confusion later.

Territories, Exclusivity, and Form of Presentation

What is the *geographic territory* in which the agent will represent the show? Is it the US only, or North America? If North America, does that include Mexico or only the US and Canada? Does it include New York City or not?

Hand in hand with this is the question of *exclusivity*—whether all engagements in a given territory must come through this agent or not—bearing in mind that it is possible for a producer to grant an agent exclusivity in one territory and authorization to represent the show on a nonexclusive basis in another.

Why would an agent want a nonexclusive relationship anywhere? Though he might prefer exclusivity worldwide, if the producer is unwilling to grant that, by having at least *non*exclusivity in some territories it gives the agent a foot in the door and precludes the producer signing an exclusive agreement with a different agent for that territory.

And directly related to the issues of territory and exclusivity is determination of the *type of engagement* covered. The most restrictive will be live publicly announced performances in front of paying audiences. There are three important qualifiers here: that performances are 1) live, 2) publicly accessible, and 3) have an admission charge. Notably, what is *not* on this list are corporate engagements for private events, television, radio, and film engagements, teaching residencies (though usually workshop activity linked to live public performances would be included), promotional tie-ins, and concerts offered free to the public.[3]

Once again, the agreement could segment by exclusivity and nonexclusivity: an agent could have exclusive representation for live public and paid admission performances, and nonexclusive representation for corporate events, media-transmission events, and activities, etc. This may seem like splitting hairs and not worth the effort to sort out up front, except that if a high-paying television or film opportunity comes along for the show, the agent will care a lot about what got agreed to in the agency agreement!

Agent's Exclusivity Minimum

Generally an agent will at minimum require exclusivity for markets and engagement types in which he is most connected and may seek nonexclusivities for other territories and activities not already held by other agents. A US-based agent specializing in live public performance touring in the US may seek exclusive live public performance representation in the US and nonexclusive representation in all other parts of the world, for private events, and for all other media activity. With increased reliance on the World Wide Web as a means of promotion, while the focus may be in one territory, unexpected opportunities may arise from different parts of the world via global Internet exposure of which he would like to be able to take advantage. He would like to be a spider in the middle of the largest possible web to maximize the potential for catching bugs. But like the widening threads on a spider's web, the further afield the agent attempts to represent, the less comprehensive and in-depth his clout is likely to be.

Producer's Perspective

The producer must decide how important different parts of the world are for her show and how likely it is that audiences in different territories will appreciate the production. If a producer feels strongly that Italians will love this work, then it may be in her interests to hold off granting even a nonexclusivity for Italy to an American agent with few Italian contacts and instead offer exclusive representation to a Rome- or Milan-based agent who knows the territory intimately.

Some shows may have separate agencies for media and other work that specialize in those fields, which falls outside of the scope of our book.

An Offer is an Offer

In practical terms, when it comes to territories, an offer is an offer. If an agent does not formally represent a show in a certain country but receives an unsolicited offer for the show from that country, there is generally no harm in taking the offer to the producer for consideration. The agent will ask the producer for "protection" for this potential engagement, which means the producer grants this agent authority to pursue this specific engagement on a limited, one-time basis and guarantees him a commission if it goes forward. By doing so, the producer does not cede the territory to the agent on a longer-term basis.

If the producer has no representation in the territory, he risks no downside in protecting the agent to seek the engagement. If the producer does already have representation for the show in that territory, she may alternately refer this agent to the other to sort out a potential shared commission relationship if the offer is from a presenter with whom the in-country agent is not already in communication. This, of course, is where the communications can get a bit dicey if the in-territory agent claims that he was already in conversation with that presenter and therefore should not share any commission with the other agent. And it is difficult to determine that until the first agent has revealed the identity of the prospective presenter, which he is normally loath to do without being protected first.

Promote with Clarity and Honesty

Regardless of what is worked out on territories and exclusivity, it is imperative that it be made crystal clear among all parties and to the presenting field who represents the show in what territories for the purposes of live theatrical touring. All of this should be clearly spelled out in the promotion by both the producer (who should list respective territory and activity contacts clearly on the show's Web site, promotional video, and literature) and by the agents (who should be explicit as to the territory and activity they represent). A show's credibility can be severely damaged by its appearance on the rosters of more than one agency, creating confusion and loss of credibility in the field. Likewise, it is highly unethical as well as being illegal for an agent to actively promote a show to a territory in which he does not have representation.

Multiple Shows from the Same Producer but Different Agents

Note that some producers of multiple shows have different agents represent-ing different productions, presumably chosen based on the agents' strengths. If it is a producer who is in the background on the different productions (i.e., whose name itself is not part of the branding and identity of the productions), this can be okay as long as no two agents represent the same production. But if the name of the producer is central to the brand, such as a renowned dance or theater company, this can be a very bad idea. It would create enormous confusion to have two different dances performed by the Martha Graham Dance Company or two different plays produced by the Royal Shakespeare Company represented in the same territory by two different agents!

Transferring Agents

If an agency is assuming representation of a show from another agency, engagements in a state of advanced negotiation through the departing agency are often reserved in the contract with the new agency for completion by the old. A time limit—normally one or two performance seasons ahead—will apply to this exclusion, at the end of which the departing agency loses its reservation of those relationships on which deals have not been concluded.

Clarity and Good Will

Clarify as much as possible in the agency agreement and establish a basis of good will, integrity, and good communication on which unexpected sur-prises can be reviewed and sorted out. It is not unusual that at the start of a producer/agency relationship, the scope of representation will be relatively restricted and then broadened over time as the relationship gets tested, trust increases, and the agent proves himself.

A NOTE ABOUT NEW YORK CITY

As an agent, unless a production with which I am entering a rela-tionship already has exclusive representation in any part of the world, I generally require an exclusive worldwide with the one exception often being the five boroughs of New York City. New York is a unique animal. It is one of the toughest cities in the world to get a show into and the most charged with significance for the life of the show. In my experience, with the exception of a few pro-ductions that make it big in concert or long running commercial theater contexts in New York City, the great value for most produc-tions playing New York is not the profits to be made—which are often little or none at all—but the benefit to touring demand else-where from good New York press. As an agency, we stand to make

very little money from a New York engagement by one of our productions but will benefit from touring demand enhanced by strong
New York critiques. So it is in our interests to leave the producer all
possible latitude to find a means to play New York if we are unable
to do so, as long as we have the touring rights thereafter.

Term of Agreement

It normally takes at least two seasons for the field to become fully aware of a
new show/agency relationship. During the transition time there is danger of
some visibility of the show in the field being lost. So for that reason, an initial
two-year relationship is recommended to allow the relationship to stabilize and
become fruitful. It is also not in the interests of a producer or show to be viewed
as *bed hopping*, moving between agents too rapidly, and of course when a significant artist leaves an agency there is inevitably the question, why? Regardless of
the reasons for the change, such moves can be viewed by the field as somewhat
negative on the show and raise a question of management stability.

Agency Commissions

Traditional concert commissions range from 10 to 20 percent in classical music.
Theatrical commissions range up to 20 percent. Occasionally the commissions
are based on a flat sum per performance or per week regardless of the precise fee.

If a percentage and not a flat sum is decided upon, a related question
to be resolved early is on what basis the percentage is calculated. There are
two alternatives, with a subtle but important difference in financial results:
the commission added on top of the producer's net fee (which favors the
producer) or calculated within the gross to be paid (favoring the agent).

- *Added on top of tour costs.* Using 10 percent, and assuming the
  production's expenses to tour are $20,000, this commission will be a
  percentage of the base costs, $2,000, added on top of the $20,000,
  calling for a total fee to be paid of $22,000 and commission to the
  agent of $2,000.

- *Calculated as a commission on the gross fee paid.* In this case, if the production costs are $20,000, in order to derive a 10 percent commis-
  sion one must calculate with $20,000 representing 90 percent of the
  total to be paid. One approach is to divide the production costs by 9,
  as this sum will represent one ninth of the gross fee, and then add
  the results to the production costs. In this case, $20,000/9 = $2,222.
  Added to the production costs, the total fee to be paid is $22,222,
  with $2,222 going to the agent.

While $222 differential in agency commission may not seem much to quibble about, as fees increase and in agreements with higher commission rates of 15 and 20 percent, this differential can become significant. Using production costs of $100,000 and a commission rate of 20 percent, the difference to the agent is between $20,000 in the first instance and $25,000 in the second.

Net or Inclusive of Freight, Travel, and Accommodations?

Another important financial issue to agree on early is whether the value of these expenses is included or excluded from the commission calculation. In some cases fees paid are *all in* and include the producer paying for travel, freight, and accommodations from within the fee received; in other cases those are paid separately by the presenters. The question of whether or not the costs of travel, freight, and accommodation are commissionable must be spelled out in advance.

Back End and Royalties Included?

If there is a back-end percentage payable in addition to a base guarantee, it is normal that this percentage payment is also commissionable. It is less common that an agent will receive a commission on royalties.

Who Gets Handed the Money and When?

A big one: to whom does the fee get paid, the agency or the artist? Most large agencies require that all fees go to the agency, with payouts to the producer at the time of the engagements. Smaller agencies are often more flexible. Note that if payments are split, with the agent receiving his commission directly and separately from the fee balance being paid to the producer, it is important that the presenter's finance office distinguish the tax identification numbers associated with each payment. If a payment to one entity gets reported to the tax authorities as having been paid to the other, this will cause problems at tax time!

If fee deposits are made, it should be decided in advance if the agent receives commissions at the time of each payment or wait until the end. Typically, either the agent gets paid first or receives commission amounts corresponding to the percentages of the fee received according to the contracted payment schedule.

Difference for Agent as Tour Producer

Our discussion has been almost entirely on the basis of an agent receiving a commission on gross fees paid. It should be noted that in certain circumstances—often international shows being brought into a country and requiring minimum guarantees in order to be able to come, as well as many music tours—the agent becomes a tour producer or promoter instead (discussed in our chapter on taxes). In this circumstance, the agent/tour producer is assuming financial risk by guaranteeing the show a fee plus defined tour expenses and keeping what is left over. Obviously the agent/tour producer hopes in this instance to make at least as much as he would have on a straight agency commission plus extra as recompense for having assumed financial risk and for assuming the work of coordinating the tour itself beyond an agent's core responsibility of bringing the engagements through contract.

Agency Telltales

As producers are researching agencies, there are various telltale signs to watch for in forming opinions about the agents' effectiveness and appropriateness for their productions. These include a) What artists or productions are currently being represented by the agency in consideration? b) Where are those artists in their careers relative to yours or how do those productions compare to yours in size and stature? and c) How long have those productions and/or their producers been with the agency?

Assessing One's Own Strengths and Field Position

Difficult as it might be as a competitive artist or producer, one must critically evaluate the work of the other artists and producers on the rosters of prospective agencies and consider the position of one's own show in relationship. Is your show hotter with bigger stars than those? Do the other shows have the same performer union status and related cost structure as yours? Does your show have the real potential to be a hot new name; is it an established artist or show on a plateau, or will it always appeal to a niche market? How does that compare with those on the rosters of agencies under consideration?

Applying the analogy of the married couple to its purchase of a home, think of the agency as the show's home in the touring field. Is your show the equivalent of newlyweds seeking a starter home, a family with growing children where size and availability of fringes like schools are issues, or an empty-nester looking for a steady home base? Are you buying for the long term or looking to get started, knowing that you are going to be moving on at some point? Or are you an investor looking for a quick turnaround? This might affect whether you want to be with a hungry new agency looking to make its mark in the field versus an established name with clout.

Check the Recent History and Status of the Agency

Is it on the move up or down? You don't want to be the only classy house in a downscale neighborhood, though being the up and comer in a desirable area or a leader in what is clearly becoming a trendy upscale neighborhood is not bad at all. Two potentially desirable positions for the producer's show are: 1) to be among productions that are a little ahead of where yours is right now in overall name recognition and demand on the theory that the image of your show will be burnished by slightly more upscale company, or 2) to be the big name on the roster of a hungry agency that will make you its star and work extra hard to keep you.

What Time Horizon Are You Considering?

If your show is expected to have a short life due to a big star name with limited availability, then your goal will be maximum impact over a short period (quick turnaround). If you are a young theater company hoping to grow over the years and establish a solid niche in the field, you are thinking longer term. Assess the longevity of prospective agents' relationships with their client producers and artists.

Agencies Choosing Artists or Productions for Representation

While a code of ethics says that an agency should never actively solicit an artist or show to leave another agency and sign with it, there is no barrier to responding positively to an inquiry received and to being open for producer-initiated discussion. Since most producers don't want to completely cut current agency ties until they know they have another agency that will take them on, these inquiries are often confidential and occasionally placed through mutual acquaintances or other producers, sometimes artists or producers already being repped by the new agent.

For an agent there are two positives to having a new show recommended by an artist or producer already on his roster: 1) if he signs the new show, the one already on the roster is less likely to be jealous and resentful of potential competition, and 2) it signals that the current producer is happy with the agent's work or he wouldn't be recommending him to friends.

Can I Sell It?

Since an agent makes money only from commissions on booked engagements, the first question he must ask is whether he thinks he can sell the producer's show and to whom? That doesn't mean every show has to already be famous to get agency representation; some agents enjoy the challenge of working with unknown shows and artists they believe in and introducing them to the field.

But an agent will be looking for the *hooks* in every production represented. If he has two minutes of a presenter's attention during a conference in which the presenter is besieged by hundreds of agents with thousands of shows, are there hot bullet points about this one that will stick in the presenter's mind? Just as a presenter, in considering a production, will ask herself, "can I sell this to my audience?" the agent is doing the same thing in considering whether to take a production onto the roster, his "audience" being the presenters.

Additional Bases for Consideration of a Show by an Agent

After the obvious first questions above, agents will be considering some or all of the following.

Growth or Replacement?

Does adding this show means growth for the agency or replacement of a show that is leaving? For a large agency with hundreds of productions, adding or subtracting one or two is a relatively minor choice. But for a smaller agency with one to fifteen productions on the roster, a shift by one or two can have a more substantial impact on the agency's often delicately balanced allocation of resources.

Field Communication Efficiency

This relates to both artistic genre and scale, and how easily the new show will fit into the agent's ongoing dialogues with presenters. If the agent is working almost exclusively with theatrical presenters, does it make sense for him to suddenly offer one orchestra to these presenters who are unlikely to present it? If the agent's entire roster is made up of shows in the $10,000–$25,000 fee range, does it make sense for him to take on a $75,000 show realizing that it will be out of the price range of most of his current presenter contacts? This is not to say that an agent might not be open to expanding his buyer profile, but in the example of the theatrical agent with only one orchestra, it will probably not be cost effective for him to undertake developing a database and relationships with large-scale classical music buyers for only one orchestra unless it is part of a larger strategy to open a music division of the agency.

Cash Cow versus Heavy Lift?

An agency will inevitably look at the ease of sale for the show as another perspective on resource allocation within the agency.

Certain shows are not only well-known names but have a high *return rate*, with presenters bringing them back on a regular basis. These shows are somewhat crassly referred to among agents as *cash cows*. Agents will be most eager to add them to their rosters and may even be willing to negotiate down on the commission rate to get them. Such shows on the roster not only en sure a steady stream of relatively easy income but will make the agency that much more attractive to similar artists seeking to change agencies in the future.

The opposite of the *cash cow* is the *heavy lift*—a show with no name recognition that the agent will be working hard to introduce to the field from scratch with questionable return in the short run. Agents' appetites for such shows vary considerably. In an apt comparison to presenters taking risks, in their hearts most agents know that it is important for the field to continually source new shows, and of course many dream of getting in on the *ground floor* with a new show that will rocket to stardom and reap big returns in the future.

An artist or production that is known in the field, but with a bad reputation to overcome, is another form of heavy lift. A common reputation attached to a production may stem from it having technical demands that presenters consider unreasonably high and expensive in the context of the public demand and revenue potential for the show. A committed agent in a good relationship with the producer of such a show will convince the producer to reduce the tech requirements and promote the "new, streamlined" show structure to the presenting field.[4] Another example of a black mark might be an artist with a reputation for cancelling after contracts have been signed. Such reputations can be difficult, but not impossible, to overcome with concerted effort and commitment on the parts of the artist, producer, and agent.

It is telling that several of the major agencies, traditionally representing only the best known and most easily salable artists, have divisions dedicated to newer and more experimental work that function as incubators of lesser-known talent in the marketplace. How much of that work can ultimately be *mainstreamed* and made consistently profitable for the agencies is, of course, a gamble.

Smaller agencies, generally founded and run by individual entrepreneurs, are often the first agency homes for hot young shows. These are choices the agencies are likely to make as much out of infatuation with the artists and shows as from any real business sense, and with the early costs of introducing such shows to the field often borne on the backs of more established names on the rosters. Agencies view their early work to bring these shows to wider presenter audiences as longer-term investments.

The Reality Quotient in the Producer's Expectations

The agent will evaluate whether or not the producer has a realistic sense of where his show is in public awareness and whether he seems ready to do what it takes to become better known and help sell the show. (This reflects back on the advice to producers above to attempt an honest self-evaluation.) And are the producer's and the agent's evaluation of and expectations for the show aligned? The parties will have a hard time in a relationship if the producer thinks his show is really hot and should be playing major urban arts centers in big cities for extended runs when the agent knows that at this stage they'd be lucky to get a series of one night stands in secondary markets!

Financial Expectations

Are the financial needs and goals of the show in line with what the agent thinks he can deliver from tour engagements? This, of course, relates to how well-known the show is, the kind of audience and ticket price it can command, and the size of theater it can reasonably be expected to fill. Is the producer realistic in the adaptation of the show to touring or is there an expectation that every engagement will have the full scale production values and cast size of the Broadway or original home version with resulting costs beyond what the market will bear?

Conversely, does the show need to be *enhanced* or enlarged to play the Broadway-sized theaters on the Road; does the producer think that the show developed in a cabaret is ready for an arena? There are certainly examples of relatively small-scale Off-Broadway productions that have been hits and been scaled up to play large Broadway-sized venues on tour, the example of *Stomp* by now legendary. Likewise, as popular musicians move from clubs to performing arts centers to, in some cases, arenas, the scale of production is ramped up around them. Not all productions, of course, can withstand this increase in scale: classic drama, for instance, often needs more inti-mate theaters for reasons of artistic appreciation. This limits the potential revenue relative to comparatively high production costs, and contributes to why there is so little good drama touring regularly compared to other art forms.

Show's Touring History and Previous Agency Relationships

If a producer takes a show away from an agent whose work is respected and who is known to work hard for his clients, one must ask why the producer is moving the show to another agent. It can be purely personality differences, of course, but at the core, producers usually leave agents because they are not getting enough of the kind of work they think they should be getting, which they come to believe another agent can deliver. Sometimes they're right, but if the real problem is the producer's own lack of realistic perspective, no amount of changing agents will solve the problem. And a lot of *bed hopping* by the show among agents can taint the show's reputation, and savvy agents and even presenters will view it with suspicion.

Similarity to Artists Already Represented

In considering a new show, an agent will carefully consider the contrast and balance with shows he already represents: too close and there will be internal competition; too far away and he will run into the field communication efficiency issue discussed above. Agents' communications with most presenters are continuous season after season. When a presenter has successfully presented a production purchased through an agent and begun to trust the taste and business sense of that agent, she may well ask, *What do you have for me next season?* That is when the agent wants another show ready to offer that is different enough to bring back the audience, but with the same overall appeal.

FOR MY OWN AGENCY, OTHER FACTORS COME INTO PLAY

Active Creativity

While we began the agency with the great Marcel Marceau at a time when he had all but ceased creating new solo productions,[5] we have evolved since his retirement to working almost exclusively with artists and producers who are in creatively active phases of their careers. That being the case, and by announcing new productions each season, the artist's and producer's creative dynamics synergize with our promotion as an agency that buyers feel they must routinely check in with to hear of exciting new offerings.

Representing Producers versus Isolated Productions

We sell more than the productions themselves. Our agency identity is defined in part by the creators and producers with whom we are associated season after season despite changing productions. We are marketing the creativity and reputations of those artists and producers as well as their individual productions. Given a choice between an ongoing relationship with a highly talented and active director or producer, or with a one-off production with great press but with diminishing returns and no sequels, I'll usually choose the former.

Questions I Consider

- Am I moved by the production? Would I spend money and an evening to see this work? Are my staff members moved by the work?

- Does the production have something unique? Does it feel fresh and relevant, or old and dated? Is it the best of its artistic genre or are there better out there already touring?

- Will our buyers like the work and will they feel that their audiences will like the work? To what presenters would I make the first five calls about this show?

- Does the producer seem open to having us as part of his over-all strategic planning team or is he looking for a by-the-numbers, hands-off agent? (If the latter, there are some out there, but not us!)

- Do I like him/her/them as people? I like to think of these relationships as long lasting. Will we like each other in six months or three years? Important to my enduring relationship with Marcel Marceau were our lengthy and very enjoyable games of chess at all hours!

- Is the show really ready to tour? Some artists talk about touring, but when actual offers come in are surprisingly reluctant to commit to accepting the dates. Touring is not for everyone and not all artists are emotionally ready to take on the Road. It is important to know this *before* actively promoting their work for tour.

Important Relationship Issues

Many of the relationship issues of concern to agents parallel those of concern to producers.

Geographic Territory and Exclusivity

The agent wants to know that he has a clear field in which to work, with the geographic scope of that field an important part of the agreement. And while competition might keep him sharp in the broad sense—if he doesn't deliver engagements for the producer, the producer will take the show to another agent—it can be counter productive if other agents are simultaneously con-tacting the same presenters about buying the show or if buyers are seeking to bypass the agent and negotiate directly with the producer. Two things that can undermine an agent's effectiveness are 1) confusion in the minds of buy-ers about who the authorized agent is for a show in their territories and 2) worrying that the producer, if approached directly, might work a deal behind his back to avoid paying the booking commission. For agents, these should be considered deal-breaking issues with the producer. Without contractual clarity on these points, the agent should walk away from the show no matter how tempting.

Clarity on Agent's Responsibilities to a Booking

As a rule, an agent obtains the engagement offer and, subject to acceptance by the producer, brings it through signed contract and receipt of initial deposit due, at which point his active participation ends and the producer takes over to deliver the show. The negotiating process, of course, involves brokering the myriad details of the agreement that end up in the contract. The contract, prepared with care and thoroughness, provides a clear map and schedule for the producer to follow in exchanging the necessary materials and information with the presenter (technical exchange, marketing materials and support, program copy, further fee payments, etc.) and having the show arrive, set up, and be performed on time and on budget.

COMMUNICATIONS WITH PRESENTER THROUGH THE NEGOTIATIONS

As a rule as an agent I insist on being the prime communicator with the presenter through the negotiation process so as to avoid any confusion and as I am responsible to the producer for the outcome of negotiations. A common exception to this is that I often ask the tech reps from the presenter and the show to communicate directly on technical matters to be sure the show can fit in the stage, to assist the presenter in budgeting, and to make any adjustments particular to this venue and engagement in the technical rider *before* the contract is executed. If the engagement involves complex residency activity, I might arrange conference calls or meetings between the presenter and artist to save time in sorting out a residency plan that works for both parties.

Otherwise, once the contract is signed by both parties, I do the *hand off* in which I introduce the producer to the presenter—usually by e-mail—and advise them that from this point forward their communications will be direct. I thank the presenter for her work with us and let her know that a) we are available if we can assist in any communication or clarification as the engagement approaches, and b) that we look forward to working with her again in the future. Our relationships with presenters are among the most valuable to us and keeping that door open for future presentation proposals is critical to our business!

Clarity on Financial Terms

Nothing messes up a good relationship between a producer and agent more than distrust around money. So it is very important to confirm such details as the amount of the commission and on what precisely this is based (Net of travel and accommodation expenses? Net of withheld taxes?) for every engagement. It is important to know how the cash will flow and, if a foreign engagement, in what currency. When agents perform as tour producers the financial relationship becomes more complex. Rather than receiving a commission, the tour producer generally receives the gross fees, pays the production and related tour expenses, and retains the balance, and clarity on who is responsible for what expense areas is extremely important.

COMMISSION DEPOSITS

As an agency we often request a deposit from the presenter with contract execution, which is the same amount as our commission, and have that money sent directly to us. We then ask for the next and all future payments to be made directly to the producer. This allows us to know precisely when the deposit is in, assists with our cash flow, and minimizes the effort and expense of transferring funds to or from the producer. Finally, in a worst-case cancellation situation in which the deposit is returnable (normally cancellation due to *force majeure* or for reasons in the control of the producer), it puts us in the position of expediting at least a portion of that return without waiting for the producer, thereby insuring our continued good relationship with the presenter.

Access to Decision Makers

The booking process can sometimes become quite frenetic with a fast back-and-forth flow of questions, answers, and discussions about what is possible, all under a deadline to finalize (usually determined by marketing needs). It is vital that the agent have immediate access to the artist, tour producer, manager—whoever are the primary people on the producer's team responsible for decision making and delivering the show on tour.

Duration of Agreement

A minimum two-year starting relationship with an option to extend by mutual agreement is reasonable in order to have time to build an awareness of the relationship in the presenting field. Keep in mind that the cycle of booking is quite extended. Typically an agent is finalizing an agreement in the spring of Season I so as to include the show in the design and printing of his roster brochure that summer for engagements that will start in September of Season II and go through the summer of that Season. Of course tours south of the equator mirror these times of year with the theatrical seasons getting under way in February, March, and April. The opera and large-scale classical music fields work further ahead than that.

In the US we are supported and to a large degree guided by the regional booking conferences that take place in the fall, starting in late August or early September (Western Arts Alliance), leading up to the national conference of the Association of Performing Arts Presenters (APAP) in New York in January.

Clarity on What is Being Represented

This may seem obvious, but watch out! Many artists have solo shows as well as larger productions, some suitable for clubs and small venues and some for larger. Does the agent represent all, and if not, which? Many dance companies maintain second *feeder* or *incubator* companies—which is being offered to an agent can make a huge difference. Musical theater productions are sometimes offered in both concert form and fully staged. If the agent doesn't represent them all, what assurance does he have that he will not be competing with another agency in trying to sell the same production in different format, or the artist in a different production, in the same market? As the agent, be crystal clear as to which you are representing and which not. If the producer's name impacts the brand identity of the show, know in what other productions the artist and/or producer is involved to avoid nasty surprises.

EXCLUSIVE TOUR OPTION TO A PRODUCER'S SHOWS

My current agency represents some production companies that produce one or more shows a year. Often we begin the relationship because we like the overall work of the production company and one or two specific productions in particular. But of course not all of the productions are equally tourable. So our agreement in such cases usually stipulates those initial productions that we agree to offer for tour *and* gives us a first option on all future productions by the same producer that we mutually agree should be offered for tour. This gives us and the producer an out. If we really don't like the next production but the producer loves it and thinks it can tour, if we pass on our option the producer can seek another agent for that production.

More commonly the decisions of what to offer for tour are the result of what we think will sell, what the competition is doing, production size and flexibility, and touring economics. New productions each season are important for us as an agency. We must bring new shows to the field or we quickly become seen as stale in our offerings and start to lose the attention of the buyers.

Once Agency Agreement Is Reached

Reaching an agreement between producer and agent ends one complex process but is the beginning of an entirely new relationship!

Producer's Role and Responsibilities to the Agency Relationship

Some producers, especially solo artists or small companies with limited staffing, after finally reaching agreement with an agency breathe a sigh of relief and proceed to ignore the agent through the booking process and await the results at the end. But producers will benefit from a more proactive ongoing relationship. This might include:

- Asking for periodic updates on the status of bookings, the periods in the calendar in which there appears to be the strongest demand, and initial feedback being received from presenters about the show. This feedback can be on the fees being asked, on the effectiveness of the marketing materials, and on the overall perception of the show from the presenting field (This is the feedback that many artists are most reluctant to hear, but from which they would receive the greatest benefit!).

- Sharing the budgeting that underlies the fee requests with the agent for confidential feedback. Agents are experts in touring and see many such budgets. They should be considered part of the producer's team and not some outside stranger, and their feedback may be of great help.

- Letting the agent know of newsworthy activities related to the show that may provide talking and sales points in conversations with prospective presenters. This might include special television appearances or feature articles, cast changes, a new book being published by one of the performers, awards won, and touring activity in territories other than that being represented by the agent. Though an agent may only represent for North America, it makes a good talking point to mention that the show has just been booked for a hot London engagement!

- Discussing collateral marketing material with the agent *before* it is finalized and put in print or posted on a Web site to allow input from a booking perspective. Remember that the agent is the producer's eyes and ears to what the presenting field sees, thinks, and needs related to the show.

- Inviting agency staff, and particularly the sales agents themselves, to rehearsals and performances.

- Sharing the history of the show's touring and thoughts on where there may be return demand.

Many producers consider booking agencies to be a necessary evil that takes away income through commissions that would otherwise come to the producer, and they end up treating the agents this way. They often consider any bookings that come their way their divine right and only pay attention to the agent when there is a lack of bookings. They may not be aware that for every booking finally contracted, the agents will be involved in hundreds of conversations and negotiations that do not lead to bookings. And they forget that though the agents may consider their work a job, they are often in this field through love of the art and appreciation of the work of the artists and producers. If the producer's concern is to make sure that the agents keep her show front and center in presenter conversations, honey goes a lot farther than vinegar. A personal note from the producer to the agent thanking him for a particularly successful engagement goes a long way to encouraging that agent to extol the show's virtues in future presenter conversations.

On their side, agents can consider producers who hover over their shoulders to be intensely annoying and distracting. *Producers:* Give them some space! *Agents:* Remember that these productions are often the *children* of these artists and producers and the results of considerable blood, sweat, and money invested, and show some understanding. *Both:* Work to find a mutually satisfactory basis for ongoing communication.

MANAGING EXPECTATIONS

As an agent I am constantly managing the expectations of producers who are eager to hear what buyers have expressed interest in their shows and which are in active negotiation and likely to confirm, in addition to what deals have closed. Some producers and artists operate in a rose-colored world. A reported first inquiry from a presenter gets transformed in their optimistic minds into a sure thing, only to cause them disappointment later when it falls through. Other producers can handle the difficult roller coaster ride of possibilities and occasional rejection that is the booking process. While I attempt complete clarity in all reporting, it is inevitable that I am affected by what I know to be the stamina of each producer for the whole truth as the process rolls forward.

Agency's Role and Responsibilities: Know the Show

Regardless of how many artists and shows the agency may represent, the good agency—and the agents themselves—will have done its homework before the booking process begins.

What are the performers' tastes, willingness to interact with the press, public, and the presenter (and often the presenter's donors), overall friendliness and tone? If a star is involved, is she a diva, expecting limos and suites, who feels that she is most appreciated when demanding the impossible and making someone else miserable, or is she an artist of the people who would rather walk to the theater, is okay attending receptions with the presenter's donors, and will stay until all hours after the show to sign autographs? The agent needs to know where the hot buttons are: the things the performer likes and those she finds upsetting.

Go to rehearsals, study videotapes and reviews, figure out what the strong selling points of the work are. Read the tech rider, and be prepared to rattle off some basics of minimum stage dimensions and the time needed to load in the show even if you don't have a technical stage background. It is a waste of time spending an hour talking about a given production with a presenter with a thrust stage if the show can only be performed on a traditional proscenium stage.

Special here is whether the show freight can fly as excess baggage or must go by air or ground freight, which invariably takes longer. This will have a tremendous effect on the tour schedule if the personnel can fly but would then have to wait an extra day or two for the freight to arrive by truck. And unaccompanied air freight generally drives costs through the roof!

If the artist or production is unionized, how do those rules impact the show's touring? It is not enough to know that a theater company is an Equity signatory, since there are different levels of Equity contract with pay scales varying according to a number of factors. Also, many Equity companies have slight variations in the applicability of the rules that can significantly affect touring and with which it is helpful for the agents to be familiar. And many nonunion companies operate under strict work rules and give union-level pay to their performers. Learn what you need to know in order to set up tour schedules without having to call the producer at every turn.

One of the toughest tasks of an agent is to bring feedback to an artist or producer about how his work or production is perceived in the presenting field when it does not fit with the artist's or producer's own view of his work—what a film producer friend refers to as *serving reality burgers*. This can be an excruciatingly difficult task, as the agent is addressing the heart and soul of the artist's life. There is a huge temptation on the part of the artist to deny what is being said, and further to *hang the messenger* and assume that the agent is wrong and ignorant of the deep meaning in the work. If choosing an agency is like the real estate market, the booking business itself shares much with the stock market: an artist can wish that the value of its stock were X, but it is ultimately the marketplace that will determine the value and it may not be close to what the artist believes. Notice the reference here more to artist than producer—this is an area where working directly with the performing artist can be notably different than working through a more business-based producer.

Promotional Materials: What's Needed?

At minimum, the producer must expect to provide a good quality DVD—this may include a full length recording, a nonbroadcastable recording edited for sales to presenters, and short, broadcast quality clips that can be used as b-roll in the presenter's retail promotion. For international touring, know the format of the country to which you are sending so that a disk sent to another part of the world can be viewed there.

The artist, producer, or show must have an effective Web site, with the agency clearly identified as booking contact and a hyperlink to the agency's Web site. Press quotes, tour history, upcoming viewing opportunities, and good photos are the other backbones of the press kit. Testimonials from significant presenters and well-known artists, and a listing of credibility-building items such as major awards, film and television appearances, and other notable activities, can be important.

All above materials, including an operational Web site, must be ready at the *start* of the normal booking cycle so that once the agency makes its announcement of the show's availability to the field, the agency is prepared to respond promptly to expressions of interests and requests for materials.

There is an increasing and welcome trend for artists and producers to have press, photos, touring history, calendar of upcoming performances, technical requirements, and even video clips available for viewing on their Web sites, which speeds up getting materials to distant presenters and cuts down on shipping costs. Often higher resolution materials such as printable photos and broadcast-quality video are accessible for download only with a password the agency provides to the presenter. This is done only after the contract or deal memo is signed so as to protect abuse of the show's images and to induce the presenter to execute the contract before starting public promotion.

Keeping Expectations Aligned

It is vitally important that after the agency agreement is signed, both sides continue to communicate on a regular basis, both the news to be shared and the touring goals. Relationships that have most consistently not worked are based on nonalignment around expectations, usually as the result of insufficient time spent talking between agent and producer.

MY CLIENT *FAMILY*—CLOSE INVOLVEMENT

Intentionally keeping my agency relatively small and focused, I regard the producers and artists with whom we work as part of our family, seeking informal opportunities to talk and keep in touch with their new ideas and projects in development. This is partly selfish as I like these people and admire their work. I also find that the producers and artists often have keen insights about where their work can be effectively promoted that it is important for me to hear.

A trusting personal relationship also allows me to share some of the more difficult feedback I have picked up from the field that the artist needs to hear. Telling Marcel Marceau that many American presenters felt that his show was too long, when I knew how hard and lovingly he worked to prepare each program, was hard. Telling a theater company that if they don't find ways to reduce their treasured technical requirements they are going to lose bookings can be one of the hardest tasks of an agent. But if we don't tell them, who will?

I encourage and even require our producers to share their underlying tour budget work with me in confidence so I can see their assumptions in quoting a performance fee and provide feedback if I think it will be beneficial.

I insist on signing off on the final form of their technical riders, looking for as much clarity as possible for our presenters as we are the ones usually sending these out early in the booking process.

Regarding marketing materials, I am astounded at the number of producers who approach us for representation but who, after spending large sums to create the productions, claim that they can't afford to edit videos or set up Web sites. In other instances, they claim that the unions forbid videotaping the work. Though I recognize the legitimate concerns of image misuse underlying the union rules, understand the cost challenges, and am aware that good collateral materials cost money, I will refuse to represent a show for which these important sales tools are not available. Unless the show can be seen, at least on video, how can it be sold?!

Endnotes

1   The term "partner" is used here very loosely to illustrate a point. Note that from a legal perspective, the agency/client relationship is expressly not in any way a partnership.

2   ICM Artists recently rebuffed a buyout by another large agency and was instead bought by a group that included a number of agency employees. This closely watched new development in the field brought control of the agency into the hands of individuals with a stake in their own company and years of experience in performing arts touring. The name of the company has been changed by the new owners to Opus 3 Artists.

3   This last point is of less significance than the rest in most cases, except where some artists like the latitude to be able to appear *pro bono* as part of fundraising events, etc., without the agent being involved. Agents don't usually care since they make no money if the artist is not being paid.

4   This was particularly common among a group of dance companies that, in the heyday of dance touring in the US in the 1970s and early 1980s, when funds from the National Endowment for the Arts' Dance Touring Program were subsidizing domestic touring, expanded their lighting and production expectations. The harsh fiscal realities of dance touring since the demise of the DTP have caused many of those dance companies that have survived to review these expanded tech demands and find ways to create great production effects with less. Fortunately, the timely advent of computerized lighting and digital sound generation has contributed to an increase in technical theater efficiency, as will be discussed in chapter 17.

5   Mr. Marceau continued to create new multiperformer company productions for *La Nouvelle Compagnie de Mime Marcel Marceau* until into the early 2000s.

CHAPTER 3

Agent/Buyer Relationship—the Seller's Perspective

As previously noted, the "agent" might range from one of many in a large agency to a part-time booking person in house with a small artist or production, or occasionally even the artist him- or herself. But many of the same dynamics apply to all, and for our purposes we'll refer to the person in this role as the agent.

Agent of Two Masters

An agent really has two clients: the *artists* on his/her roster (or the producers of shows on the roster) and the *buyers*. It is the agent's ability to navigate between the two that is at the core of his/her trade. In the excellent book *Guide to Producing Plays and Musicals* by Frederic B. Vogel and Ben Hodges[1] experienced producer Mike Isaacson describes this relationship thusly: "The agent also serves as a critical conduit between the show and the presenter, feeding both with each other's information and insights that often help shape critical marketing, financial, and production decisions. They are often in effect translators, helping each side understand the other's business."

Having addressed the agency's relationship to the artists and producers in the previous chapter, let's look at the particular relationship to the buyers.

Having Access/Building a Rep

A primary goal for an agent and a first test of his effectiveness is his *access* to buyers. Can he get to the ears and eyes of the decision maker(s) at presenting organizations to make a pitch? This can be *borrowed clout* as an unknown agent calling on behalf of either a well-known agency or artist uses their names to get the call through the secretaries guarding the decision maker. But ultimately, over time, an agent's goal is to build a personal reputation within the buying field so that regardless of what agency he is with or what production he currently represents, his calls will be taken or returned by the people that count.

MY OWN AGENCY'S HISTORY

When starting my agency in the mid-1990s, I had two points of borrowed clout: my own reputation as a former presenter running increasingly well-known arts centers, and the name of our first artist client, the famous French mime Marcel Marceau. Mr. Marceau had not toured in the US in about five years, and our timing turned out to be excellent as audiences were interested to see him again, and buyers took my calls and responded to mailings based to a large degree on his name. By the time Marceau retired some years later, my agency had established *presence* in the field, and we were able to segue to other artists and productions based on the agency's evolved reputation.

Having Something to Sell

Obviously getting through to the buyer is only half the battle. The agent needs something saleable to talk about. The sad fact is that much as the agent might love a show—and his personal enthusiasm means a lot—to get sold, a show must have strong sales points (*hooks* or *credentials*). The most obvious is name recognition and attraction of the artist himself or, if a production, the name recognition of the star. But assuming a show with no name recognition is being offered, other options can be:

- *Press.* Especially important is New York City press, and in particular, the *New York Times*. Say what one will, and argue all one wants for the importance of other newspapers and media, the *New York Times* still holds the #1 position for press clout in reference to selling shows on tour. In the memorable words of the Lifestyles Editor at the *Burlington Free Press* to me some years ago, when insisting on seeing what the *Times* had to say about an artist I was presenting, "If I'm going to be wrong, I want to be wrong in the right company!"

- *Television presence.* Buyers make the assumption that if the talent scouts for the *David Letterman Show*, the *Tonight Show*, etc., found this artist to be sufficiently appealing to bring to their multimillion member audiences, they should perhaps take a similar chance for their theaters.

- *Testimonials.* Praise from other presenters means a lot, preferably from markets and venues of roughly the same size as the current target. Saying that an audience in a large urban center appreciated a show to a presenter in a small rural community may have less impact than reporting good response from audiences in markets similar in size and demographics to the presenter.

- *Sales reports from other markets.* Especially relevant to presenters who consider past performance to be a predictor of future sales, there is nothing with the same weight as reporting that the show sold 90 percent or 100 percent of available seats, in a venue with similar seating capacity, in a city of the same size and demographic, grossing a sufficiently large number to get attention. And don't assume that the prospective presenter won't call the former and verify any claims the agent might make!

- *Awards, grants, and fellowships.* Obviously Tony Awards and Grammys are great sales legitimizers. Attention-getters such as Guinness World Records, Command Performances for the Queen of England, and receipt of MacArthur Foundation *genius* awards can turn heads. Receipt of major grants from name foundations and the National Endowment for the Arts provide at least some talking points with the press in consideration of advance coverage.

- *Show history.* Television exposure, of course, generally wins the day. Broadway is great. Carnegie Hall, Lincoln Center, and almost any major New York City venue, London's West End and even Las Vegas carry clout. As programmer for the Flynn Center in Burlington, Vermont, attempting to introduce the work of composer/performer Steve Reich to our audiences in the 1980s—at the time considered highly risqué—the fact that the production was coming "direct from the Brooklyn Academy of Music's Next Wave Festival" made a big difference in the final decision to present, in gaining local press attention, and on ticket sales. Likewise, the Paul Winter Consort's Winter Solstice Concert "direct from The Cathedral Church of St. John the Divine in New York City." While it is unlikely that the name of the agency or producer will ever add significant appeal for the general public ticket buyer, it is not uncommon that a presenter will get mileage from reporting that this show is "brought to you by the same people who brought you the sold out, smash hit, XYZ!"

To Whom Are Agents Really Selling?

John Luckacovic, then a vice president with Columbia Artists Management Inc., once wisely advised, "Remember that you are not selling *to* the presenter, but *through* the presenter to his/her audiences. The presenter is a middle-man." I have never forgotten those words as they continue to ring true, and more so as, within the nonprofit presenting world, presentation subsidies shrink and greater pressure is placed on box office income to make presenting viable. And in most cases, the flow through of accountability does not include only the public audiences. Long before the shows get that far, most presenter programming contacts have a boss or committee to which they answer and that must sign off on their selections—the show's first critical venue in a community may not be the theater but a board room! The relevant message here is not, *You're going to love this show.* Rather, *Your audiences are going to love this show.*

The presenter programmers—those individuals who go to conferences, attend performances, and make it their business to stay abreast of developments in the field—tend to be more sophisticated in their tastes than those to whom they must report and the bulk of those who might buy the tickets. So a deep, meaningful artistic discussion for an agent with a buyer at a conference can be deceiving since her initial enthusiasm for a show often has high hurdles to get over before a presentation commitment is made.

Do the Homework

With the advent of Web sites, it is relatively easy to see the artistic lineup a given venue and presenter has programmed. With careful study by an agent before making contact, a lot of information can be gleaned from this source. Important elements include:

- Do they prefer to present on weekdays or weekends only?

- How is their presenting profile different at various times of year?

- What is the typical number of performances offered? How far apart are they spaced?

- Does the presenting appear to fall inside or outside of certain time periods (on holidays or avoiding holidays, during the academic year or outside of the academic year, affected by climate patterns, etc.)?

- What is the seating capacity of the venue (or venues, if a complex)? Outdoor or indoor seating? Can the venue accommodate the scale of the production the agent wants to offer this presenter? This type of information can often be found in the *Venue Rental* section of the Web site.

- What is the ticket price range normally charged? Multiplied by the seating capacity one can determine an approximate gross potential revenue[2] against which a rough estimate of reasonable artist fee range can be made. Remember that the presenter is going to look at the total artist costs, so a high fee can to some degree be offset if the technical requirements, freight and travel, or accommodation requirements are low and vice versa.

- What is the nature of the programming, and how does it compare with that of your agency and of the production you want to offer?

- What are the strong selling points being made to ticket buyers? Is it star names only? Hot quotes from the *New York Times*? Beautiful photographs? Does your production match up?

Presenters appreciate agents who do this homework before calling. It saves time and impacts results on a first call, and helps to build long-term trust and respect in the relationship.[3]

Get In their Faces

Remembering that this is very much a *people business*, the most influential element of access is to provide a name to the secretary answering the phone or in the subject line of the e-mail that will be recognized and responded to by the presenter. If that name is of a famous artist that can be enough, or if you are an agent with a universally known agency such as a William Morris or CAMI, the call will probably be taken or e-mail read. But for agents representing less well-known artists and whose agencies are not door breakers, the key is to seek opportunities to establish personal relations and build up history with the person you are calling.

This "in their face" philosophy basically says:

- Be proactive in getting your name in front of buyers.

- Try for introductions to new contacts, but in their absence don't be afraid to *cold call*. If you can't get through to the top man or woman on a call, chat up the secretary or gatekeeper—these people often have tremendous influence on what messages get on the top of the piles on their bosses' desks.

- Always carry a business card and a spare brochure in your pocket, especially to events where you may encounter presenters.

- Don't feel that every point of contact must involve a sales pitch. With patience, persistence, and correct targeting, sales will be made.

- Keep notes on every contact made, including relevant personal and unique contextual information. A presenter with young children, for instance, is likely to be more sensitized to good family and youth programming. An active sportsperson may be more attuned to highly kinetic productions. A good snow base on the ski slopes in Vermont, drawing locals to the slopes on the weekends, suggests that ticket sales may be stronger on weekdays than weekends. In certain parts of the US, one night of the week is *church night* and a bad evening for theater attendance.

- Seek opportunities for humor in the relationship. A good laugh over a shared joke at the outset of the relationship gets remembered longer and more positively than anything else.

A TIP FROM THE JAPANESE

It is worth studying the Japanese concept of *aisatsu*, literally *a greeting* or *greetings*, as applied to first business meetings. The convention is that at least at the opening of the first meeting, despite the fact that both parties may know exactly what business is of interest to both, before business is discussed an effort is made to establish the framework for a working relationship. The *aisatsu* tend to be rather formal, ceremonial occasions. In some cases, the senior executives will be on hand at the beginning of the meetings to deliver (or receive) *aisatsu*, and will then leave, allowing the real business to be carried on by underlings.

As described by Japan expert Peter Grilli, currently the President of the Japan Society of Boston:

> *Aisatsu means "greetings" in the most general sense. It can be a spoken "welcome" or "greeting" by a VIP at the beginning of a conference or meeting or performance—or speeches by friends of the bride or groom at a wedding.*
>
> *The Japanese do tend to place greater importance in aisatsu than Americans might. Often such a prelude in the US is thought irrelevant, unimportant, or even a distraction before a performance or other event. But in Japan it is often considered useful in setting the stage for a meeting, getting everyone feeling "in synch" and fully understanding of the reasons that they are present.*

While the rush of booking conferences and the distance of e-mail relationships may not often permit the luxury of such formality, the concept serves as a reminder that efforts made to build trust and goal alignment into relationships play a vital role in successful business over the long term.

Multiclient versus Single-Client Agencies

A note is warranted on the subtle but important differences in presenter relationships for agents representing only one production or artist (including in-house agents) and those with a multiple-production roster. Both agencies will attempt to establish and maintain ongoing trust relationships with past and prospective buyers, calling them periodically, sending holiday cards, e-mailing news related to the production(s), socializing at the booking conferences, etc.—relationships that sets amicable contexts for doing business. But the task is somewhat different between a multiproduction agency and a single-production representative.

The Multiproduction Agent

This agent is able to share his roster of productions in a neutral (though presumably, enthusiastic) tone, discussing which productions fit best into the presenter's venue and series, audience preferences, and the artists' and producers' visions and goals. For many presenters, this context of discussion is more comfortable than feeling that the agent is representing—and probably being paid by—just one producer or artist, and fearing that rejection of the artist will result in hurt feelings.

Producers working with multiproduction agents might be concerned with whether their productions are receiving the same attention and push as other productions on the agents' rosters, presumably offset by the idea that more presenters are willing to talk with this agent. It is certainly true that from time to time in conversation with a presenter an agent may emphasize a particular production from the roster. This might be to support a tour developing for this particular production in this presenter's region or because the agent truly believes that this is the best production for this presenter in the season under discussion for valid artistic and other reasons.

A Single-Production Agent

This agent has a greater challenge, having only one show to sell, in setting and maintaining a broad, low-pressure context for ongoing dialogue with presenters since the focused interest on the part of the agent to sell only that production is the constant elephant in the room. Unless the presenter is already open to the idea of presenting that production or it is a new relationship with a presenter hearing of this production for the first time, many presenters will find spending time with that agent to be somewhat uncomfortable since as many times and creative ways as the agent brings up the idea of his presenting the production, the presenter has to find ways to say *no* that will not permanently offend.

Balance the Long and Short Views

As noted above, despite the seemingly aggressive *in-your-face* attitude, and while eager to make sales now, the good agent views the field from a long-term perspective. At what point is it better to lose what will be a bad short-term sale in the interests of gaining trust for the long haul? With the help of files or perhaps contact management software (see the chapter on technology), agents should keep track of ongoing relations and communications with presenters on the expectation that sooner or later there will be an appropriate fit of one of his shows with that presenter, and a sale will be made.

This plays out for the agent in various ways:

- If a presenter says, *I love that artist, but we're not ready for him*, or, *Not this year but maybe next*, take that seriously and set up a *tickler note* to remind yourself to repitch the artist for the subsequent season.

- If an individual with whom you have been corresponding leaves one presenting organization and goes to work for another, keep track of the move and that person's tastes for discussion in her new job (also watch for announcements on who has taken over her former position).

- Follow up engagements with a call to ask how everything went, listen to the complaints as well as the praise, and make sure that door is ajar for future conversation of both a return of that show and consideration of other shows from your roster on the presenter's future seasons.

- Seek to broaden your contacts at presenting organizations. Often marketing directors will be important in the decision-making process on what shows to bring in. Larger organizations have CEOs in addition to program directors. Get to know them in addition to the primary programming representatives and include them in brochure mailings as you can assume they will be involved in internal discussions about program choices. If the presenter is at a university that has dance, drama, and/or music academic departments and you can determine the chair people of those departments, mail to them as well.

- Remind presenters of your existence and provide news of your productions through periodic e-mails or news announcements. Find the right balance of routine communication that stops short of annoyance. Keep it lively and don't assume that every communication has to include a hard sell.

Booking Calendar

US tour booking operates on quite rigorous timetables. This is plural here intentionally as tour booking of different types of production breaks down into—very roughly—three groups:

- *Long-lead booking, two years ahead and more.* Primarily the large-scale classical music organizations, including both symphonies and opera companies. These organizations do not tour often, but the planning involves the touring of major conductors, singers, and guest musicians, and the scope of such touring can be monumental. Likewise international tours of large theatrical productions, such as a US visit by a Golden Mask Festival or Maly Theatre production from Russia, the National Theatre from London or the National Bunraku Puppet Theatre of Japan, will often be planned at least two years in advance.

- *Lead of approximately one year.* This group, among larger presenters, often begins with the Broadway productions, which will tie up large date windows in the venues, and is followed by scheduling other attractions for which subscription sales are critical. Since subscription offerings must generally be announced in the spring prior to the performance season beginning the following fall, and contracts must be signed and marketing materials developed before the subscription is offered, the booking process must generally be completed by February/March or less than one year before the start of the offered performance season but more than a year before it ends.

- *Close in and "opportunity" booking.* This group encompasses those productions that do not rely on subscriptions to sell and that, for various reasons, cannot be planned far in advance. The biggest subgroup in this are popular musicians whose on-sale dates are sprinkled through the season and, depending on their fame and draw, may only require a matter of days or weeks (or in some cases, hours!) to sell out. Additional will be *fill dates* for productions offering lower-priced engagements late in the process in order to not have holes in the tour calendar. Festivals also tend to operate on their own marketing timetables, some of which can be quite close in. While the major festival *anchors* will be booked early, it is not uncommon to see shows still being booked for summer festivals as late as the fall and winter prior.

Spiral of Life

One can almost visualize the spiral course by which a production moves from the producer into the hands of an agent, who sells it to a presenter, who offers it (quite often) first on a subscription program and then on a single-ticket sales basis to the public, a process that can easily take two years from the time the agent and producer negotiate for the production to join the agent's roster in one season, to the sales, contracting, and early subscription phase in the second season, to the single-ticket sale and actual engagement in the third.

And as the spiral is under way for one production with one engagement, new spirals are beginning with other productions entering the process, and existing productions being returned for second engagements by presenters or spinning off for further engagements in other communities.

While the timetable and process have been affected by the advancement of digital technology, including Internet-based promotion and ticket sales that require less lead time (and cost) than brochure mailings and mailed responses, the desire on the part of most presenters to offer some form of subscription or membership tied to early ticket buying for the fall in the spring prior, and its effect on the booking timetable, is unchanged.

Endnotes

1   Frederic B. Vogel and Ben Hodges, *Guide to Producing Plays and Musicals* (New York: Applause Theatre & Cinema Books, 2006).

2   Without knowing the "scaling" of the house—ticket pricing and number of seats at each price—one cannot calculate a firm gross potential revenue. Further variability is made possible by computers, which can adjust the pricing of seats according to the demand, making the concept of a fixed gross potential figure meaningless. For this rough calculation, an average of high and low multiplied by the total number of seats should give a conservative gross potential since presenters will try to weight the house toward the higher end tickets if justified by demand.

3   I find it curious that so few presenters include lists of past presentations on their Web sites, given the importance of this information to the cultural archives of their communities' and to the presenters' identities. Obviously, it would also allow agents an important research tool that might save both agent and presenter valuable time. Presenters, please take note!

CHAPTER 4

Agent/Buyer Relationship—the Buyer's Perspective

Presenters' relationships to agents range from close working relationships, which serve as pipelines for production after production to flow through the agents to the presenters' stages, to distant relationships for the occasional booking. Some presenters view agents with hostility, stemming from the idea that, if the presenter could work directly with the artist's manager or show producer, he could negotiate more favorable terms. There is presumably some truth to this: among the roles of the agent are protecting the interests of the production and obtaining the most favorable terms (for the producer) possible, and the participation of an agent inevitably drives up costs with agency commission. Hostility may also derive from a bad business experience in the past between the parties that has engendered distrust. But most participants in the process recognize that the services provided by an agent justify the added expense.

According to Trav S. D. in his book on the history of Vaudeville, *No Applause Please—Just Throw Money*,[1] the first agency was created by William Morris in the late 1800s in an effort to break the dominance of performer abuse by the large presenter conglomerates. Presumably, Mr. Morris did this only in part out of concern for the welfare of artists. He also saw an opportunity to sign enough of the most desirable performers to force the buyers to work through him to secure the services of performers, and thereby earn revenue through commissions. His battles with the conglomerates of the day are the stuff of legend, but it is notable that the William Morris Agency remains as one of the dominant agencies in the field and that Morris' early work laid the groundwork for the role of agencies today. Since those early days, of course, artists' unions have evolved as protectors of the rights of artists, and agencies focus more attention on obtaining book-ings. While bulk buyers are still with us in the form of Live Nation, the Independent Producers' Network, and regional promoters, they are focused almost entirely on the two live-entertainment areas that profit the most from popularity: Broadway and pop music. There are no conglomerates booking months of work for dance or opera companies!

Regardless, it is a safe bet that for the foreseeable future agents are here to stay as part of the equation. Most presenters *and* producers would report their relationships with most agents to be positive and that agents provide an essential service in obtaining and providing information on productions to presenters, coordinating dates and schedules, negotiating contracts, and sometimes sorting out entry visas, taxes, and other issues that would otherwise add extra burden to the presenter's often lean staffs. Presenters recognize that certain agents, who have invested the effort to become acquainted with their venues, community demographics, and institutional profile, actually pro-vide value as curatorial advisers in proposing productions well suited to their programming.

While obviously it is the mandate of presenters to obtain productions on the lowest possible terms, and of agents to sell the productions at the highest, most agents and presenters acknowledge that within this framework there is a mutual interest being served in coming to agreement and arranging bookings.

Presenters' Styles Vary

Presenters range from the very passive to the very active or aggressive, and from the formulaic to the creative, and it behooves agents to get to know the individual styles.

Armchair Presenters

There are presenters who consider it their entire function to book a list of the biggest possible star names that can be obtained within budget. While not without challenges in obtaining desired dates and acceptable terms, this programming approach is essentially formulaic in nature. The traditional *modus operandi* in the purely profit-driven, for-profit touring field, since the late 1990s this has increasingly become the program pattern among non-profits as well for reasons discussed elsewhere in this book. Previous funding tied to *risk taking* and the introduction of new artists to communities has largely disappeared or been replaced by corporate marketing money, which often shares the same focus on big star names and has little incentive to spon-sor unknown artists performing for unsold seats. See the discussion of pre-senter motives above and the introduction of Next Wave fever below.

One-Stop Shoppers

There are presenters whose rural locations, and limited staff and travel budgets, force them to become the pliant customers of a few agents whom they get to know and trust, and they will book their entire seasons directly from only a few agency rosters, often without being able to see the acts in person before booking. In such cases, in limiting the number of different conversations by the presenter, the agencies involved will tend to be those with the largest rosters. And while generally one can assume that most productions represented by a CAMI, IMG, Opus 3, or William Morris will be of good quality, this approach nonetheless limits the presenter's field of choice.

One subtle advantage for the one-stop shopper is the institutional memory and sense of loyalty associated with buying through the same agency (or few agencies) season after season. If a presenter accepts a production in one season based on the strong urging of the agent and it does not sell as expected and the presenter loses money, that fact can affect negotiations in the next season with the same agent for another production. The wise agent, eager to keep the special relationship with this presenter, will remember (or be reminded of) the bad experience and seek to arrange a special opportunity for a highly saleable production to hopefully allow the presenter to profit and make back some of the lost money. This informal back watching characterizes the personal aspect of long-term relationships in this industry.

Bellwether Presenters

At the opposite end of the spectrum are presenters who are aggressive in their search for the hot new productions that will establish their organizations, not only as dynamic locally, but as leaders nationally and internationally. Such presenters will push agents to add exciting new productions to their rosters. In some instances, presenters have been known to initiate a direct relationship with the producer or artist and then help the producer find the right agency for representation to arrange a tour based, in part, on a promise by the presenter to bring in the show. This type of presenter can also have an important impact in statewide and regional block-booking associations that virtually cover the US, as these presenters can galvanize and lead their regions in learning about new artists and productions.

Festivals

Festivals both in the US and more so abroad have long been the vehicles through which new work has been introduced to audiences. This includes not only annual festivals such as the Jacob's Pillow Dance Festival, the Spoleto Festivals (in the US and Italy), and festivals in cities such as Avignon, Vienna,

Singapore, Melbourne, and Hong Kong, but special occasions such as the Cultural Olympiads and the program in Europe initiated in 1985 by the then-Minister of Culture of Greece, the actress Melina Mercouri, of designating two cities every year as Cultural Capitals.[2] Under this program, the designated cities expend large sums on culture, often building new theaters and exhibition halls, as part of a major civic promotion. The critical mass of funding, programming, and the audiences, many of whom travel to these festival sites specifically for the occasions, enable these festivals to be leaders in bringing exciting new productions to the stage as well as promoting their home regions internationally. Indeed in some regions, such as Australia, where various cities host annual or biannual festivals, a sense of competition has arisen for world attention and acclamation as the most adventurous and exciting. The annual Edinburgh International Festival in Scotland and the concurrent Edinburgh Fringe have become significant global showcases for productions before gatherings of international presenters that often expand their touring lives as well as obtain opportunities to move to London and New York as a result of that exposure.

Presenters' Curatorial Roles: Next Wave Fever

In the early 1980s, Harvey Lichtenstein, at the helm of New York's Brooklyn Academy of Music (BAM), developed a unique presenting construct titled the Next Wave Festival. BAM is a glorious historic performing arts facility living under the shadow of the Manhattan entertainment centers. It had long sought a distinct attention-getting role for itself in the crowded New York City milieu. The deceptively simple concept of Next Wave was that, in the face of the then-classically focused programming of institutions such as Lincoln Center, BAM would create a festival that exclusively celebrated the very newest and edgiest in the international performing arts—literally the *next wave* of creative ideas for the stage. With significant leadership funding from the then-titled Philip Morris Company, the early years of the Next Wave Festival saw presentations of groundbreaking new works such as Peter Brook's *Mahabharata* and Lee Breuer and Bob Telson's *The Gospel at Colonus*, and brought the work of seminal artists such as Pina Bausch and Philip Glass to wide attention.

The Festival impacted the general public, but perhaps of greater ultimate significance, it forced the cultural press to educate itself about entirely new forms of and approaches to live performance, and it forced the international presenting world to wake up to the power of the new in programming. The Festival drew a glitterati crowd and audiences found their way to BAM. By shear volume, diversity, and commitment to provocative new work, the Next

Wave lived out its mission as a generation was taught to celebrate and seek out new work instead of relying simply on re-presenting of the old.

BAM's Next Wave Festival is arguably one of the most deft and significant applications of festival programming in arts presenting history. The Festival not only gave BAM a reenergized identity but empowered presenters throughout the US and the world to address their local curatorial roles in introducing new productions and the work of new artists to new audiences. The Next Wave Festival encouraged the training of audiences and critics to celebrate the discovery of the new instead of attending theater only out of nostalgia for the familiar and to deepen their appreciation of contemporary performing art. Through the boom 1990s, to some degree inspired by Next Wave, US arts centers nationwide expanded their commitment to new arts/new audiences, including the Yerba Buena Center in San Francisco, the Portland Institute of Contemporary Arts, the Walker Art Center in Minneapolis, the Chicago Museum of Contemporary Art, the Wexner Center in Columbus, Ohio, the Miami Light Project in Florida, the Massachusetts Museum of Contemporary Art in North Adams, Massachusetts, and additional New York City institutions such as Arts at St. Ann's, New York Theatre Workshop, the Miller Theater at Columbia University, and even Lincoln Center in the creation and programmatic daring of it's own new summer festival.

Sadly, as we write in the cold grey morning of a deficit era, with greater emphasis on ticket sales than adventurous programming and a national mood fed with uncertainty leading to a demand for nostalgia, many such bold ventures are being forced to retrench and fight to stay alive, hopefully to blossom again in coming years.

Broadway-Based Presenters

Many of the larger venues in the USA have a primary commitment to offer Broadway series, whether on a presenting, copresenting, or venue rental basis. The basis on which the shows come to the theaters may vary and is complex, and the costs are high. Regardless, due to the need for a clear block of dates for these productions and flexibility as the routing process is being worked out, the venue operators cannot commit anything else in the potential dates for the Broadway series until it is locked in, which can end up being quite late in the booking cycle. With the lion's share of their budgets and the prime dates in their theaters committed, presenters then (often hastily) scramble to fill in their seasons with other fare in time for a subscription marketing deadline. Traditionally, profits from the Broadway series have enabled the presenters to also offer higher cultural attractions, which do not break even at the box office. Many such presenters report this business model to be in jeopardy, however, with costs rising and a dearth of the megahits at which audience members will throw their wallets in droves. One hopes this is only temporary. See more on the national touring of Broadway shows in chapter 14.

Popular Music Presenters

As will be noted in chapter 15 on this high-volume element of show touring, many presenters depend on the significant presence of popular music in the season as a source of profits, which will subsidize the higher cultural fare. A certain number of music acts that book early will be committed in time for the core subscription offering, with others added as their availability is announced. As many music tours are not announced a year in advance, and can be put on sale quite late and sell without benefit of subscription, programming popular music can serve to fill in around the more monolithic Broadway programming.

Role of Bulk Purchasers: Conglomerates or Promoters

While it is addressed in more detail in the separate chapters on popular music and Broadway touring (chapters 14 and 15), in looking at presenters' relationships to agencies, one cannot ignore the role of the conglomerates and, in the case of pop music touring, the regional promoters who can play a significant role. These are organizations that in essence *bulk buy* the acts and control their routing within a given region and time period. Their relationships to the venues in which the acts play can range from a) purchase and presentation by the local presenter, b) copresentation with the local presenter with risk shared, or c) *four-wall* rental[3] of the venue and complete presentation and risk assumption by the promoters.

The involvement of the middle people—the conglomerates or promoters—results in two important benefits: 1) the promoters bring bulk-buying power to the relationship with the shows, making productions and artists available to presenters and venues that would otherwise be unattainable, and 2) depending on the nature of the deals made in each venue on the tour, the promoter spreads his risk so that a financial loss in one market might be compensated in another. The negative, of course, is that local venues and presenters have less impact and access to the agents and artists, and on program choice. In markets with more than one venue, this can be particularly challenging to those theaters considered less attractive to promoters for conducting business (smaller seating capacity, worse location, insufficient parting, high priced labor, etc.). Promoters like copresentation relationships with local presenters and venue operators who have strong membership or marketing programs in place as they are often better able to reach and obtain the audiences than the promoter, who may be based elsewhere.

In situations involving promoters, these people serve as the middle people between the agents and the presenters, and in this case the presenters and agents will have little or no direct communication. If the promoter/presenter relationship is ongoing and one of shared risk, the presenter will usually have a voice in deciding which productions will come in, but the emphasis will be on those productions the promoter has secured for the season.

Obviously another implication of promoter involvement is that there is another player in the relationship expecting a piece of the profit from the engagement, thereby splitting the pie into more pieces and reducing what might otherwise have been available to the presenter. As access to potentially unattainable artists is provided to the presenters and risk is traded off, so is potential reward.

Presenters' relationships with agents are comparatively simple: agents are the people whom presenters approach to obtain the services of the productions they want on their seasons unless forced to work through middlepersons instead. We will now progress to the process of negotiation between the two.

Endnotes

1 Trav S. D., *No Applause Please—Just Throw Money: The Book that Made Vaudeville Famous* (New York: Faber and Faber, Inc., 2005).

2 See *http://ec.europa.eu/culture/eac/other_actions/cap_europ/cap_eu_en.html*.

3 As the name implies, *four-wall* rental refers to the rental of the venue, often not including equipment or staff, all of which is paid for in addition.

CHAPTER 5

Negotiating the Deal

Negotiating is an art of its own, with many books written on this subject alone. There is no one style, and individuals will use different techniques according to the situation.

And there are those who will say that art is not a mere commodity, and it is wrong to even think of booking the performing arts as negotiation in the same manner as buying or selling a house or a used car. It is not a house or a car, of course, but it is negotiation nonetheless, and an understanding of some of the basic forces at work in the process is an essential part of tour booking.

What's Being Sold: The Element of Time

The essential commodity being purchased in a tour booking transaction is not only the show itself, but the show in the context of a calendar. What the producer has to sell are dates. And time (at least for our purposes) only moves in one direction! So booking an engagement to take place yesterday is of course absolutely worthless. And paradoxically those dates get more and less valuable the closer they are, with the determinant of the value range being how badly the buyer needs to buy or the seller to sell.

The *Need Quotient*

The degree of need is what we might call the *need quotient* or the amount to which one side or the other is under pressure to conclude the deal being negotiated.

For the buyer this might be based on factors such as this being the really hot show this season with his audiences clamoring to have it come to town, perhaps the show is only touring this season with an artist about to retire, the presenter might have a date open in the theater calendar that must be filled to complete a series with this show being the perfect fit, or there is the possibility that if she does not conclude a deal for this show another presenter down the street will get it and create competition in the market. And there are those artists who are so phenomenally famous and hard to get and easy to sell to the public that the buyer will feel privileged to be on the artist's calendar whether one month or three years in advance.

For the agent, the *need quotient* will most likely be determined by some combination of date and geography—the need to fill a hole in a tour with the show already in a certain geographic territory—though there may be other issues such as the need for a show to preview and work out technical issues before coming into New York, or the fact that the artist has demanded to play that particular community for some personal reason. The prominence of the presenter will also be an important factor. Working on the assumption that this show will play this market sooner or later, the agent will place a premium on selling the show to the higher-class venue or the one with the best location and audience accessibility.

Who Called Who? What's the Goal?

Whichever side first contacted the other generally gives the one being called a very slight negotiating advantage by offering the first expression of interest—like white opening in chess—though depending on the balance of need quotients this advantage might be very slight indeed.

If the presenter has called the agent, it is likely that she knows enough about the show to want to hear more or that she is ready to book it, knows dates that could work in the theater's calendar, and has some sense of what she is willing and can expect to pay. Assuming she has done some homework and has more than a passing interest in the show, she is calling to try to get the show or at least see if her available dates and budget match with the producer's expectations and availability. On a first call she's usually willing to mention dates, but less willing a) to reveal the true extent of her interest for fear it will tip her hand and weaken her bargaining position and b) to admit to the highest fee she will pay as it would leave no bargaining room (and because of course she'd rather pay less if possible).

If the agent has called the presenter, all the reverse is true: the agent knows up front he'd like to sell the show to this presenter, with some sense of date availabilities (*avails*), and on what minimum terms. But he is probably not likely to reveal how much he needs this engagement in his tour plan as it will weaken his bargaining position, nor is he likely to let the presenter know his real financial bottom line in the first conversation.

Following the rule that everything we say here has exceptions, of course the initial disclosure on both sides can work the opposite. Working on the presumption that the artist will choose to go where he knows he is really appreciated and will be well cared for—in addition to getting a good financial deal—the presenter might say up front that he is absolutely *dying* to have the artist in and is calling to make that happen. Or the agent might take a plunge, put all his cards on the table, and admit that he desperately needs this date to fill a hole in a tour offering the prospect of a discounted fee as a carrot to induce the presenter to take the artist on one of the dates offered.

PERSONAL HISTORY COUNTS

Realizing that many presenters and agents do business together season after season, negotiating for various artists, it never hurts for either side to be seen as having done a favor for the other side—the agent making a special effort to adjust a tour to suit a presenter's calendar, or a presenter accommodating an agent's need to fill a hole in a tour. Remember that the international touring world is a "small town" and favors get remembered!

Doing Homework

The Internet has made doing one's homework in advance of the first call so easy there is no excuse for not doing it.

Before an agent calls a presenter to offer a show, there is no longer any excuse for him not to have spent a few minutes on the presenter's Web site to determine the scale of show being offered by this presenter, the venues being used, and the configuration of engagements (one nighters, multiweek runs, weekends versus weekdays, etc.).

Likewise the presenter, through the show's Web site, can quickly determine what fellow presenters have recently brought in the production and can often get advice from presenter colleagues about the suitability of that production for his community before calling.

As an agent, if I sense that a presenter's pattern indicates potential to bring in my shows beyond just one booking, I will call and get on the mailing list (e-mail and/or post) of the presenting organization as a means of keeping tabs on their programming to track volume, scale of productions, ticket pricing, and run configurations. As a presenter, I often talked with other presenters about their experience with a show before calling the agent.

First Conversation: Places to Start

Assuming both sides are reluctant to reveal their financial bottom lines early on or how high their need quotients are, an important element they can and should discuss early on is the calendar. Regardless of who called first, a discussion of dates available (in the theater and on the show's tour calendar) or even times of year is safe as it won't reveal too much and might even allow each side to position itself more strongly for the negotiation to come.

In an effort to achieve some negotiating advantage, the presenter might say, "Well, my season is almost complete but I do have just these one or two dates still open," or the agent, "We've had such demand for this artist all over the world, but let me see if I can possibly squeeze you in" (of course there is the question of how far from reality either of these might be!).

Likewise, a discussion of how many performances over how many days, the seating capacity of the theater, and the ticket price range and gross potential income provide an exchange of information important to the financial discussions to come. It also allows a sense of whether run configurations preferred by this presenter are aligned with the producer's preferences for the show. If the venue has 400 seats, and the presenter would like to consider fourteen performances over a two week run (or longer), a high-profile artist used to a series of higher-paying one-night stands in 3,500-seat performing art centers at high performance fees would probably find such an engagement unacceptable as the per-performance fee would be much lower, while many theater companies (and dance, if the stage is big enough) would be delighted. Conversely, the agent for an intimate drama will say no to an offer of a one-night stand in a 3,500-seat theater as the audience experience would be unacceptably compromised by the size of the venue.

Finally, a discussion of recent presentation of like shows (by the presenter) and of past engagements in like markets for this show (by the agent) give other areas of early discussion, though also holding potential for exaggeration— the presenter often claiming that similar artists did not sell all that well as a justification for a lower fee and the agent claiming exaggerated sell outs in similar markets as a justification for higher fee.

Best Alternative to a Negotiated Agreement (BATNA)

In the informative compendium of articles on negotiation titled *Winning Negotiations That Preserve Relations* published by the Harvard Business School Press,[1] business writer Anne Field, in her essay titled "How to Negotiate with a Hard-Nosed Adversary," advises:

> *When you're desperate to make a deal, that weakens your bargaining position. To strengthen your hand, think through what would happen if you were unable to strike a deal. In other words, what's your BATNA? (That is, your Best Alternative to a Negotiated Agreement.) The key here is to remember that you may not be the only one who needs the deal. Do some research beforehand to see what would happen to the other side if you were to back out.*

She continues:

> *Knowing your BATNA makes it easy to determine the worst-case terms you'll accept, which means that you're much less likely to be browbeaten into an agreement that you'll later regret. Plus, when your opponent digs in her heels, you'll know it's time to do the same.*

This is another way to look at the need quotient described above and is an important concept in relation to the booking of shows for two reasons: 1) it encourages both sides to explore all the possible alternatives on dates, venues, etc., pertaining to having the show in, and 2) it helps each side think through its real bottom line. The agent should know, going into the negotiations, if he has alternatives for this show to this engagement in this venue on these dates, and the presenter should know all her alternate dates for this show and her alternate shows if this negotiation does not succeed—or is it okay for the theater to stay dark?

Who Says the First Number?

Being the first to put out a fee quotation is hard—sometimes the hardest part of the process. And who should propose the first number is a hotly debated point among the experts. John Ilich in his book, *The Complete Idiot's Guide to Winning through Negotiation*,[2] advises that if someone has to, let it be the other side. Max H. Bazerman in *Negotiating Rationally*[3] counters that putting out the first number can set the overall financial frame and influence the final outcome, and it should be you and offered early (whichever side you're on).

As a rule, the side that made the first call can reasonably be expected to name a first number. If the agent called the presenter, it is reasonable for the presenter to ask, "How much?" and the agent to provide an asking price. Likewise, if the presenter called, it is reasonable for the agent to ask if the presenter "has a figure in mind." Most shows have already worked out a pricing chart with the agent in advance: how much for a single, a split (half week, presumably shared with another half elsewhere, and skewed for weekend versus weeknights), a single full week, a multiple-week run. Unless there is a compelling reason to quote otherwise, this is normally the best place for the agent to start.

When Should the First Number Come Out

Roger Fisher, in his landmark book *Getting to Yes*,[4] suggests delay, cautioning that offering a number too early might close off exploration of interests and possibilities of other factors that will influence the final deal. Whether that is always true in our case is up for debate, but it serves as a reminder that one should never be hasty in getting a number out.

The timing of quotation (if from agent) or offer (if from presenter) in tour booking is in part influenced by the complexity of the engagement being discussed and when what details are put forward. If a presenter calls an agent and says, "How much for that show?" obviously the agent can't answer the question without knowing how many performances, over what amount of time, and whether the presenter is seeking an *all in* deal or expecting to pay a fee plus providing add-ons such as travel, freight, accommodations, royalties, and perhaps per diems. So in this instance, the agent has a valid reason for a delay in quoting. But if the presenter says, "I'd like an all-in fee quote (inclusive of travel, freight, accommodations, and per diems) for a single performance of this show in my 2,000-seat theater, with a projected average ticket price of $30, on (specific date)," there is not much reason for the agent not to quote as long as the show is available on the requested date.

Tips on Quoting the First Number

The following early dialogue, or much like it, is common.

The Agent Might Say:
This artist generally receives guarantees in the range of XXXXXXX, plus accommodations, freight, and travel (remember to quote all the money and cost items up front!). But if you can accommodate this or this date, we can save some money on travel and amortize rehearsal and I can work with that fee.

An alternate ending after the "But" is: . . . *if you can commit early and allow us time to build a tour around you, we can . . .*

Or even better: . . . *if you can help us find two more dates to fill up the week, we can offer you . . .*

Any of these, of course, will be preceded by something like: *This artist just performed at ABC Theater in X community (similar size theater and community to that of presenter with whom talking) and sold 95 percent. The audience was on its feet, the press raved and the presenter is thrilled—call and ask!*

And it will be followed with something like: *[Artist's name] would really like to play your community as he has a deep emotional connection with (the south, horses, the desert, mountains, chocolate, open pit mines, rich people, acid rain, etc.).*

The Presenter Might Say:

I realize this is below what an artist of his stature is worth, but given our limited budget and policy of low community ticket pricing, I hope he might be able to accept in the range of XXXX.

An opener such as this is often framed with lines such as:

- *Our mountains (seaside, skiing, open pit mine, etc.) are so fantastic that many artists are willing to come for below their normal fees and take extra rest time here.*

- *The acoustics in our theater are so fantastic that musicians practically pay us for the pleasure of playing this stage.*

- *I shouldn't tell you this, but famous Artist Y was willing to accept a fee in that range just to play here.*

- *Ask any artist who has played here—we will take such good care of him, he will fall in love with it here. Artist Z wants to buy a house here!*

- *With our location, we are accessible to so many places and can fit into almost any tour in the region.*

- *We have a good track record of bringing artists back once introduced successfully to our audiences, so if you can give us a price break on the first engagement to help us introduce the artist to our audience, it might lead to a long-term relationship.* (Sometimes that's true!)

Another way around the first number issue, especially in late-cycle negotiating, is for one side to invite the other to "make your best offer." If said by the buyer to the seller it might be "name your lowest price." This puts the onus of first number mentioned on the other side of the table. It also signals that the side saying this is ready to work seriously toward a deal if the price is right.

Tonal Difference between Commercial and Cultural

There is a tonal difference at this stage between commercial negotiations, where the expectation is that the show should generate profit in the engagement, and nonprofit or "cultural" negotiations, where it is clear that no matter what the fee, the presenter is likely to lose money against the box office income and will be arranging to subsidize the presentation.

In commercial negotiations, there is likely to be discussion of a "split of the back end" (a share of profits in addition to guaranteed fee) versus a "buy out" (a flat fee with no percentage) involved, and it is expected that the seating capacity of the venue and planned ticket prices (multiplied to determine gross potential income) will have been shared by the presenter early in the discussions and that the terms—fee and, if appropriate, percentage payable to the artist—will be discussed in that light. It is not unusual for the agent to invite the presenter to "make an offer," which is often done in writing, showing an outline of the gross potential, the presenter's other costs, such as the venue rental, tech, and marketing, and then showing the proposed fee and back-end split, if any, to the artist in the total context.

In nonprofit negotiations, where there may be no hope of a back end or profits of any nature, it comes down to how much the agent really needs the date on the tour and whether the presenter can and will pay it. This is not to say that there is never a back-end split in such deals, but far rarer. Such would be the case if the presenter is planning to put the show in a large house, but expects to sell only a relatively small percentage of available seats. In this case there might be a hypothetical profit (or "excess revenue over expense" in nonprofit parlance), and it sometimes gives the producer or artist a warm fuzzy feeling to think that in an ideal world the show will break all expectations and sell out and a percentage will kick in.

But the sad fact is that many higher cultural shows simply do not sell the percentages of more popular entertainment, and the notion of a split of the back end is illusory. Most presenters are happy to offer a back-end percentage in such circumstances as they are not budgeting with any expectation of profit anyway. And most nonprofit touring organizations such as dance companies are not in a financial position to take a risk on tour dates and likewise do not go into most engagements with any expectation of or reliance on back end to cover costs.

International Differences: Weekly versus Per-Performance Fees

Presenters in many countries outside of the US, notably in most European countries, are used to paying for shows on a per-performance basis rather than per week. While this corresponds to expectations among many American musicians, it does not align with most American dancer and actor contracts, which are based on guaranteed weekly salaries with a maximum number of performances possible in a week.

The precise definition of a week, especially in international touring where distances are often greater, must take into account the extra travel time. Getting from the US to Asia generally takes two days just for travel over and one day back, and most artists require a day to recover from jet lag once they arrive. Many artists are reluctant to travel the distance across the Atlantic or Pacific for only one performance and would require a minimum of one, two, or even three weeks of work to justify the trip. In the case of musicians, they also might have a minimum number of dates in order to undertake the effort of long-distance travel.

Artists foreign to the US and traveling to perform in the US may start by quoting based on fee per performance, as they are used to in their home territories. But if the visit is to include week-long runs, they can expect insistence by the tour producer on renegotiation to the weekly fee expectations in the country.

Thus in foreign negotiations, the fee basis to be sorted out before the agent starts quoting terms to presenters has special considerations both of differing expectations of fee structure and extra travel time.

What Besides the Money?

Keep in mind that in every deal, commercial or nonprofit, there are additional considerations besides the money that can be big factors in the negotiations. Often in discussion are a) technical stage costs (What theatrical equipment is the show carrying and what is expected to be provided by the presenter?), b) accommodations (How many single and double rooms, and who pays?), c) travel and freight, and d) availability of marketing support materials.

Negotiators may establish the framework for all of these elements before getting to the money. Alternately, the first fee quotation (from the agent) or offer (from the presenter) should be qualified with these early in the conversation or there will be the risk of a perception of bad faith in the negotiations. If the presenter is offering a fee and does not want to deal with accommodations, freight, and travel, he should say that the fee is offered "all in, inclusive of . . ." Likewise, if the agent quotes a number, in the same breath or page he should clearly state what other considerations he is expecting that will cost the presenter money. Quoting a fee today and adding tomorrow, "Oh, by the way, that is in addition to travel, freight, and accommodations," for a large troupe can significantly (and negatively!) affect both the negotiations and the trust between the negotiating parties.

Most producers will establish a budget for their touring, including what is expected to be covered from within the fee, and what is needed in addition, to serve as a guideline for the agent as he goes into negotiations. This budget normally establishes the minimums needed for the show to go out, with the producer and agent hopeful of obtaining higher.

Formal Offers from Presenters

Some producers and artists' managers take the position that all financial discussions must start with an offer from the buyer, usually including an analysis of the gross potential revenue for the presentation, so they can see how the offer relates as a percentage of the presenter's potential income. This is especially true in commercial entertainment but carries over into nonprofits as well.

There is logic to this from the producer's side in that in one stroke he is putting the pressure of first number on the presenter and insisting on seeing the revenue context, putting him in a much stronger response position. The negative to this approach early in the negotiation is that it tends to cut off discussion and force the presenter into a programming decision early—perhaps prematurely—since once a formal offer is made, if accepted, it is considered binding.

There are sometimes advantages to keeping the negotiations less formal for a while as each side feels the other out and also determines what its BATNA or need quotient really is.

The issue of formality leads to the question of when in the negotiating process written exchanges should begin. The answer is *as soon as actual terms are being mentioned.* The primary reason, of course, is so you have a track record of the back-and-forth exchange on terms and don't end up in the game of "oh, I thought you quoted . . . !" Additionally, some people get uncomfortable talking about numbers and find it easier to exchange in writing.

E-mail is of course well suited for this purpose. So if you are pressed to offer the first quote or at any point in the negotiations, don't hesitate to offer to send it by e-mail.

History Helps

There is no question that a positive history between an agency and presenter helps in this process—remember that it is a people business! Not only does it help one side getting the other on the phone, but successful engagements booked between the parties previously can serve as reference or basis of comparison for the current discussion. The buyer can use reference arguments to try for a lower fee: "compared to X last year, this show has only Y number of people traveling and has not appeared on the *Tonight Show*," to which the agent might respond, "yes, but it is a simpler show technically, and your lower technical costs coupled with the lower accommodations you are being asked to provide free up more money for a higher fee. *Plus* this show has further to travel to get to you and it *has* been featured on the *Today Show*." Of course killer arguments based on history may include the presenter saying, "I lost my shirt on that last presentation and you owe me one . . . " or the agent saying, "you made a fortune on that last artist without any back-end sharing with the producer, and my artists will start leaving me if I don't get them deals that are more fair!"

The Walk Away Offer: Go Right to the Bottom Line

Throwing all the negotiating techniques aside, there are buyers and sellers in certain situations who are refreshingly candid. Their candor fits into the concept of the *walk away offer*, which involves going right to the bottom line to cut off negotiation and either get the deal on the offerer's terms or walk away. Of course the risk in this is that both sides miss out on exploration of variables that might make the difference in closing a deal, but if the need quotient is low and both sides have other options, the risk in this approach is not so dire.

A buyer might say, "I am prepared to present the show on any one of the following dates and I can pay this much." As we will examine later in analyzing the exchange of documents, such an offer will usually have an expiration date.

An agent might say: "I really need to fill this date on this tour for this show. You are perfectly located and an ideal venue for us. The normal fee is $X but I will take $Y if you would agree to present the artist on that date. That's the lowest I can go."

This *bottom line* style of negotiation is most meaningful late in the booking cycle when the agent and producer already know they are unlikely to end up with a deal that is highly profitable based on guarantee (at least to the producer) and also when time is short to conclude a deal. They are primarily concerned with filling dates (in the venue calendar or the show's routing) and, at a minimum, trying not to lose money, rather than (for the producer) paying the artists to sit in hotels and lose money and (for the presenter) having a dark day in the theater or a hole in the season.

As the producer in this situation is likely to be receiving below what he wanted, the agent may push hard for some back-end split in hopes that the show sells well and makes up on the percentage. In such circumstance the presenter, recognizing that her downside risk is being attenuated by a lower up-front guarantee, will most likely agree to share any upside.

Bottom Feeding

On the buyer side, such last minute booking is the opportunity for what is known somewhat crassly as *bottom feeding*—taking advantage of other presenters who have already arranged to bring a show into the region and then seeking a low-price, add-on date late in the process. Unless the bottom-feeding presenter is highly compelled to fill a date in the theater, faces direct competition, or must lock in early for a subscription deadline, she may troll through shows passing through the region with last minute dates to fill at lower prices, knowing that the agents' rates at this late stage will be highly negotiable in order to fill open dates in the tour.

There are presenters who book this way on a regular basis, especially in smaller and/or poorer communities where they cannot afford to pay asking fees. Such organizations will often structure their marketing to allow for later public offers than the normal spring subscription renewals to permit last-minute, low-priced bookings. And in fact there are some booking agencies that specialize in buying up unsold dates on shows' tours and selling them off at discounted prices.

In this business there are people who will try to turn a profit from almost anything!

Nonnegotiable Fees

There are some producers in the enviable position of saying, "That's the fee for my show and it is not negotiable." This of course works if the show is in great demand, if the fee quoted is reasonable for the show being offered, and/or if the producer is prepared to accept the potential consequence of not obtaining a lot of bookings, opting for higher revenue per engagement than a volume of engagements. It certainly makes negotiation easier for the agent as he has nothing to back-and-forth about. It also relieves the parties on the issue of who says the first number.

It's a *walk away* quote every time!

Take your Time

It is important for neither side to rush into a decision if he or she is unsure of his or her position, and to be wary of a presenter or agent who tries to hurry the deal. It is a common negotiating tactic for one side to attempt to control the negotiating dynamic by setting a deadline and threatening to rescind the offer if not accepted instantly.

Obviously there are factors such as deadlines for printing season brochures (presenters) or deadlines from alternate presenters who would otherwise take the date, albeit at a lower fee (agent) when haste is needed and legitimate, but be wary of the "offer expires at 5 PM today" tactic.

Personal Hints

At the risk of "never being able to work in this town again" and without naming names, I will reveal a couple of tactics I have observed or experienced that
might add to the reader's negotiating tool kit.

From Shared Agent/Presenter Perspectives

The further ahead of the performance dates the negotiations are taking place,
the more both sides can afford to *shop* dates and fees and seek alternatives.

The agent, if being asked to commit an isolated date for the show very early
on, without knowing what other activity may build around it and without pressure to complete an impending tour, will expect to receive a higher level fee.

The presenter will be aware that by making an early commitment he is
providing an *anchor* date around which the agent will have time to build a
tour, and therefore may try to argue for a lower fee.

Perception of Name Recognition and Expectation of Audience Appeal

The public awareness and appeal of a show or artist, of course, underlie much
in negotiation. If the presenter can be convinced that the show is already
known and in demand by his audience, he is far more likely to book it, give
it prime placement on the calendar, and pay good money.

But keep in mind that the *perception* of public awareness is half the battle,
especially in performance genres with poorly quantifiable public appeal
criteria, and perception is often subjective. In popular music, for instance,
there are highly quantifiable statistics to quote having to do with number of
radio plays, CDs sold, and iPod downloads as well as the number of fans in
specific markets and the artist's position on popularity charts.

Public appeal and awareness is far less easy to determine with most other
genres, however; and much will depend on the means by which the agent and
producer bring the show to the attention of the presenter and the legitimizing elements available. If the artist appeared on the *David Letterman Show* or
Prairie Home Companion, it can be assumed that a lot of people saw or heard
it. But did they love it? And does it matter if they loved it, or is the simple
fact that the artist appeared on a nationally broadcast program known to be
experienced by millions sufficient to attract the requisite number of people
to buy tickets?

An old adage in the public relations business says, "Ink is ink" (coming from the old days when the printed page dominated the transmission
of news), the theory being that having one's name known had value regardless of whether it was viewed in a positive or negative light. Certainly some
celebrities may be reviled by the public (I promised not to name names!)

but continue to draw public and media attention and would probably sell a lot of tickets to live stage appearances. But if you have a ballet that is widely known but universally detested, are you going to have an easier time selling it if everyone has heard about it but most don't like it than if they have never heard of it at all? (Would that the art form of ballet should draw such public discourse and controversy!)

Field Strength of Agency or Presenter

Obviously the biggest elephant in the room is the fame and salability of the show or artist. But in the selling process the reputation and clout of the agent, presenter, and producer count as well, if in more nuanced and less quantifiable ways. Of course the clout of these three players ultimately reflects the weight of the artists with which they are currently or recently affiliated.

A presenter will take a call from an agency representing some heavyweight artists and listen to a pitch on a new artist more attentively than he might if the agent was not affiliated with the other artists.

Artists will want to be seen at arts centers that are known for presentation of the very best as such engagements send a message about the artists to other such venues.

The influence of the producer is more complex as there is such a large variety. But certainly a theatrical production coming from known and respected institutions such as the American Repertory Theatre at Harvard University, Los Angeles' Center Theatre Group, or The Acting Company will automatically attract attention by dint of the producing organizations, as will a music ensemble touring under the name of The Juilliard School or Jazz at Lincoln Center, or an event from The Apollo Theater or the John F. Kennedy Center for the Performing Arts.

Interplay of Scale between Presenter and Agency

A presenter in a smaller community, perhaps a bit out of the way geographi- cally, will be eager to earn the attention and respect of agencies—especially the big ones—to have an early opportunity to book their shows and not be offered only the fills and leftovers. Such a presenter might do an influential agency a favor in filling a tour date for a lesser known artist offered by that agency to earn an informal promise of earlier dibs on more significant artists in the future.

In the reverse, smaller agencies may have a hard time getting the attention of the "big girls" of presenters, taking several years of mailings, calls, and seek- ing opportunities to meet at conferences. Once broken through, the agency will work hard to earn the trust and respect of such presenters, seeking that perfect balance between how much to stay *in her face* without abusing the welcome.

Some Specific Suggestions

The Power of Silence, Especially on the Phone. A long, pregnant silence in response to a number from the other side is often interpreted as displeasure at what has been quoted (or offered), eliciting a fresh upward (or downward) quotation.

Respond Promptly; Keep the Dialogue Moving. I am amazed at the number of bookings I have concluded, both as presenter and agent, by simply being prompt in response and keeping the negotiation moving. It certainly beats out those agents and presenters who apply the technique of not calling back, thinking they are somehow strengthening their negotiating position thereby! I have attempted to maintain a *24-hour rule* wherever I have worked, which means that calls to my office will be responded to within one business day, even if the response is to say "not interested" or "I don't have the answer yet but I'm working on it."

Write Down Terms Discussed. As a venue manager I had a producer who occasionally rented my theater. In the second conversation about an engagement, he inevitably would start off with "I understand your fee is X," which was lower than I had quoted. He did it with such sincerity, and as I was younger and more naive, I would often immediately feel guilty for seeming to switch my quotes until I realized that this was his standard negotiating tactic to try for lower rates. Whether you are buying or selling, and whether the terms mentioned are from you or the other side, *always* keep notes at the time. As elsewhere recommended, a follow-up email or other written confirmation of what was discussed, even if final agreement has not yet been reached, rarely hurts.

For Agents Only

Experience shows that saying to most presenters, *The artist will be in the area. Would you like to take a date?* has far more appeal than saying, *Would you like to take responsibility for bringing the artist to your area?* The first booking commitment has special value; seek the leadership anchor date(s) first and then approach the followers on this basis.

Prioritize Target "Anchors" versus "Fills" in Advance

Who are the leaders among presenters and who the followers? Whether selling single-night engagements or multiweek runs, you will end up setting scheduling priorities based in large part on whether a presenter will commit early and hopefully pay the full fee, or will string you along and seek a discount. As noted above, those anchors are critical to getting the show into a region. And you will want to maintain the greatest degree of scheduling flexibility for the higher-paying presenters, which means you will not want to commit a prime date to a discount payer only to later find that that is the one date the higher payer can take! Presumably, part of buying at discount is that the presenter waits longer for date confirmation, and also in many cases takes weeknights instead of the more generally desirable weekend dates.

While the agent may list all his targets and make initial contacts at once, he should know ahead of time who will get the priority on filling dates. There is a premium on early commitment by a presenter so the agent can peg a time frame and region for the show's tour. The question, of course, is whether on the one hand the presenter should receive a discount for early commitment (and especially for early fee deposit) or, conversely, should pay the highest price for the show to commit a date early on. In most cases, if the presenter needs to know that the date is locked early, she will expect to pay the asking price, and since the agent doesn't know yet how well coordinated the tour will end up being, he is less willing to negotiate down at this stage. If the presenter needs a discounted price, the agent may ask her to hold out her offer longer while surrounding engagements are secured.

Every presenter works on a slightly different planning timetable. It is never too early to call or e-mail and ask when it will be appropriate for you to bring something to their attention for presentation consideration. They will either give you time frames in which to contact them, invite you to pitch now, or tell you its too late for next season but open the door for the following. Either way, you have moved an important step forward. At the point that you do send materials, it can mean a great deal that your cover letter sent with the marketing materials can now open with *"Per our phone conversation . . . "* Hopefully this will have a positive impact on obtaining a response and follow up from the presenter.

Do your Homework about the Presenter's Program Pattern and Context

As previously noted but worth repeating: get to know everything you can about the size of the venue, the ticket price range, the types of shows typically presented by this presenter, the suitability of local audiences to your show, the number of performances normally booked of a given show, and whether bookings only take place on weekends or weekdays, all *before* you make contact. Be prepared to make your case based on appropriateness of your show to the presenter's pattern. An Internet lookup of the current season at the presenter's organization or venue will quickly give you most of the information you need once you know what to look for.

Along with knowing the patterns and constraints of the presenter you are about to call, try to gain knowledge of who the alternate presenters are in the presenter's community and what he is up against. Are you about to call the biggest player in town, the runner up, or the hot newcomer? How might that affect how you pitch? Do you have an alternative if this presenter declines? But *watch out* for thinking that you can call and pitch to all of them at once. Even big cities are "small towns" when it comes to information flow, and if you are calling each and simultaneously offering an "exclusive special offer," it may come back to haunt you if it turns out the presenters in the target community get together monthly for lunch and compare notes!

Filling a Doughnut Hole

If as an agent you absolutely need to fill a hole in a "doughnut" tour (one with engagements on both sides of an undesired open date) and are limited as to the date available and acceptable geographic region, you are in a weaker position and your need quotient is high. This is one of the very least desirable positions to be in since if the date does not get filled, it can mean not only a loss of revenue but lack of income against the costs of accommodations, salaries, and per diem while the company is sitting and waiting on the Road (assuming the tour is not close enough to home to make it worthwhile to return and then go out again).

This may well be a situation in which a deal structure heavily weighted to back-end sharing is appropriate, lowering a fill-in presenter's downside risk as an inducement to take the show. If the producer can get accommodations paid and a reasonable shot at some percentage of ticket revenue, she is still better off than with an empty date in the middle of a tour.

The Venue Manager is your Friend

Remember that even though a venue itself may not want to take the risk to present your show, it still wants the theater to be booked. If your show is right for the venue size and audiences, and your desired date is available in the theater, they'll want you in—just not at their risk. If a venue/presenter declines to present, don't hang up without first asking if one of your desired tour date(s) is/are open in the hall's calendar. If so, ask for advice on outside presenters or regional promoters who do business in the venue to which they would refer you. They know the local presenters whom they trust and who get involved in different artistic genres. If you can convince the outside presenter to bring your show into the venue you have done their rental job for them! Sometimes, if the date is fairly close in and not likely to be otherwise booked, the venue will offer to accept a percentage of box office in lieu of part or all of its rental fee to help the deal go forward, noting that it likely also makes money in areas such as concessions, ticket handling, and parking fees.

Shopping Price instead of Artistry

If a presenter seems overly eager to have a price quote early on, she is probably shopping *price* instead of *artistry*—that is, she has only so much budget left to work with and is trying to find an acceptable artist within that cost. If, as an agent, I sense early in the conversation that they already have a fee cap in mind, rather than shooting out a number, I might counter their request for price by asking what budget range they are working with. I expect them to start low, but if we are at all close—and of course depending on my need quotient and BATNA—I can counter with, "We're not that far off, let's keep talking."

Quote for a Larger Time Frame than Requested

This applies specifically in the case of a request from a presenter for a fee quote for a one-night engagement for an artist who will not, or strongly prefers to not, go out for an isolated single date. So if the question is "How much for this show for one night," rather than answering directly, I start my response with "For the show to go out we need to obtain income of $X for a week, but multiple single dates are possible within a week," and proceed from there.

This response achieves several things: a) it puts the presenter on notice that in order to obtain a single-night booking at a reasonable fee, she is going to have to cooperate with scheduling and routing in order to obtain the weekly fee goal, b) it invites the presenter to consider more than one night since having to find additional presenters to fill a week adds time and uncertainty to our process, and c) it invites the presenter to think of colleagues in the region she knows through local association that she might help persuade to join in the tour in order to achieve her objective. Related to the latter, I might suggest that this presenter could end up with a more favorable fee as a result of assisting in seeking neighboring bookings.

Mention all the Cost Variables in the Terms When You First Quote

Realizing that there are some costs that will vary between the time of negotiation and the engagement, such as the cost of fuel for transportation and freight, international currency exchange rates, and variable withholding taxes, it is important to identify those variables up front. If I quote a fee plus travel and freight, I realize that before we are through the presenter will undoubtedly seek a cap on the costs of travel and freight. But the later we obtain quotations on those costs, the likelier they are not to change, and of course I don't want to go through the costing exercise in depth until I know if the presenter is serious and we are within negotiable financial range.

What to Do if the Presenter Says, "No Way, Too High!"

Tone counts for a lot, and cost is relative. Listen carefully to the presenter's tone. Is she saying, "I really wish I could bring in this artist, but I just can't at that price," or is it a polite way for her to end the conversation because she is not really interested. If the former, a couple of suggestions:

- If your fee includes travel and freight and royalties, ask if the presenter has a separate line for those items in her budget. Many presenters do, but may not think of this. Money is money, so you don't care if they offer a separate amount toward freight costs and lower the fee accordingly as long as the total is workable, and sometimes an arts center or university bureaucracy will have multiple line items available to the presenter.

- Ask what the presenter projects as the likely ticket revenue from this presentation and the acceptable break point (or percentage of gross potential). Help explore other budget areas—the presenter may be budgeting too high on the technical costs, for instance, and by lowering that can increase the fee line. Likewise, in getting into a discussion of break point and upside potential (profit), you may find a fee plus back-end formula that is acceptable to the producer.

- Invite an offer. When all is said and done, and you have quoted your terms and the presenter has regaled you with how stingy her audience is, how tickets have not been selling well, how high her technical and marketing costs are, etc., bring yourself back to the role of middleman and invite her to make her best offer for you to take to the producer. You want this offer in writing. It may be less than is wanted and even than the producer will ultimately accept, but a written offer nonetheless focuses everyone's minds and brings the producer to consider his real cost flexibility. Keep in mind that while you are technically negotiating on behalf of the producer with the buyer, you are in effect negotiating between the two sides. Producers can often be creative with their budgets when they want to accept certain dates!

- Negotiate your commission. Remember that you also have the power to reduce your commission on a particular engagement if you feel it is better to have some income from an engagement than to lose it altogether and if by getting this engagement as an *anchor* you have the potential to build a tour around it that will ultimately generate more income for yourself (obviously you want to watch out for setting a precedent this producer will come to expect).

• Ask the presenter to help you secure another date in his region that will allow the producer to amortize certain costs, such as travel and freight to the region, and to accept a lower fee. Often presenters are in closer touch than you are with area presenters.

• Invite the presenter to consider an expansion of activities. If it costs the producer the same to offer one or two performances or throw in a master class, suggest that instead of lowering the fee the artist do more for the same money.

Think of your Relationship with the Presenter as Long Term

Always keep your eye on the fact that whether or not this deal goes through, you will want to have access to this presenter in the future. Related advice is that you will always serve your producer client best if you are able to share your passion for the artist's work while maintaining a dispassion about the business side. *Love the show, but never fall in love with the deal!* There is again a delicate balance here. Don't sell this show short to curry favor with the presenter, but at the same time attempt to conduct your negotiations in a manner that insures that the presenter will feel comfortable to work with you again in the future. Part of this is listening to the presenter carefully. If she says, "I like this artist and will present him but not this season," if you feel you've exhausted your arguments in favor of this season, accept it, flag it for follow up a year from now and move on. If that market is critical to a tour this season, seek another presenter.

Don't Over- or Undersell

Depending on your style as an agent, by all means be persistent and aggressive in pursuit of your client's interests, but never wear out your welcome with the presenter. You do not do yourself or your clients any service by that. One approach I find effective is to refer to the presenter's *consideration list*. This is a list most presenters have more or less formally—those shows under serious consideration for a season, which they will winnow down and from which ultimately select their final choices. It is often gentler and more comfortable during the process, instead of asking, "are you going to book my show?" to ask "do you have my show on your consideration list?" You can even follow by asking the artist's *standing* on the consideration list. This is to some degree a euphemism, of course, for "how seriously are you thinking about booking my artist," but effective nonetheless.

At the same time, remember that presenters have dates to fill in their theaters and they *expect* agents to make proposals and pitch shows. Don't be shy about it. I am amazed at the number of times presenters have complained to me about agents, saying, "He's nice and we have a great time together over lunch, but he doesn't get to the point and tell me what he'd like me to consider." Remember that to a degree, presenters consider agents—good ones—as curators who have presumably chosen with care those artists they will represent, and will value their suggestions of shows for their seasons.

Selling Through the Presenter—Find the "Hook"

As previously discussed but worth restating, you are never just selling *to* the presenter, but rather *through* her. This is done through establishing credentials, be it "everyone is now talking about this artist because he's been on the *Tonight Show* five times" or "Carnegie Hall has made a three-year commitment to present this rising star." Work to give the presenter a *hook* early on in your communications—something that will hopefully keep your artist on the presenter's mind, floating over the hundreds of other artists with which the presenter is being assaulted, and give her some shorthand to tell her committee why she thinks your artist is right for their season. Most bookings are the result of an extended process of pitching, materials review, and cost and date negotiation, which can go on over months during which the presenter will consider hundreds of shows. Anything you can do to keep yours *top of mind* through that process is vital.

For Presenters Only

You really want a show but you are not a large presenter with deep pockets or big clout. Here is the nub of things. Of course it is possible that the show is just out of the price league of your presenting organization and you should just give up. But if you are a determined sort, and the differential doesn't seem that insurmountable, in addition to much else discussed in this chapter, some thoughts:

- *Be patient.* Don't assume you have to book the artist *this* season. Open the dialogue. Let the agent know that if not this season then perhaps the next. Ask to be notified if the artist is going to be in the area with a date available to be filled in a tour. (It took me three years to get the great Ella Fitzgerald to our jazz festival in Burlington—her first and only Vermont appearance!)

- *More than one performance.* Consider multiple performances, even on the same evening. This was the way many name pop artists successfully played the 1,450-seat Flynn Theater for us in Burlington with an early and late show, thereby generating enough revenue to pay the fee. Several smaller venues in midsize communities have had success booking five performances over a long weekend, allowing them to offer package fees that many artists will accept. Be creative in your exploration of configurations and don't assume your only option is a single performance.

- *Loss leader.* If the artist is a big name and sure seller, and will arguably strengthen your overall subscription sales, change the basis on which you normally project numbers for presentations. If you normally require a 60 percent break even, for example, you might shift for this artist to 80 percent or 90 percent or even higher. If you make no money at the box office but don't lose, and have increased the rep of your theater and overall subscription sales, along with making money at the concession stand, depending on your organization's mission you may still be ahead! Remember that venue reputations are ultimately made by the artists and productions that appear in them.

- *Offer to assemble a block booking.* You may well have relationships with fellow presenters in the region that the agent doesn't and those relationships can have value in the negotiations. If you can put together a cohesive block of work for a show in the region by inviting your colleagues to join you, not only do you get the show but the presenter who organizes the *block booking* commonly gets first pick of date as well as a discounted fee.

- *Offer to make an early fee deposit.* The *time value of money* will help the producer by allowing him to earn interest on those funds. Producers are looking at their *cash flow* for tours as well as at *bottom lines.*

- *Extend your firm offer for as long a time as possible and permit the agent to announce to the field that a firm offer from you is on the table.* This will assist the agent in building a tour around your date and make your offer more attractive to the show's producer.

- *Offer as much flexibility on dates as your calendar will allow for as long as possible.* This also helps the agent to secure tie-on dates.

- *If it is an artist, production, or producing company with which you might like a multiseason relationship, bring that into the negotiations.* A producer may be willing to cut fee and consider you a priority if the potential for a multiseason agreement exists.

- *Don't hesitate to inquire, even if you don't think you can afford it.* It never hurts to ask, even if you are a modest-sized theater in a smaller community and it is a big expensive star. You never know when there may be a hole in the artist's tour passing right by your area!

Early versus Late Booking

The timing of booking can be critical. You will always be strongest at either the front end of the cycle—when the agent is first determining in what regions the show will tour in what time periods—or the back end of the cycle if the agent has a hole to fill in the tour in your region. At the front end, of course, you have a lot more say in obtaining the show you want on the date you want if you can afford to pay the asking price. At the back end, you risk no dates being available. Your marketing stratagems also play a part: if you are bound to a single year-long subscription selling program that mails in the spring, you have less flexibility to take advantage of the late-cycle deals that come along. Some presenters break the season in half with a fall subscription offering followed by another in the winter/spring, in part to allow some flexibility for later bookings for the winter/spring version.

Be Clear about Zones of Exclusivity

Zones of exclusivity are measured both in travel distance, normally a radius around the presenter's venue, and time, normally an amount of time before and after the dates of the engagement. Since this is generally something the presenter will require and not something the agent will volunteer, it is important for the presenter to be clear about her wishes early in the process, even naming those other venues in which she does not want to see the show appear if she feels them to be a conflict.

As with almost everything else, this can be a point of negotiation—if by allowing a performance at another theater within your normal comfort zone you can have a reduction in show fee of greater value than the potential ticket sales lost to the other venue, it can be worth it. Be reasonable. If you are booking a single performance in a 500-seat theater in a community of over half a million souls, a fifty-mile zone with no dates prior to yours and for three months after should be plenty.

Know the Agents

Agents are not all alike, even if they seem like a teeming mass at first. The good ones have keen eyes for talented artists and develop a good sense of what might work for you. These warrant listening to. You also want to be sure to be on the radar of agents so they will think to contact you with special opportunities.

So while, yes, you are the buyer and therefore in a strong position, realize that with competition, budget, and other factors, that strength is often illusory. Keep your door ajar to agents to contact you at any time and signal that you want to hear from them if they have a show coming into the region.

Once you know what agents have tastes that are aligned with yours and who you can work with, maintain the relationships. Don't hesitate to call them if you are starting to plan your season and have not heard from them. If you are traveling to where they are based, give them a call for lunch or coffee when you are going to be in town.

Remember that whether you book this particular show in this season from this agent, you want to keep a good communication with the agent. If you can't present the show this season but like it for potential presentation in the future, be sure to communicate that.

Other Presenters

You can assume that even the best agent is out to make a sale and so may not give you the unvarnished truth about a show on his roster. But fellow presenters in other communities have no reason not to share candidly with colleagues their experiences of shows—and their agents—and can even add the all-important information about how well the shows sold in their theaters and at what ticket prices. Look for and make contact with presenters in communities with similar tastes and demographics to yours with venues of the same size that you feel are good at their work, remembering that those presenters may be one hundred miles away or on another continent!

Of course while presenters in other communities may be your friends providing support, local presenters may be competitors. Know who they are and, if possible, build bridges or at least be on good speaking terms. Opportunities for competition as well as collaboration will arise. It is better to know the competition and be able to reach out when needed than to sit behind walls and book blindly, hoping you won't end up competing with similar artists on the same dates.

> *Hold your friends close and your enemies closer.*
> —Sun-Tzu
> (Chinese general and military strategist, circa 400 BC)

Contacting Artists Directly

Some adventurous or aggressive presenters seek to communicate directly with the artists and/or their managers, thinking to work around agents. Motivations range from a genuine desire to have a meaningful artistic conversation about a project idea before plunging into negotiations, to hoping to save money by cutting out the agent's commission. Since presenters are not privy to the details of the agent/producer agreement, they don't know if the agreement calls for an exclusive or a nonexclusive relationship—the one requiring that a booking with this presenter go through the agent, but the other allowing latitude.

This can be explosive, depending on who is the agent, since the agent may feel threatened by the effort to cut him out, and even after presenter–agent communication gets under way, there may now be an element of distrust to overcome. A good agent, asked by a serious presenter, for an opportunity to have an artistic dialogue with an artist about a project idea prior to moving into detailed negotiations, will relay this request to the artist and, if she is interested, will arrange such a dialogue, whether in person, by phone, or other means.

As a rule, if there is an agent clearly defined as representing the artist in the territory, it is most appropriate for the first approach by the presenter to be through the agent.

Get to Know the Show and (hopefully) to Love It

In all our talk of buying for your audiences, don't lose sight of the fact that ideally you will also really love this show. This will be important to put your heart into selling it to your committee, your staff, and ultimately your audiences. Go see it live if you possibly can before committing. Listening to your head and your heart (or both sides of your brain) at the same time is a trick shared by the best of presenters, and works differently for different people, organizations, and circumstances.

Of course you must do your due diligence and determine to the best of your ability how many tickets you can sell at what price, and whether the proposed deal makes business sense. But if this were only a numbers business, you probably wouldn't be in it. And assuming you are the person who will be telling your marketing department, board of directors, and the local press what you are bringing in, the more personal enthusiasm as well as knowledge about the show you can bring to that process, the more tickets you are going to end up selling.

THE KEY IS LISTENING, LISTENING, LISTENING!

The one point on which all the negotiating experts agree is that by listening you can a) establish a higher level of trust with the other party and b) pick up the unstated signals being offered you in the negotiation process.

Endnotes

1   Published as part of the *Results Driven Manager* series © 2004 Harvard Business School Publishing Corporation.

2   John Ilich, *The Complete Idiot's Guide to Winning Through Negotiation* (New York: Alpha Books, 1996).

3   Max H. Bazerman and Margaret A. Neale, *Negotiating Rationally* (New York: The Free Press, 1992).

4   Roger Fisher and William Ury, *Getting to Yes* (New York: Penguin Books, 1991).

CHAPTER 6

Terms and Deal Elements

Having reviewed the negotiation process, let's take a look at some of the elements that may be *on the table* in the negotiations and in the final deal, generally referred to as the *terms*.

A primary reason for using *terms* instead of *fee* is that many deals involve more than the fee to be paid. Elements that might be paid or provided by the presenter to the producer in addition to the base fee could include some combination of a percentage of box office income calculated in one of several ways, provision of accommodations, intercity and local travel, freight, per diems, and royalties. International engagements might have added considerations such as the cost of visas and/or work permits, translators, carnets[1] for international freight movement, and the cost of translation and projection or simultaneous transmission of the text of the performance into the local language.

Some presenters seek *all-in* deals, in which they pay a flat fee and let the producer deal with travel, freight, accommodations, and delivering the show to the theater door. Others prefer or will accept *fee-plus* deals, with some or all of the added elements listed above and perhaps others not mentioned.

Guaranteed Fee

This is the most obvious element: the amount of money the presenter guarantees to the producer for the show, an amount to be paid regardless of how much revenue comes in through ticket sales. The presenter is taking the full financial risk for this amount of money if the box office income doesn't cover it. In some deals, the guaranteed fee is all that the producer will be provided by the contract so 100 percent of any profit in the presentation will remain with the presenter. Deals in which this is all the producer is provided are often referred to as *buy outs* since the presenter is paying for the services of the show on a flat fee basis and is buying out any claim to further income or box office participation by the producer.

Two important details related to the guaranteed fee:

1) Payment Schedule

The producer generally wants a portion of the fee paid at the time of contract signing, another portion at some point in advance of the engagement, and the balance prior to the final performance since the producer's most effective leverage to compel the final fee payment is to hold up one or more of the performances.

In the case of a production traveling abroad, and especially to countries not easily accessible to the producer's home country's legal system and/or in first-time business relationships, it is not uncommon for producers to require that the full fee be transferred prior to the production's departure from the home country. Alternatives to paying the full fee to the producer in advance are to have some placed in *escrow*[2] for release at the time of the final performances or for the presenter to provide a *letter of credit*.[3]

The presenter of course generally wants to pay as little as possible in advance of the show's arrival, and prefers to hold back a share of the fee until delivery of all performances has been completed. This latter may be justified in certain circumstances based on the potential for damage to the venue or a hint of reputation on the part of the artist for not showing up or completing her shows.

The issue of damage to the venue tends to be more true in the rough and tumble of a rock music setup, for instance, than a more sober classical string quartet where the greater concern is often in the reverse: the care and protection of artist's property such as valuable musical instruments.

The concern of nonperformance might arise if the artist has a reputation for not showing up or skimping on the shows,[4] which is sadly true of more big name artists than one would like to believe.

PAYMENT OF FEE BALANCE

The timing of the payment of fee balance can be a contentious issue and needs to be sorted out early. Assuming the presenter is unwilling to release the final payment until after the last performance and the producer is unwilling to offer the last performance without being paid first, a compromise can sometimes be struck by agreeing that the presenter will show the check to the producer's representative on-site before the start of the last performance and hand it over during intermission. The more formal solution is a form of escrow or bank letter of credit, wherein the money is held by a neutral third party for automatic release to the producer when the final performance obligations have been met.

2) Taxes and Other Withholds

For shows touring internationally, and in many states in the US, there is a mandatory tax to be withheld on the fees to artists visiting and performing from outside of the state (see chapter 9). Additionally, the contract may have stipulated that the presenter could withhold funds from the fee for certain expenses incurred by the producer in the presenter's community. This might range from the cost of long distance phone calls made by the producer from the touring production office to the cost of renting special equipment arranged by the presenter but payable by the producer. It is very important that the parties are extremely clear on what, if anything, may be deducted from the final fee payment—the more so because the people who negotiated the contract (the agent and senior official of the presenting organization) may be asleep in bed at the time the final payment is made after the final performance or completion of load-out!

Percentage of Box Office

Whether in addition to the guaranteed fee or in lieu of it, the concept of the producer receiving a percentage of the box office or *gate* embodies variables that break down loosely into two categories:

1) Percentage of Gross

This means that the artist receives a share from the first dollar (euro, yen, etc.) received by the box office, or perhaps from the NAGBOR (net adjusted gross box office receipts). This might be as an alternative to a guaranteed fee, presumably whichever is greater.

2) Percentage of Net or Profits

The broad concept is obvious: if profits are made, the producer gets a share of all income remaining after expenses have been paid. But the application is again nuanced and various questions must be addressed up front.

- Is it profit over the actual presentation expenses, which involves a complex sharing of all presentation expense receipts by presenter to producer and often a long delay after the close of the show for all final bills to come in, stage labor costs to be tabulated, etc., or against a preagreed presentation expense figure, usually based on a budget proposed by presenter and accepted by producer?

- How does an allocation of proratable expenses that apply to more than just this presentation get calculated—a share of the costs of subscription marketing, for instance, in which this production is included, or a share of lighting equipment leased for the season by the presenter?

- What is a reasonable allocation for the presenter's administrative overhead (often somewhat misleadingly referred to as "promoter profit")? Assuming a range of 10–20 percent is acceptable, on what is that percentage based? If based on the core expenses, it would provide an incentive for the presenter to drive up presentation costs; as a percentage of gross income it would provide an incentive to maximize revenue, but without regard to keeping presenting costs under control. A *promoter profit* based on a percentage of net income over presenting expenses would incentivize the presenter to maximize revenue and minimize costs and is preferred by producers, but it is not usually acceptable to presenters as it places their administrative overhead income at a higher level of risk.

Stepped Percentage Deals

It is not uncommon for the splitting to have several tiers. The agreement might be that the presenter keeps the first X percent or a fixed amount over the break even, that the producer keeps all of the next Y percent or a fixed amount, and then the parties split.

Or it might be that the initial split is weighted in favor of one side or the other up to a certain gross, after which it shifts the other way or goes to a 50/50.

There are an infinite number of formulas the parties can come up with and no proscribed or standard pattern.

Net Adjusted Gross Box Office Receipts[5] (NAGBOR)

An important detail in any calculation of percentages is on precisely what revenue basis the calculations are made. There are certain expenses related to the cost of selling tickets that, under US law and standard practice, are not considered expenses per se, but rather downward adjustments to income. This may seem to split semantic hairs except when it comes to dividing up the profits! Such adjustments to income notably include fees paid to credit card companies, fees to group sales agents, and fees to ticket sales agencies (those paid by the presenter and not the ticket purchaser). The adjusted gross on which percentages are commonly calculated has been defined by the Actors' Equity Association and titled NAGBOR, but it is in general use regardless of whether the production tours under an Equity contract.

SHARING INCENTIVE

Unlike a strictly guaranteed fee deal or *buy out*, where the presenter is taking all the financial risk and receiving all of the potential profit, in a *percentage deal*, assuming the guaranteed portion of the fee is less than it would have been in a buy out, the presenter is at somewhat less risk if ticket sales go badly but also doesn't get to keep all the profits. It has the effect of increasing the shared incentive on both sides to keep costs down and sell more tickets.

Separate Payment of Expenses

Certain expenses such as the cost of travel and freight for the show to get to the performance location and, in some cases, rehearsal and preproduction expenses are often treated separately in the agreement, paid directly or reimbursable to producer by presenter upon presentation of either firm cost quotations or receipts from qualified freight agents, airlines, etc. There are two reasons why it might be in the interests of the deal to separate out such expenses from the fee and treat them differently: *price volatility*, especially on travel and freight costs, and *taxes*.

Price Volatility

Highly volatile costs may increase or decrease between the time of contracting the engagement and the time the expenses are actually incurred. If the expenses are going to be high and even a small percentage fluctuation could be costly, both sides will have trouble agreeing on a locked-in price early on. Recent volatility in global oil prices and increases in the costs of obtaining visas for international artists have significantly affected travel and freight costs and brought new attention to this issue. Presenters now almost always insist on establishing a cost cap in areas of freight and travel so they can firm up their budgets. Producers, fearing rates may go up before purchase, are wary of agreeing to caps and usually insist on including a contingency to cover unexpected increases. Both parties often seek cost quotations to be sure to get the best prices.

Decreasing Tax Basis

Some—but not all—taxing states and countries do not consider reimbursed expenses incurred outside of their territories to be part of the basis on which tax is calculated. By separating them out from the fee contractually it can lower the *basis* on which tax withholding is calculated. As of this writing, the State of California, for instance, has often been willing to overlook reimbursed expenses falling within very specific categories such as advance production work prior to the artist's arrival in the state, and the costs of travel and freight to get there, whereas the State of Missouri has not. Most non-US countries are willing to consider guaranteed fee only in calculating tax with-holding. Most taxing entities treat royalties as nontaxable for withholding purposes, which is important to note in negotiating the deals and structuring the contracts.

Supplies and Services Provided Directly

Various cost areas associated with a show performing on tour are often paid directly by the presenter and not by the producer. This varies according to the nature of the tour and the show, and the preferences of the presenter and producer.

Onstage Tech

The most obvious supplies and services normally provided directly by the presenter are the onstage technical staff, equipment, and supplies, which are addressed more comprehensively in chapter 7 in the discussion of the techni-cal rider.

- *Stage labor.* It is nearly universal that presenters will provide a certain number of stagehands for a defined number of hours to work under the direction of the touring technical supervisors to set up, run, and strike the show.

- *Production Equipment.* Most smaller shows, structured for faster touring with shorter engagements in more locations, require the presenters to provide standardized lighting and sound equip-ment, which most theaters involved in such presentation have available—either owned or leased for presenting seasons. Larger productions, notably rock-style concerts and Broadway shows, will tend to travel with fully rigged lighting and sound equipment ready to roll into theaters on a *four-wall* basis, making it possible to set up a more sophisticated production on a stage in less time than if each light has to be individually circuited, colored, focused, and cued in each venue. It is often more cost effective for such shows to lease and prepare lighting trusses for an entire tour than to have each presenter provide locally, with cost benefits both in the bulk rental rates (shared among all tour presenters) and crew efficiencies at load-in since the lights generally travel prehung on trusses and precircuited.

- *Disposable Items.* Items such as gel color and gaffers tape are often provided by the presenter.

Accommodations

It is common to ask presenters to provide a certain number of rooms/nights of accommodation in a defined minimum class of hotel or apartment, though some presenters will insist on paying an *all-in* fee and have this cost paid by the producer.

The advantages to the deal to having it provided by the presenters is that often arts centers have access to local hotel sponsorships that would not be available to the producer directly, and the local presenter, if a nonprofit in the same state as the accommodations, is exempt from some if not all local and state taxes that would otherwise have to be paid by the producer based in another state, thereby lowering the total costs of presentation.

In instances in which the presenter requires the producer to pay for accommodations, the presenter is still often willing to use its local leverage to obtain the best possible price. Note that some organizations, notably LORT members used to bringing actors to town for limited periods to appear in locally produced productions, will have access to—and even in some cases own—artist housing that they can make available to the touring productions they present.

Local Transportation

Aside from the question of intercity travel, local airport transfers and, if necessary, travel between the accommodations, theater, press interview sites, etc., can be a cost factor normally left to the presenter to provide. Some have volunteers to do this, which, as long as proper insurance is in place, is normally acceptable to touring artists. Obviously this ramps up in the case of large companies requiring busses to move, or diva artists requiring stretch limos!

Per Diems

More applicable to international travel than domestic, it is quite common to ask the presenter to pay per diems directly in cash (usually in local currency) on arrival of the show in the presenter's community. In certain circumstances, where the tax basis is on fee or salaries only, this can lower the tax by being separated out of the fee. Also, the use of local currency saves the presenter the cost of converting the funds. This obviously becomes a discussion point for a show touring into a country whose currency is not easily internationally convertible, meaning that any per diem the company members have left over at the time of departure from the country is worthless outside of the country. To address this, *buy-back* agreements are sometimes built into contracts to allow for show members to sell unspent per diem currency back to the presenter for the artist's home currency at the end of the engagements.

Royalties

Royalties are not on this list as they are not always considered an expense of the production, but rather an obligation of the presenter directly to the rights holder of the work being performed. The exceptions are those dance, theater, and other companies that make agreements with their resident directors, choreographers, and other creators to pay royalties directly and then seek it within the fee to be paid by the presenter. But as we have attempted to clarify above in the section on taxes, this is not always to everyone's best advantage if the royalties thereby become taxable by the host region since some regions (the States of Massachusetts and Connecticut as examples) do not tax royalties but do tax gross fees. In this instance it would be better for the producer to identify the royalties in the contract separate from the fees so as to avoid this taxation.

Rights Guilds. Many countries have strong guilds representing the interests of artists, which will often seek to collect royalties on behalf of the artists and to then distribute the funds. An organization like SACD (*Société des Auteurs et Compositeurs Dramatiques*—Society of Dramatic Authors and Composers) in France is a good example, SOCAN in Canada and APRA in Australasia. The Web site of Australasia's APRA defines its role as:

> *Since 1926 APRA (the Australasian Performing Right Association) has been making life a little easier for song-writers, composers, and music users. Australian copyright law makes songwriters and composers the exclusive owners of their original music and lyrics. Nobody else can use their work without getting their permission first, and if necessary, paying a royalty for this use. This is where APRA steps in. APRA is a not-for-profit organization that collects royalties on behalf of its 42,000 + members, and by agreement, for all the copyright owners around the world.*

While the organizations serve the interests of their member artists admirably, many nonlocal touring artists prefer to have their royalties paid directly by the presenting organizations and/or the venues, both because they usually receive the money faster and because there are no administrative fees removed for the guilds.

For music being performed in the US, royalties are often paid by presenters as part of an umbrella licensing agreement with either ASCAP or BMI.[6] In the case of theatrical productions they are often payable directly to the producers of the shows and either directly or indirectly to a number of potential claimants such as the publisher (music and lyrics) and guilds representing actors, directors, choreographers, designers, etc.

For shows that may run multiple performances or weeks such as dramas or musicals, royalties are often calculated as a percentage of the gross box office income, ranging as high as 10 percent in some parts of Europe, and requiring a report on such income from the presenter and payment usually within thirty days of the close of the engagement. Shows that perform for one evening on tour will often negotiate a flat fee per performance for royalties. This is more typical for dance companies paying for the rights to use a certain work of music.

Visa and Work Permit Costs

As the costs for gaining entry and working on foreign soil have increased worldwide, it is increasingly common to see them separated out for reimbursement by the presenter or tour producer. In some cases outside of the US, where the presenter is a government agency such as a major government run festival, the presenter is able to get these costs waived.

For foreign artists inbound in the US, these costs include not only the fee to the US Citizenship and Immigration Service (USCIS—formerly INS) payable within the US, but fees are now required by advisory organizations for their "no objection" letters such as Actors' Equity and AGMA, and there are fees per person to be paid at the US consulates abroad where the visas are actually issued.

Agency Commission

It bears noting that occasionally an agent will make arrangements to have his commission paid directly by the presenter as a separate expense outside of the fee. This also is primarily driven by what offers the best tax advantage, though might also reflect a concern on the part of the agent over delay in getting the commission paid by the artist or over the commission being at a rate or amount that for some reason he does not want known to the artist.

Sponsorship Percentage

In a case in which the presenter has been able to obtain a financial sponsor for the presentation of the show based in part on its name and reputation, in the same spirit as percentage of box office, the producer should receive some commission on this sponsorship.

Obviously most agents and producers will agree with me on this point and presenters will disagree. And in fairness, it does open up the argument by presenters that the reverse should then be true: that if the producer is able to obtain a tour sponsor based in part on the commitment of a presenter to be part of the tour, the presenter should then obtain a commission on the sponsorship or a fee reduction. One way I have seen this matter resolved, rather than considering a specific commission on the sponsorship, is to treat the presentation sponsorship as revenue to the production in addition to the box office income. So if there is a *back-end* percentage payable to the producer based on profit (or in nonprofit parlance, *excess income over expenses*), the basis of income used in this calculation includes the amount of the sponsorship in addition to box office revenue.

Endnotes

1   *Carnets* are effectively passports for freight. They are international customs documents that simplify customs procedures for the temporary importation of various types of goods. The most common type of carnet issued in the US is called the ATA Carnet, developed in 1961 by the then-named Customs Cooperation Council, later the World Customs Organization. The name is an acronym for the combined French/English: "Admission Temporaire/Temporary Admission." ATA Carnets ease the temporary importation of theatrical goods and facilitate international touring by helping to avoid extensive customs procedures and the payment of duties and value-added taxes, and replacing the purchase of temporary import bonds.

2   *Escrow* is funds placed in the hands of a third party, often an attorney or a bank, with stipulation that they will be paid out automatically when certain conditions are met. In the case of theatrical performances, this would be most commonly when the performances have taken place. Though rarely assets other than money when used in the theatrical business, escrow can be any form of property or deed to a property and need not be only cash.

3   A *letter of credit*, typically issued by a bank or financial institution, authorizes the recipient of the letter to draw amounts of money up to a specified total according to specified terms and conditions. In the case of theatrical presentation, it means that the presenter has supplied the funds and they are being held secure by the bank for automatic release to the producer once the performances have taken place. Once issued, the presenter can't change her mind and take the money back! It functions similarly to escrow but is often somewhat easier and less costly to set up.

4   Most contracts for live performances by pop musicians will specify a minimum number of minutes for which they are to appear on stage.

5   Actors' Equity Association defines NAGBOR (net adjusted gross box office receipts) as "the gross box office receipts in a given week, as adjusted for certain accepted deductions. These may include, but are not limited to, city and/or state taxes, credit card charges and group sales discounts" (*http://www.actorsequity.org/docs/rulebooks/Production_Rulebook_League_04–08.pdf*).

6   *ASCAP (American Society of Composers and Performers)* and *BMI (Broadcast Musicians Incorporated)* are performing rights organizations. They represent some 95 percent of all music under copyright in the US. Rather than negotiating individually for each musical work presented, presenting organizations often sign blanket licensing agreements with ASCAP and/or BMI involving the payment of one annual licensing fee, which allows presentation of most US copyrighted music without further detailed accounting.

CHAPTER 7

Documents

This chapter will introduce three essential documents that are integral to formalizing the agreements that have been reached: the *Deal Memo* (also sometimes the *Accepted Offer*), the *Engagement Contract*, and the *Technical Rider* (sometimes called the *Technical Addendum*). We will discuss the functions of and broad issues related to all three, and will look into deal memos in some detail as they are shorter than contracts and contain the essential elements. For detailed examinations of the contents of contracts and technical riders, the reader is referred to appendixes I and II respectively.

IMPORTANT DISCLAIMER

I am not an attorney, and this section and the appendixes should be used as guidelines only and not as formal legal advice.

The thoughts shared are gleaned from three decades of working with thousands of contracts from both the buyer and the seller sides, and from input over the years from a variety of attorneys in both the US and abroad. My intention is to empower the reader to think carefully and logically about the functions of these documents. If a detailed analysis is wanted, the appendixes are added to assist the reader in preparing a draft contract, hopefully reducing the number of billable work hours of an attorney to review a draft instead of starting from scratch.

Formalizing the Deal

So you have reached agreement by phone and perhaps e-mail exchanges. But while a case could be made, and possibly won in court, based on the spoken and e-mailed word, none of that can be safely considered binding on either party without a document signed by both parties (or *fully executed*). This is generally accomplished initially by one of three things: A formal written *offer* from the presenter that is signed and accepted by the producer or agent, thereby becoming an *accepted offer*; a document issued by the agent (a *deal memo* or *deal confirmation*) confirming the terms of the engagement and signed and accepted by the presenter; and/or an engagement contract issued by one or the other party and signed by both.

There are surprisingly few actual court trials over performing arts engagement agreements. While the high cost of such trials is an obvious deterrent, it is also due to the care often taken in the negotiation of agreements and the written documentation of those agreements. Ideally, both parties to a contract will view it as a list of what each side agreed to and a road map to use in the case of trouble.

Keep in mind that if the court battle is over interpretation of language in the contract, the e-mail exchanges and even meeting notes prior to contract execution may have relevance in clarifying the intentions of the confusing text.

So the deal memo and contract serve not only as objects to fight over in court, but in fact, if prepared well, they will help keep you out of court.

> **Rule 1:** No matter how pleasant the relationship between presenter and agent, and what may have been promised verbally during negotiations, keep in mind that it carries little or no legal weight if it is not written into the contract!

The Documents

We will focus on three documents.

The Contract

The centerpiece of course is the contract, which is the comprehensive documentation of the agreement. It may or may not have attachments to it called addenda or riders, but for our purposes we will refer to the overall document. This is an essential document and no professional engagement of a live touring event would take place without one.

The Deal Memo (also called Accepted Offer)

This document precedes the issuing of the contract and is a short version intended to quickly confirm the points of the deal to allow both sides to consider the deal firm. This allows the presenter to make the public announcement of the show and put tickets on sale, the producer to contract the performers, and both parties to lock the dates. To be meaningful, deal memos are binding agreements carrying the same weight as contracts. Deal memos are not necessary or always used. If time permits or under certain circumstances, it may be appropriate to go directly to the contract.

It is not standard to issue deal memos for international agreements where two different languages are involved. Given the linguistic challenges, it can be confusing and add unnecessary time and effort to issue a DM and then a contract, and it is often preferable to issue a full contract from the start and spend the translating and negotiating time and energy on the one document only. Many foreign presenters, however, will begin the formal documentation with an official letter of invitation, which will often confirm the basic dates and terms of the engagement along the same lines as an offer.

DMs are also not issued by presenting institutions that are forbidden by laws or internal policy to sign more than one binding agreement for an engagement.

Technical Rider (or Tech Rider, or Technical Addendum)

This document will end up as a formal attachment to the contract. But it is of such importance in outlining the technical requirements of the show that the presenter often uses it as a stand-alone document for analysis even before the agreement is reached. As with the contract, our comments here are general, and appendix II offers a more detailed analysis of tech rider content points.

The Process

Negotiation is often about process, and so is formalization. You may think you have resolved the deal for the engagement—the basics of show, venue, dates, and terms presumably have been worked out. But it is only as one side is issuing the first contract draft and the other side reading it that details emerge. When are portions of the fee expected to be paid? How many people are actually traveling and who's paying for their hotel rooms? Do this many people really need to fly first class and who is paying for that!? If we do have to go to court, are we going to fight about it in your state's (or country's) court system or mine?

You thought the negotiations were over when the basic agreement was reached, but in many cases that was only the prelude—the big picture items. Through the process of exchange of contract drafts, the smaller, subtler issues will be teased out and hopefully resolved.

Keep the Wording Understandable

A first objective I encourage the reader to undertake is to have the one issuing the contract write it so that intelligent nonlawyers can understand it, and if you are the one receiving it, make sure you understand what it all says and means.

In my experience over the years, I have been astounded at how many lawyers, given the opportunity, will choose a complex wording that is only understandable by lawyers instead of plain language. Lawyers, of course, wear a certain glow of authority and one hesitates to challenge them if one is not also a lawyer. But when challenged to make wording more understandable, they often can. This lesson becomes more poignant when you are the one—perhaps the agent, presenter, or producer—whose name is on the contract and who will be signing it. Suddenly it becomes very crucial that you understand what all that verbiage means about indemnity, warranties, and insurance.

Don't get sucked in by excessive *lawyerese* or you are doomed! Remember that the lawyer works for you and not the other way around (though that can be difficult to impose if the service is *pro bono* and, worse, if she is on your board of directors and technically your employer). Likewise, if you are the recipient of a contract from the other party, don't be embarrassed to demand explanations of what you don't understand.

The need for simple language is of added importance if you are asking a presenter in a non-English-speaking country to sign an English-language contract.

Rule 2: If you don't understand it, don't sign it!

The Game of Lawyerese

The tyranny of overcomplicated legal language instead of simple prose, presumably holding over from the day when Latin was used so the peasants would not learn the Great Mysteries, has been overthrown! The game of lawyerese is insidious and does great harm to a field with often very thin financial margins as attorneys show off their erudition by writing in language that other lawyers then have to be paid to explain, thereby feeding the endless spiral of increasing legal costs.

As a rule, if I can't understand what has been sent to me and my counterpart cannot explain it to my satisfaction and offers to have me speak with his attorney, my response is that it is my counterpart's responsibility to explain it to me since he issued the contract. If we have to speak with his lawyer to understand what has been written, then I threaten to bring in my lawyer for the conversation at my counterpart's expense since he and his attorneys are responsible for the gobbledygook in the first place. That usually brings the needed attention to the matter.

Rule 3: Don't be embarrassed to admit what you don't understand and ask for clarification. It is better than getting legally screwed for putting your signature to something you didn't understand.

Be Thorough

While these documents will ultimately be at the center of a battle if you ever go to court, on a more practical level, the written agreements serve as documentation of all the understandings, large and small, that the parties came to through the negotiation process. In larger organizations, they are the guidebooks by which various staff members will do their work related to the engagement—in marketing, artist services, ticketing, accounting, production, etc. The more thorough you are in negotiating and preparing the documents, making sure that all conceivable eventualities are anticipated and schedules and areas of responsibility clarified, the smoother the engagement will go. Likewise, the more prepared you will be to address problems if they do arise and the less likely that you will ever go to court.

For example, if you are the producer, don't hesitate to spell out the precise way in which you want the name of the show to appear in the advertising, or the form and date on which you wish to receive portions of the fee. If you are the presenter and the inclusion of a certain actor in the play is essential to your decision to bring the show, write that into the contract.

Rule 4: Be very detailed in the contract on issues of importance to your side.

Be Patient

The process of contracting can take a long time and challenge your patience. Stick with it. It is when you lose your patience that you are prone to make mistakes or to accept wording in the contract that you shouldn't.

Often the negotiating process is one of exchanging the document, or a set of notes related to the document, back and forth—sometimes what seems endlessly—winnowing down the issues, attempting different wording, jousting back and forth around what is ultimately acceptable and what is not. You may encounter a negotiating partner who is herself, or by instructions from her bosses, extremely nitpicky to the point of exasperation.

The result of such a detailed process, however, is that by its conclusion there is not one detail of the engagement that has not been examined and agreed to.

Rule 5: Be no less patient than your negotiating partner throughout the process. Go word for word, line for line, as long as it takes to complete the process. Stay positive throughout.

Who Issues the Agreements and Why it Matters

It is always preferable to be the one issuing the deal memos and contracts because you can be sure that all the points you want to see are in there. Though you should want to end up with a fair and balanced contract, if it is to be skewed in any fashion you will want it skewed in your favor, which is more likely to happen if you issue it.

Having said that, if you are in the position of issuing the contract, you are strongly encouraged to issue *fair and balanced contracts* from the beginning. Hold in mind the spirit of building positive relations that will hopefully last for many engagements.

Many big presenting institutions will insist on issuing their contracts. It's not the end of the world, probably just more work on your part to negotiate adjustment of points for your side. Some institutions, recognizing this but obligated to have their contract on top, will invite you to issue your draft anyway and will attach it as an addendum to their contract.

Rule 6: Given the choice, always issue the first contract draft.

The Result

The result of this, if done thoroughly, is a document that covers every issue the producer and presenter can expect to face in preparing for the arrival of the show at the venue, setting up, running, striking, and leaving. And it will hopefully also cover eventualities—such as cancellation and the roof of the theater falling in—that you don't expect to come up.

Sometimes it is the unlikely eventualities that one can feel almost uncomfortable talking about: not only the roof falling in but the dancer breaking his leg, a war breaking out during the engagement, or what court you will fight in if you have to go there. But it is the task of the agent and presenter to cover all these eventualities in this document so all are ready in a worst-case scenario.

Details of Deal Memo or Accepted Offer

We will delve into the essential points recommended for inclusion in a deal memo in detail. This is a) because these are the very core elements of the deal and b) because the deal memo is comparatively short. For our purposes we will refer to the document as the deal memo or DM, noting that it might alternately be an accepted offer (AO). Both documents serve the same basic function of securing the basics of the deal quickly, with the DM normally having been issued by the agent and the AO issued by the presenter.

The DM is a shorthand version of the final agreement, identifying the contracting parties and the production, and outlining time, place, and terms. While it is assumed that a full contract will follow, it is important to recognize that if for any reason a contract does not follow, the DM will serve in its stead. The DM is not absolutely necessary if the parties agree instead to go right to contract.

The deal memo should state that this is a firm agreement that is *binding on both parties.*

A Nonbinding Alternative

There is occasionally a need for a document that confirms the serious negotiations but is not binding. Most common is a memo of understanding (MOU). A presenter may be applying for a grant to help underwrite the season and need to prove that she is in serious negotiation for an artist, even though the deal has not been concluded.

Conditional Offer

There may be occasions when a nonbinding offer or a conditional offer is of value. A not uncommon example is an invitation to an artist to appear for which an engagement subsidy must be sought by one of the parties. In this case proof of a sincere invitation and offer from the presenter and acceptance by the artist to appear are required to support the request for subsidy. There may be an understanding in this case that if the subsidy is not forthcoming, the parties are not obligated to proceed with the engagement and that conversely, if the trigger condition is met (i.e., the funding approved), the deal is considered confirmed and binding.

The Primary Items in a Deal Memo or Accepted Offer

Almost all elements in the offer or DM have to do with defining the parties to the agreement, precisely what the show is, when and into what venue, and what each side is committing to, with focus on issues that cost money and issues that affect calendars.

Most deal memos and accepted offers will include the following items in one form or another:

Identity of the Contracting Parties and the Authorized Signatories

The first step is to formally identify the presenter, the producer, and, if appropriate, the agent who are part of the agreement. These are generally corporate entities of some nature, though occasionally artists will sign as individuals

After identifying the names and addresses it is customary to assign each a one word "moniker" in parenthesis for reference later in the document, an example being "(*hereinafter referred to as "Producer"*)". The same may be applied to the "Presenter," the "Engagement," the "Production," and to any other entity whose name appears repeatedly (the "Venue" or "Agent" for instance).

Define the "Production"

Identify the show that is to be presented, plus any salient related identifiers that are conditional to the agreement such as the participation of certain cast members. Remember the importance of production distinctions such as between a fully staged production of a musical versus a concert version, a first versus second company of a dance troupe, or an appearance of a musician solo versus in the context of a quartet, band, orchestra, etc.

Define the "Engagement"

Name the venue in which the performances are to take place, including address and seating capacity, and the start times of the performances. List any related activities agreed upon for inclusion in the engagement including workshops and lectures. If the technical preparation of the stage will require time before the day of first performance, it is a good idea to show that as well so the total calendar scope of the engagement is made clear.

Producer's Obligations

Keeping in mind that deal memos should be short—generally not more than two pages—this basically states that the producer will provide the production on specified dates and times, plus such additional activities as have been agreed to, and will support the presenter in marketing efforts.

Presenter's Obligations

Again, maintaining brevity in the deal memo, the presenter's obligations are normally listed as:

Terms. That which is payable by presenter to producer, both as guaranteed fee and box office split. If there is to be a split, identify the basis on which the split will be made including, if appropriate, the ticket scaling, gross potential, and split point or revenue amount above which the split goes into effect.

Other presenter obligations. This may include some or all of the following, depending on the deal and the nature of the production, and listed as brief bullet points:

- Technical requirements (tech rider can be attached)
- Accommodations, specifying the number of single and double rooms for how many nights (*# room nights*)

- Transportation (intercity and local) as agreed to be provided by presenter

- Freight, if being provided by presenter

- Royalties due, if applicable

- Any other items that are of special importance to the engagement, and especially those that affect the calendar or will cost either party money!

Less Obvious Items that Might be Included

- *Attach the Budget.* If a presentation budget has been discussed and accepted by the parties as the framework for a box office split, this can be attached as an addendum with the specific notation that "The budget appended hereto is considered an integral part of this agreement" and with space for initials of both parties on the appended budget. Note that if there is no box office split, the presenter is under no obligation to show the producer his presentation budget or provide a box office statement.

- *Taxes and withholds.* Specify that the fee is "net of any taxes or other withholds," or if you know and both accept that a certain tax must be withheld, better to stipulate it now than fight about it later.

- *Marketing control and announcement restriction.* Assuming that the presenter will expect to announce the engagement based on the deal memo, it is important to stipulate that a) the presenter may not make any public announcements of the engagement until the DM is fully executed and b) that any announcements must use descriptive copy and images of the show provided by or approved by the producer.

- *Exclusivity required by presenter and agreed to by producer.* Often this is defined by an amount of *time* before and after the engagement and a *distance* expressed as a radius in miles or kilometers from the venue within which the producer will not allow the production to appear without prior consent of the presenter. This can be important and better to get clear early as the agent is often in midbooking process at the time the DM is executed and will be looking for tie-in dates around this one. The agent needs to know the agreed upon geographic limitations in that regard.

- *Sign-by or expiry date.* Whether issued as an offer by the presenter or a deal memo by the agent, the issuer should include an expiry date by which she can expect the document to be executed and the deal confirmed, and after which, if not confirmed, the offer or commitment can be considered void (notice I said *can* and not *will*, allowing wiggle room if the issuing party wishes to extend the offer a bit). Otherwise, in theory, the issuer is holding the dates (in the venue or the artist's calendar) indefinitely without a commitment on the other side.

- *Not binding until both sign.* Along with the expiry date is the important caveat that the offer or deal memo is not binding on the parties until fully executed by both parties. This may seem obvious, but again relates to the question of at what point an issued document is considered binding on either party.

What's *Not* Typically in the Offer or Deal Memo

- *Cancellation terms.* You will note that documents don't usually include cancellation terms. As the contract is expected to follow reasonably soon after the DM is executed, it is rare to encounter cancellation before the contract is signed. If you anticipate a long time between when the offer or deal memo is executed and the time a contract will be issued, it may be a good idea to put something in about cancellation.

- *Reference to pending contract.* One thing you do not want your offer or deal memo to say is that the document is pending or otherwise relies on the future execution of a contract for the engagement. This weakens the power of this document by implying that it is not a binding agreement until the contract is signed. It is important that the language convey that the signed accepted offer/deal memo is a binding agreement between the parties, implying that, should a contract never get executed, this document would carry them through the engagement.

Contracts

Whether being issued following a deal memo or as the sole agreement document, the *big kahuna* of documents is the contract. To be more precise, we might refer to this as an *engagement contract*, to distinguish it from an agency agreement, a royalty agreement, a licensing contract, an artist's employment contract, or any of a number of other contracts that might surround a production.

An engagement contract has two primary purposes:

- To identify what each party is agreeing to provide in funds and services, including everything from insurance coverage to lighting to local transportation, as well of course as the funds to be paid and the show to be provided

- To provide a guide and agreements to come into play if needed to resolve disputes, minor or major, that may arise, and to cover the unexpected

Don't Delay the Contracting Process

No matter how much you have discussed the engagement details with the corresponding party before the contract is issued, there are often points that come out in written form that require further discussion and negotiation. For this reason, it is a mistake to delay the contracting procedure on the blithe assumption that "we have a deal, so there's no rush." Even the friendliest of relationships can be strained when it comes to certain detailed points related to payments and responsibilities that may only surface though the contracting process.

Contract Structure and Boilerplate

Both presenters who bring a variety of productions to town and agents representing various shows want to see certain points standardized in all contracts. Other points, by necessity, will be particular to the needs of individual productions. Issues related to cancellation or insurance, for instance, might be standard for all engagements, whereas the number of hotel rooms required, particular artist needs, or special rules in a particular theater will be unique to each production or presenter.

For this reason, it is normal that each side will have its standard paragraphs—often referred to as *boilerplate*[1]—in a ready-to-send form. The items specific to the show or unique to a venue are then addressed in one or more addenda or riders that are appended but treated as integral to the contract. This can do much to speed up the often time-consuming contract process, hopefully keeping to a minimum those points on which extended negotiation are necessary.

Differentiate between Tough Negotiation and Fair Contracts

You should negotiate the very best deal for your side that you can. But once the negotiations are complete and an agreement is reached, don't attempt to renegotiate the core points through the contracting process. There will be enough details to work out as it is. Despite the "cowboy" reputation earned by some segments of the touring business, this is by and large an amicable field in which the parties expect to do business again and legal trickery has no place.

It is also important that the team working on contracting for each party, perhaps a staff person responsible for contracts, an advising attorney, and the signatory, be "on the same conceptual page" in contracting. The *good-guy/bad-guy* routine where the front person says, "I'd agree to that but my lawyer made me be nasty" (which goes along with "I don't know what it means either, but my lawyer made me put it in"), is a little old and irresponsible, wastes a lot of time, and builds bad vibes into relationships that can haunt later. How much better to gain respect and trust by issuing contracts that are sensible and fair to both parties, and that are clearly understandable to the nonlawyers who will be acting on them throughout the engagement.

There are many, sadly, who on their own or advice of counsel, issue contracts that, while protecting their own organizations' interests, do little to protect the other sides'. Presumably this is done on the theory that the other side can take care of itself and will respond to and challenge points that it feels are unfair. The implied assumption is that if the other side doesn't spot the points of imbalance, "too bad for them"—the performing arts equivalent of *buyer beware* in the real estate world. This *win–lose* attitude, while defensible from a purely legalistic perspective and probably deemed admirable in more cut-throat human enterprises, represents a mean-spirited attitude that is counter to the spirit in which most live-entertainment touring takes place in the twenty-first century. The inevitable results of this approach are either that one side "loses" in a game in which the intentions are for both sides to work together to get a successful presentation on a stage, or that an inordinate amount of time is wasted while the receiving party responds to the contract issuer on a detailed point-by-point basis and negotiations continue for weeks over something that should be resolvable much faster.

That being said, of course there will be points on which the balance is not going to be easy to find, and I don't ask anyone not to protect the interests of his client. With both sides approaching the issue with a *win–win* attitude, mutually acceptable resolutions can be found.

Ask for Advice

The contract you are negotiating will probably not have issues that have not been addressed before by others. Call colleagues, service organizations, and your own attorney to ask how others have handled the tricky questions.

Written Contract is the Final Word

Regardless of your friendship with the opposing party or private understandings that may have been made, always remember that at the end of the day the written contract needs to reflect the full and complete agreement. If there are any discrepancies between the contract and the deal memo that was issued previously, the later document—the contract—will generally prevail. Imagine that the contract is being disputed by attorneys before a judge in a court of law without any of the original negotiating parties, including you, involved, and make sure it fully and accurately reflects your client's interests and the agreements made about the engagement.

Technical (and Other) Riders Integral to the Contract

Riders and addenda are effectively the same thing. They are special sections added to the contract that are to be considered integral to the agreement. Depending on the form, some presenters and agents prefer contracts where, with the exception of some basic boilerplate, most of the *meat* of the contract is in the form of riders.

Riders can be added by either party during the course of negotiation. The primary rider issued by the agent on behalf of the production is the tech rider. Presenters often add riders related to subjects such as marketing procedure and materials requested from the producer; artist services having to do with accommodations, backstage amenities, and other on-site operational issues; and a procedures or rules rider that often outlines standard procedures for presented productions on matters such as comp and house seats available to the artist, procedure and percentages taken from the sale of merchandise, policies related to late seating and delay of performances, and rules such as no drinking or smoking on the premises.

We will address the tech rider in greater detail below and in appendix II. What is important to note here is that in order for riders to be considered valid parts of the contract, a statement to that effect must be inserted in the contract *above the signature line.* Added confirmation of acceptance by both parties is often indicated with initials on the riders.

Resolving Discrepancies between Riders and Main Contract Body

Most riders that get added to contracts after the initial issuance will state that, in the event of discrepancy between the main body of the contract and the rider, the added rider will overrule. This will typically be in a circumstance in which the agent has sent out the first draft contract with the show's addenda attached and, rather than making point-by-point changes, the presenter will send it back with its own standard addenda added stating its policies with respect to everything from the number of comp tickets offered to the percentage it expects from merchandise to what it will offer in number of lighting instruments. It usually includes the blanket claim that it overrides the same areas in the main body of the contract. Unless the agent challenges, this rider thereby becomes the controlling part of the final agreement in those areas.

Riders are important, and as the contract goes back and forth it is important that both sides read through the riders as they are added and/or changed and consider their fine points in the negotiations.

Production's Technical Rider or Addendum

While much of the marketing and artist's services information might be in the main contract body or in riders, the one area of information that is almost always attached and almost never included in the main body relates to technical production: the requirements of stage labor, theatrical equipment, electrical power, etc., to mount the show in the venue. This is because this information is so specialized to the technical directors, stages managers, production managers, master electricians, and other technical experts engaged by each party that most administrators and lawyers prefer to have it isolated in its own document for review and discussion between the technical experts associated with the show and the presenter or venue. What the presenter wants to know is "How much time in the theater will it take?" and "How much will it cost?"

Depending on the size of the production, this rider can run to many pages and become a source of considerable negotiation in and of itself. This negotiation often takes place parallel to the primary negotiations by surrogates, technical experts who represent the agent/producer and the presenting organization. They represent both the interests of the production, to insure that it gets in and up and works the way it is supposed to, and the interests of the presenters, to insure that all is being done in the most cost-effective manner. This often represents one of the largest variable elements of the presentation budget and should be conducted concurrently with the overall contract negotiation, and largely completed before contract execution.

Realizing the importance of this cost area for a large production, a wise presenter considering bringing in a show of any production size will request a copy of the technical rider early in the negotiations, even before a presentation commitment has been made, and have his technical director cost out what is being required of the presenter to provide the necessary technical resources.

Tech Needs versus What's Available

The show's technical rider will guide the discussion and frame the negotiation since it outlines what the producer claims to need in order to mount the show. But presenters will make available the tech specs for the venue in which they are contemplating presenting the show, which will include dimensions of the stage area, an inventory of the lighting, sound, and other technical equipment available in the venue, notations about standard repertory light plots they keep hung over the stage, union rules applicable in the theater, notes about truck and backstage security access, and other technical matters unique to the venue.

It is in the comparison between these two documents that crucial issues are addressed and the basic viability of the engagement gets sorted out. If lighting instruments are needed for the show beyond what are available in the venue's stock, they can generally be rented in. But if the show requires a minimum proscenium arch width of forty feet and the venue's arch has only thirty feet between immovable plaster, does the presenter seek a different venue, does the producer restage the production, or does the engagement not go forward?

Sequence of Approvals and Analysis—*Due Diligence*

For all but the simplest technical presentations being contemplated, there is a technical analysis sequence by the technical representatives of producer and presenter that parallels the negotiations under way between agent and presenter.

1) The first question is, "Can the show work in this theater?" This is a broad brush question having to do with the most basic parameters of the show: is the playing space on the stage big enough, is it configured acceptably in relationship to the audience (i.e., proscenium, thrust, etc.), if the show requires an orchestra pit and/or a fly system, does this venue have them, and can the set get through the loading dock onto the stage? This question is normally determined by the show's production manager from a set of technical specifications for the venue, which the agent has arranged to have sent early in the process or that are available for viewing online.

2) At the same time as, or soon after, the show's production manager has given the initial green light and confirmed to the agent that the show will fit, the ball is in the presenter's court as she determines what the technical needs of this show will cost her and for how much time it will occupy the theater. For this, the agent provides a copy of the show's tech rider (not the contract yet, only the rider) to the presenter to pass on to her technical director. He now conducts his

analysis of stagehand needs, equipment that may have to be rented, and other cost factors involved in bringing the show in, and delivers a preliminary production budget to the presenter. During this process the presenter's technical director and the show's production manager may well be in direct communication to clarify points, discuss equipment substitutions or cuts if needed, and work together to determine the most cost-effective approach to getting the show in and up.

Note that during those discussions, agreements made on the part of the show to amend the standard tech rider for this particular engagement and venue get noted, as an amended version of the tech rider will end up as part of a contract for the show in this venue.

3) With the show green lighted from a production viability standpoint, and a budget now in the presenter's hands, she proceeds to work with the agent in negotiating an engagement (or stops if the costs are just too high!).

Obviously for simple shows, the process may be trimmed or fast-tracked. But it is a naïve presenter who will enter into an engagement contract without technical due diligence and a production budget in hand, as this—along with the artist's fee and the cost of marketing—is generally one of the biggest cost items in a typical presentation.

International Touring

Rider differences for US shows touring abroad often include showing dimensions in metric instead of feet/inches, differing gel color references, requiring translators, showing schedule times by twenty-four-hour clocks, and most importantly, substitutions of sound and lighting equipment to what is generally available in the host country. Keep in mind electrical power differences for any equipment being carried by the artist. Details such as internationally acceptable flame proofing on soft goods being brought by the production, and whether or not the show can be performed on a raked (sloped) stage—common in Europe and South America but nonexistent in the US—are also important. Avoid American colloquialisms that may be misunderstood by a reader for whom English is not the first language. If a large amount of touring is anticipated in a region with a first language other than English, the investment in a translation of the rider to that language may be worth it.

This is the Road, not Broadway!

Productions should keep their road technical requirements as simple and flexible as possible, while still insuring that the core artistic needs of the production are met. Producers generally want their shows to tour to as many places as possible, and they don't want to bankrupt the presenters nor kill the stage crews through overwork. Remember that the vast 400-instrument lighting plot with which the show was originally created for its initial run at home does not need to be replicated in full in every one-night-stand touring engagement and should be relit with touring realities in mind.

Tech-Demand Ethics

Whether a guarantee or a copresentation deal, if the show is requiring the presenter to provide lighting, it is ethically correct for the producer to attempt first to work from within the presenter's available inventory before insisting that the presenter go to the expense of renting additional equipment. Likewise with sound equipment and any other technical and backstage requirements.

One of the worst offenses a touring show can commit is to require that a presenter incur expense to rent equipment and then show up and not use the equipment! This has caused such consternation as a disrespectful wastage of the presenter's time and money that some presenters now insert requirements in contracts that if they have rented equipment required by the show that is then not used, the rental cost is deducted from the fee.

Collaborative Process—Advance Planning is Key

While of course each side is going to be watching out for its interests—the agent insuring that the show has what it needs and the presenter insuring that the tech is planned with maximum time and cost efficiency—this is ultimately a collaborative process. Particularly in situations in which the producer receives a share of the back-end profit, she has a financial incentive to be as lean and efficient as possible in local tech costs within the framework of delivering a good quality production.

Remember that for a large show going in, involving substantial theatrical equipment and a large crew, this process is akin to a military operation where lack of planning can result in a significant waste of time and money and jeopardize getting the show up in time. Advance planning, a thorough exchange of the show's technical needs and specs on the venue between technical representatives, and communication are the keys.

Other Riders

I have focused in greatest detail, both here and in appendix II, on technical riders, as they are the most common to routinely appear with contracts. They are also often the most specialized and represent one of the highest potential presenter cost areas. But separating out various additional contract areas into riders is not uncommon. A few of the most commonly seen follow.

- *Press and Marketing.* This outlines deadlines for delivery of marketing support materials by the producer to the presenter and provides contact information for the marketing staff.

- *Production Schedule.* If the engagement is at least a week, and/or the load-in process extensive, it is not uncommon to attach a separate production schedule. This might also include the performances and residency activities such as workshops and lecture-demonstrations.

- *Artist Services.* There are a range of artist-related issues such as accommodations, complimentary tickets, backstage hospitality, and local transportation between airport, hotel, and theater that are often grouped by presenters under "Artist Services."

- *Recording Permission.* If there is contemplation on either side to record the performance, in recognition of the fact that this is outside of the core purpose of the agreement related to live performance, the details of any recordings the parties agree to are often outlined in a rider specific to this issue.

- *Residency Activities Technical Riders.* Artists who routinely offer talks, lecture-demonstrations, classes, or other nonperformance residency activities will often prepare technical riders specific to these activities, addressing issues such as the size, temperature, and floor conditions of studios for workshops, and the preference for podium, microphone type, and projection equipment for talks.

RIDERS ARE PART OF THE CONTRACT

It bears repeating that an item is no less important if placed in a rider instead of in the main contract body as long as each rider is referenced in the main body of the contract above the signatures with a stipulation that it is an integral part of the contract.

Endnotes

1   The term *boilerplate* derives from steel manufacturing where boilerplate is steel rolled into large plates for use in steam boilers. The implication is either that boilerplate writing has been time tested and is as strong as "steel" or possibly that it has been rolled out into something strong enough for repeated reuse. Legal agreements, including software and hardware terms and conditions, make abundant use of boilerplate. The term is also used as an adjective as in "a boilerplate paragraph."

CHAPTER 8

Postcontract

The execution by both parties of a contract, and often the payment of the fee deposit, is a watershed moment in the life of an engagement. From this point on the producer and presenter move forward with this engagement as a locked future activity at a time and place.

Once the contract is signed, the presenter is free to announce the show to the public and begin promotion, and the producer will firm up contracts with the performers and technical team, make sure the set and other theatrical goods are in good repair and ready to be shipped, reserve rental cars or book flights, make freight arrangements, and otherwise move from a negotiating frame of mind to one preparing to deliver the show as contracted.

End of the Booking Process

The completion of the contracting process is often the end of the formal involvement of the booking agent who now turns his full attention to securing future bookings while the producer takes over responsibility for delivering this engagement. But in the sometimes small-seeming world of performing arts touring and presenting, and in the endlessly cycling calendar of booking seasons, the relationships don't really end but rather shift.

Agent Moves to the Back

On the engagement for which the contract has just been completed, the agent would now move to the background as the producer and presenter work together on the logistics of the engagement's advance publicity and of the show arriving, setting up, and being performed in the presenter's community.

But the agent often does remain involved in two important capacities: a) receiving funds, noting that many artist/agent relationships call for some or all of the fees to be paid to the agent and not directly to the producer, and b) facilitating in the event of a contract dispute between presenter and producer. As the agent is often the person or organization that issued the contract, even if he was not a signatory, experience shows that he is likely to be the first one called to help resolve a dispute or misunderstanding between the presenter and producer *or* to help negotiate if one side seeks to cancel. A good agent will attempt to mediate a resolution agreeable to both the producer and presenter and save them the expense and hassle of engaging attorneys and going to court.

Presenter Shifts Focus to Promotion

Having completed the execution of the engagement contract—presumably one among a number that will make up her performance season—the presenter will shift her attention to the season's marketing. If, as is true for many performing arts presenters, the core of the marketing is based on subscriber sales of multiple shows (in France called *abonnement* or in the UK, variously, *combo* or *multibuy offers*), the acquisition and preparation of mailing lists and start of graphic design of the season brochure may well have been under way even before the final engagement contracts were signed.

For many performing arts centers, as with festivals, the announcement of the following season's artistic lineup is an event unto itself—some presenters will go to the added expense of flying in one or two of the more recognizable artists for the occasion in hopes of attracting greater press attention and generating early excitement and demand among the public.

Contracts for venue use are now finalized (if the presenting organization does not have its own theater) and long-lead detailed planning work will get under way with reservations on hotel rooms and theatrical equipment rental placed early to be sure of availability. Presenters may also start or continue a process already begun of soliciting sponsorships for the season or for individual artist engagements—whether as marketing tie-ins on a commercial basis or as contributions to nonprofit arts centers.

Agents and Producers Review Context of Booking

Producers and agents will look at how this engagement fits into their season plans. Is this an *anchor date* around which they hope to secure additional touring in the region? Is this a long run for which they need to block out the necessary time? Are all the essential personnel contracted so there are no nasty surprises in finding that the strongly preferred stage manager or the show's star has booked elsewhere? How much work must be done on costumes, sets, and props to prepare for the engagement? And are there visa issues if this engagement involves crossing international borders? What is the lead time required to start the visa petition process?

Next Round Already in Process

By the time a contract is fully executed for one engagement, it is often the case that all parties are in midbooking process for the season following. Though it is rare that the same production would be in consideration by the same presenter for the immediate next season, it is to be expected that the same agent and presenter are in discussion about other shows for the next round, possibly being offered by the same production companies. Of course the agent is also in search of other presenters for this and other productions for next season.

The process and outcome of each engagement can be important building blocks in the reputations of all parties. If the presenter of the current engagement is not well-known in the field—perhaps a new organization or in a less-traveled part of the world—the agent and producer involved in the current engagement may well be called by other agents and producers considering engagements next season with this presenter to find out how the presenter was to work with through the process, and how trustworthy with respect to honoring agreements.

The same may be true for the other two sides of this triangle: the presenter called by others to report on the reliability and quality of the production, producer, and agent, and the producer and presenter called for reference on the agent by an artist considering joining his roster.

TIMING OF ENGAGEMENTS IN THE BOOKING CYCLE

If the artist or production is new to the field, agents will press for more performances in the fall of the year, which is earlier in the booking cycle for the following season, to use as showcases for viewing by potential presenters. Performances viewed in the spring are often too late to serve as effective sales tools for the following season.

The Handover from Agent to Producer

Unless he has agreed to do more, once the contract is executed and the fee deposit received, the agent's formal relationship with this engagement is complete. His final duty is to properly introduce the relevant people on the production and presenter sides to each other. Depending on the nature of the organizations, on the producer side this might be the general manager or tour producer, and on the presenter side the artist coordinator, program director, or other such titles.

Regardless of whether the producer and presenter have been in direct contact prior to contract execution—and most agents will insist on limiting direct contact until the negotiations are complete—the agent should formally introduce all relevant parties from the presenting and producing teams to each other at this point and bow out of this relationship. It serves as a good opportunity for the agent to thank both sides for their cooperation in the process.

There will be a number of relevant deadlines, notably when the artist is to provide the program copy, the light plot, the rooming list; when the presenter is to make fee payments; when both sides are to exchange insurance certificates; and of course the process for arrangement of advance telephone press interviews with the artist. On departing from the active process it never hurts for the agent to remind both sides of this schedule and their obligations.

From the agent's perspective, of course, the handover is also an opportunity to remind the presenter of other artists on his roster and hopefully open fresh discussion of the next season.

Agent Check-In Along the Way

Though the agent has no formal part in the engagement once the contracting is finished, he has two important reasons to stay tuned in to the communication and planning between the producer and presenter and the advance sales of the production. *First,* noting above that the agent will likely be the first one called if there is a dispute between the other parties over the contract, it helps to not be blindsided but to see a problem as it is coming up. *Second,* if the agent wants to refer other prospective presenters of this production to this presenter for comment on how it is to work with the show and how sales are going, the agent better know ahead of time if the reports are going to be favorable!

Obviously if the producer is to receive a percentage of box office, whether of gross or of net, and if the agent is to receive a commission of what the producer is to receive, he has a financial interest as well in knowing if the income is likely to get above the kick-in level for such percentage.

AGENTS CONTINUE AS BACKGROUND COMMUNICATION CHANNELS

As agents were often central in brokering the deals, they can remain as informal back channels for communication. Presenters may have a closer relationship with agents than with producers as they work together, often year after year, on different presentations. If presenters have special requests to make of artists, ideas for unusual activities related to the engagements, or complaints about producers or productions, they will often float them by the agent first before undertaking formal communication with the producer. Likewise, if producers have a special request of presenters pertaining to booked engagements, they may seek the support and advice of the agent before plunging in.

Follow-Up to Engagement

To paraphrase John F. Kennedy, *"success has many fathers while failure is an orphan."*

JFK's statement is never truer than in the often-risky presentation of the performing arts. An engagement that is well attended by an appreciative audience, with positive press and everybody in the black financially, will have many taking the credit for the astute choice of show and excellent negotiation, marketing, and presentation.

The presenter, of course, will claim special insight into the tastes of his community—and board members and staff will feel justifiable pride in the success. The artist/producer will insist that the show is so spectacular that success was never in doubt!

Those relegated to little positive credit, and attention mostly only in the event of failure, are the *lighting designer* (whose best work is so subtly supportive of the show as to appear invisible), the *press agent* (who it is assumed was not really necessary as the press loved the show so much it would have provided all that coverage anyway) and . . . you guessed it . . . the *booking agent*, whose primary contribution took place more than a year before and is by now long forgotten.

Follow Up Anyway

Agents should always seek feedback from both the producer and the presenter following an engagement, not only as a conduit of productive commentary between those two, but so the agent knows whether to refer other presenters to this presenter for reference on this show and what to advise other producers they may send for presentation by this presenter.

The feedback sought generally breaks down to a) the financial—did the attendance and box office revenue hit or exceed the presenters targets?—and b) the softer communications and logistics issues: was the advance communication timely and clear, were the marketing and other materials provided by the artist what was expected and effective, were the technical production costs what the presenter had been lead to expect?

Noting that presenters—nonprofit community-based organizations in particular—often have constituencies such as donors and board members whose opinions carry special weight, it is important to hear whether those people were happy with the presentation.

Positive and Negative Feedback

Whether the presentation was a success or not, feedback can be important.

Positive feedback, of course, can be conveyed directly among all parties. But negative or *corrective* commentary is where the special position of agents brings them back into play: if the presenter has a critical comment to make about either the producer's operation or the show itself, or if the artist or producer wants to complain about bad treatment by the presenter, they will rarely communicate it directly but rather through the agent. Artists and presenters are reluctant to criticize each other directly for fear of souring future relationships. Somehow agents are seen as having tougher skins and can "take it," and as noted above, the agents often have longer deeper relationships with both the producer and the presenter and have built up more trust over time, allowing room for greater candor.

GOOD NEWS/BAD NEWS

As a rule of thumb, everyone likes to give good news in person— especially to artists. When there is bad news to be conveyed, agents and managers loom large in importance as the messengers!

In the Event of Failure

Obviously, if an engagement's failure was due to what one party perceives to be bad faith or contract violation by the other party, more than delicate communication through the agent may be called for.

It is rare in the nonprofit cultural sector of touring entertainment that parties go as far as legal action. Strong letters from attorneys or senior officials of the offended party often bring the other side to negotiation of the issues, and the threat of censure within the closely knit field carries weight. A presenter with a reputation for not paying as contracted will quickly find that agents demand full payments up front, and artists with reputations for not showing up or last minute demands for more money or services get marked for special caution by presenters if not passed over for presentation.

ALL INTEGRITY, ALL THE TIME

Since one never knows who talks with and respects the opinions of whom, with presenters often corresponding with colleagues a block or a continent distant, disparate artists often schmoozing with each other, and agents hobnobbing with other agents at conferences and via phone and e-mail, regardless of one's role—as agent, presenter, or producer—*pursue all dealings with maximum clarity and integrity at all times.* It is often preferable to lose one engagement, which may hurt in the short term, than to lose one's reputation or do damage to that of the client artist or producer, which can hurt for many years to come. It is preferable to have a reputation as a tough negotiator than as dishonest.

Disagreement on Definition of Success

It is not unusual for a presenter and an artist to have highly differing opinions of the success of an engagement. Good presenters often *paper* (fill with invited audiences) a less-than-sold-out house, sometimes without telling the artist. Some will have volunteers throw flowers on the stage and seek other ways to convey to the artist (and the critics) the impression of a huge success and a sold-out, adoring audience, while in fact they have lost their shirts on the presentation!

As an agent, I have had my artist call me ecstatically after a show to announce a triumph with standing ovations and flowers thrown, certain that the presenter is ready to bring him back *immediately* for an extended return engagement. Then I've heard from the presenter that sales were abysmal, the artist was overly demanding, the local *cognoscenti* hated the show, and "never again!" These are the moments one considers changing careers before relaying this bad news to the sensitive artist.

When and If a Presenter will Bring a Show Back

For the agent's and producer's purposes in planning for the show's or artist's future, it is important to hear whether, how soon, and under what circumstances this presenter would invite this artist back. If, as is often the case, the presenters say they would bring the artist back when the artist or producer has a new show, that may feed into the artist's and producer's long-term planning of new productions.

The agent also needs to know whether, if called by a fellow presenter for comment, this presenter would say good things about the artist or production.

If the presenter is ecstatic, don't hesitate to request a letter of praise for the artist, suitable for reproduction in the show's press kit. And as with the mix of press sources above, don't assume that only letters from New York's Lincoln Center and Carnegie Hall matter—presenters need to see that organizations with similar size venues, local populations, and economics were happy with this artist as well as the presumed experts in New York. And presenters—especially new organizations or venues becoming established—benefit from a growing list of artists and agents singing their praises in the field.

Financial Report

Of course if the producer is to receive a percentage based on box office income, then she can expect to receive a detailed, formal box office statement that will show numbers of full price, discounted, and complimentary seats used. If the engagement was on a *flat guarantee* or *buy out* basis, the presenter is under no obligation to provide the producer with a box office statement, though some will as a courtesy.

CHAPTER 9

Taxation

As with the section on contracts, we begin this chapter with a disclaimer:

I am neither an accountant nor a tax attorney and am not qualified to provide actionable tax advice. I will not accept legal responsibility for actions taken based solely on this book and encourage professional consultation.

This being said, this chapter will attempt an overview of the various types of taxes that relate to touring, of current trends in taxation, and of what the participants should be conscious.

Most national governments and a meaningful number of US states levy an amount of tax on some if not all of the fees to be paid to shows entering from outside and performing in their countries.

National Taxes in the United States

The US is among the more aggressive countries in regard to fees to non-US artists appearing in the country, requiring a federal tax withholding of 30 percent of the fee. And unfortunately, despite discussion between the Internal Revenue Service and the arts touring field, policies shift and confusion remains about the options available to tour producers, agents, artists, and presenters to address, and hopefully lessen, the impact of these taxes.

I will mention several of the factors that may apply, but this area, more than many, is one in which we invite the reader to undertake further research before determining a course of action.

The first advice offered, however, is *don't ignore this issue and hope it will go away or not show up.* It very likely *will* show up and, if not prepared for, can be a nasty surprise.

How the Tax Application Works

Before looking at opportunities to obtain relief from this tax, it is important to understand how it works.

Withholding Agent

Working on the assumption that the US government will not be able to easily get at and enforce a tax payment from a non-US organization, the US government seeks a US entity in the chain of responsibility that it can easily reach and compel to pay. The most obvious, and the first targets, are the *presenters* who will be paying fees. But in a tour involving numerous presenters, this can be cumbersome and a tax on gross fees represents the highest amount of tax that could be applicable. A second option is to hold a US-based *tour producer* responsible, if there is one and assuming all fees are being paid to him and he is paying the fee to the show.

It is important to understand that the government holds all participants in the chain of responsibility legally liable for this tax unless or until one party steps forward and assumes the burden. If the tax doesn't get withheld and paid to the government, the government may come back later and obligate members of the chain to pay it anyway. For this reason, if an agent or tour producer tells presenters that they will not need to withhold the tax, wise presenters will seek written guarantees that any federal tax liabilities will be borne by the agent or tour producer or have been waived by the tax authority.

As we will see, this has direct bearing on the chain of tour contracting, as well. If a US presenter contracts directly with a non-US show, the show should be prepared for the fact that the presenter will withhold and pay 30 percent of the fee to the US government.

Central Withholding Agreement

The primary government-recommended approach to determining the amount of tax for a US tour is by having the artists and the withholding agent sign what is referred to as a *Central Withholding Agreement* with the US Internal Revenue Service. This is done at least three months in advance of the tour with an estimated budget provided. An amended final financial report can be filed after the tour. Once the IRS determines the amount of tax to be paid, the withholding agent arranges for the tax to be withheld and sent to the government. The artists are expected to file nonresident tax reports at the end of the year.

Details on this process are available on the IRS Web site at *www.irs .gov/businesses/small/international/article/0,,id = 106060,00.html* with further questions asked and answered at *www.irs.gov/businesses/small/international/ article/0,,id = 149709,00.html*.

Web Site for Non-US Artists coming to the US

The Association of Performing Arts Presenters and the American Symphony Orchestra League have teamed up to create an extremely helpful and comprehensive Web site that addresses both US federal taxation and visa issues for artists from abroad. It is located at *www.artistsfromabroad.org*.

Avenues to Lessen the US Tax

There are several avenues to explore that can potentially reduce the tax impact. The approaches fall under three categories: a) to reduce the tax basis—the sum on which the tax is calculated—if this can be achieved legally, b) to invoke a tax treaty between the US and the show's home country, assuming one exists and the engagement terms qualify, and seek a tax waiver, and c) to prove and establish tax-exemption qualification in the US based on status in the producer's home country. All avenues bear consideration.

Adjusting Tax Basis

The *basis* is the amount upon which the tax is calculated. This might be legitimately reducible by moving certain nontaxed expenses outside of the taxable sum.

Tour Producer

Often when a foreign artist is to tour the US, a US-based tour producer is secured by the show's producer. Various types of tour producers are discussed in this book, including a tour producer who produces Broadway shows for tour. But in this case, it is a person or entity that effectively *buys* the show from the foreign entity and *sells* it to presenters in the US. The tour producer may also function as the agent in selling the show dates, but his legal position as tour producer is beyond that of agent (a tour producer might in fact engage the services of an outside agent for selling the dates if not performing both functions himself). As a tour producer, he is taking on higher levels of legal responsibility to the show *and* to the presenters, and is assuming financial risk. The tour producer will establish himself as the withholding agent with the Internal Revenue Service.

A tour producer is generally far more involved in all aspects of a tour than an agent, whose responsibilities normally end with booking the dates. A tour producer normally provides and supervises the travel, freight, accommodations, technical planning, etc. And of particular significance to our tax withholding discussion, the tour producer is taking some level of financial risk by receiving the gross payments from the presenters, paying out tour-related expenses and the show's fees, and then profiting or losing based on what is left. The obligation for tax to be withheld does not go away if a tour producer is involved, but the tour producer assumes the responsibility of withholding agent. The distinction between having a US-based tour producer involved or not is whether the tax is calculated on the gross sums to be paid by the presenters or on the net fees the tour producer pays the artist.

Note that the starting position of the US government is that the tax basis is all of the fees paid by the presenters to the show, but through conversations with government tax officials and experience, the government appears to recognize the risk-taking role of a US tour producer (as distinct from a nonrisking agent), accepts him as withholding agent, accepts certain tour-related expenses such as travel paid by the tour producer as outside of the tax basis, and adjusts the tax basis to the fee to be paid to the show. Again, this is an area on which to seek expert advice as you move into it.

Payment of Advance Preparation Expenses

In some circumstances, the government treats payment by the US tour producer of certain specific preproduction expenses in the show's home country in anticipation of the tour differently than performance fees and does not require tax to be withheld on these payments. A payment sent separately in advance to the show's producer to fund the construction of new costumes or rehearsals for the tour, for instance, is generally not considered within the withholding tax basis.

Royalties

Royalties are often treated differently in the international tax treaties with less or no tax applicable. If this is the case and if royalties were otherwise included in the fee to the show's producer, be sure to separate them out into a royalty agreement instead of folding them into the fee.

Invoking Tax Treaties

The US has tax treaties with a number of countries around the world and, before going further into this issue related to a tour, it is important to determine if such a treaty exists with this show's country of origin. The obligation of tax under these treaties is often based on the maximum income any one individual touring will be earning in the host country[1] during the course of an *entire tax year* (not only this tour). If below a threshold amount specified in the treaty, no tax need be withheld, though filing a claim for such exemption to the US government may still be required (see W-8BEN below).[2]

Some examples follow from existing treaties with the US.

In the US–France tax treaty dated 1996, the section on "artistes" reads as follows:

Article 17 Artistes and Sportsmen

1. *Notwithstanding the provisions of Articles 14 (Independent Personal Services) and 15 (Dependent Personal Services), income derived by a resident of a Contracting State as an entertainer, such as a theatre, motion picture, radio, or television artiste or a musician, or as a sportsman, from his personal activities as such exercised in the other Contracting State, may be taxed in that other State. However, the provisions of this paragraph shall not apply where the amount of the gross receipts derived by such entertainer or sportsman from such activities, including expenses reimbursed to him or borne on his behalf, does not exceed 10,000 United States dollars or its equivalent in French francs for the taxable period concerned.*

2. *Where income in respect of personal activities exercised by an entertainer or sportsman in his capacity as such accrues not to the entertainer or sportsman but to another person, whether or not a resident of a Contracting State, that income may, notwithstanding the provisions of Articles 7 (Business Profits), 14 (Independent Personal Services), and 15 (Dependent Personal Services), be taxed in the Contracting State in which the activities of the entertainer or sportsman are exercised. However, the provisions of this paragraph shall not apply where it is established that neither the entertainer or sportsman nor persons related to him derive from that other person any income, directly or indirectly, in respect of such activities that in the aggregate exceeds the amount specified in paragraph 1 for the taxable period concerned.*

3. *The provisions of paragraphs 1 and 2 shall not apply to income derived by a resident of a Contracting State as an entertainer or a sportsman from his personal activities as such exercised in the other Contracting State if the visit to that other State is principally supported, directly or indirectly, by public funds of the first-mentioned State or a political subdivision (in the case of the United States) or local authority thereof. In such case the income shall be taxable only in the first-mentioned State.*

From the *United States–Canada Income Tax Convention* of 1980:

> *Public entertainers. The exemptions for either dependent or independent personal services do not apply to public entertainers (such as theater, motion picture, radio, or television artistes, musicians, or athletes) from the United States who derive more than $15,000 in gross receipts in Canadian currency, including reimbursed expenses, from their entertainment activities in Canada during the calendar year. However, the exemptions do apply, regardless of this $15,000 limit, to athletes participating in team sports in leagues with regularly scheduled games in both the United States and Canada.*[3]

From the *US–Japan Income Tax Convention* of 1971:

> *Articles 17 and 18 provide that under certain circumstances an individual who is a resident of one state shall be exempt from tax on income for personal services in the other state if he is present in the other state for 183 days or less. In the case of a public entertainer who is not an employee, the exemption applies only if he is present for 90 days or less and his income does not exceed $3,000.*

In the *Convention between the Government of the United States of America and the Government of the United Kingdom of Great Britain and Northern Ireland for the Avoidance of Double Taxation and the Prevention of Fiscal Evasion with Respect to Taxes on Income and on Capital Gains* dated 2001, it briefly states:

Entertainers and Sportsmen

> *Income derived by a resident of a Contracting State as an entertainer, such as a theatre, motion picture, radio or television artiste, or a musician, or as a sportsman, from his personal activities as such exercised in the other Contracting State, which income would be exempt from tax in that other State under the provisions of Article 7 (Business Profits) or 14 (Income from Employment) of this Convention, may be taxed in that other State, except where the amount of the gross receipts derived by that resident, including expenses reimbursed to him or borne on his behalf, from such activities does not exceed twenty thousand United States dollars ($20,000) or its equivalent in pounds sterling for the taxable year or year of assessment concerned.*

W-8BEN

If a non US artist or entity is planning to tour in the US from a country with which the US has a tax treaty and seeks to claim exemption under the treaty, the primary form used to document such a claim is Form W-8BEN, obtainable on the US government's Web site. Filing a W-8BEN will often require the foreign entity to establish a tax identification number with the US government even if no tax ends up being owed.

Educational and Nonpaid Activities

If the engagements involve extensive training or workshop activity by the artist, the tax treaties tend to treat academic activity differently and more favorably than live public performance in the area of taxation.

An artist performing without pay, as an amateur artist or a professional appearing at a gala fundraising event without fee, under most of the tax treaties with the US would not be taxed as his/her income would be beneath the minimum threshold.

Tax Exemption or Charitable Status

If approved by the IRS, a producer that holds nonprofit status in its home country may receive such recognition in the US and be provided with a waiver of tax withholding. Information provided in the *questions and answers* section on *www.irs.gov/businesses/small/international/article/0,,id=149709,00.html* from the IRS includes:

> For a foreign tax-exempt organization to claim an exemption from withholding it must provide a Form W-8EXP to the withholding agent. The Form W-8EXP must be accompanied by either: (1) a copy of a tax exemption letter from the IRS, or (2) a letter from an attorney in the United States who attests that the organization would likely obtain tax-exempt status from the IRS if it applied to the IRS for such status.

A non-US nonprofit producer considering this approach to sending a show into the US is advised to undertake further research and consult a US attorney.

US Shows Touring Abroad

US producers sending shows on tour abroad will face national government tax withholding requirements in many countries. Some of these countries have more responsive mechanisms than the US for applying for reduction or waiver on the tax, often in advance of the engagement or tour. The petitions are generally based on demonstrating that little or no profit will be taken from the tour, and that no one individual on the tour is making more than the amounts of annual income from the tour specified as tax thresholds in the tax treaties between the US and the host countries. Regrettably, these treaties do not allow for cost of living increases, and as years pass without revisions to the treaties, these thresholds diminish in current value.

Of course an agent can always start by insisting to the presenter that the fee has to be paid net, thereby dumping the tax responsibility into the presenter's lap. In some cases that works, especially if there is a tour producer in the foreign country taking responsibility for a whole tour. Some large international festivals are used to petitioning for tax waivers in bulk from their governments for the many artists they bring in. Other presenters that are actually branches of or significantly supported by their governments are sometimes able to arrange this internally.

Regardless of who does the paperwork, submission of a petition and budget is almost always required, which involves the participation of the producer (or agent on her behalf)—like it or not.

Timing Conflict between Contract Signing and Tax Waiver

A timing conflict often arises in which the producer is asked to sign a contract to deliver a show internationally before the petition for tax relief can be made or is granted, with the contract necessarily stipulating that the presenter may withhold the tax if required. The producer, of course, is highly reluctant to sign such a contract unless the contracted fee is increased sufficiently to leave him the requisite net if the tax must be withheld. Working with presenters who are willing, if absolutely required, to pay this additional cost is the preferred solution from the producer's perspective.

An alternative is to sign the primary contract and execute a separate agreement that permits the producer to cancel the engagement without any obligation in the event that, by a specified amount of time in advance of the engagement, the tax has not been waived. This, however, puts both parties in difficult positions with a degree of uncertainty remaining as to whether the engagement will proceed: the producer vis-à-vis contracting artists and personnel for the engagement, and the presenter in regard to announcing the engagement to start selling tickets, and booking flights and hotel rooms.

Tax Treaties in Reverse and Form 6166 Proving Payment of US Taxes

The tax treaties discussed above work in the reverse related to US shows going to treaty countries. In order to be able to invoke the terms of those treaties, it is not uncommon for a foreign presenter to require proof from the US producer on behalf of the presenter's government that the producer is current in her US tax obligations. This is done with a Form 6166 from the US Treasury applicable to the contracting US entity (individual or corporation), which is a simple letter stating that the US entity is current in her tax obligations. The document and the process of procuring it are relatively simple.[4]

Two notes, however, from experience: a) apply as early as possible as it can take three or more months from the time of application to get this letter in hand, and b) be sure the letter stipulates the year in which the tour will take place. This latter point is confusing since the letter will always refer to the current year unless otherwise requested. If your application is submitted in the fall for an engagement the following year and the letter is issued in December, the current year will automatically appear on the letter unless otherwise stipulated in the request. In this case the tour host government is likely to insist that the producer start all over again requesting a letter from the US Treasury dated with the new year!

The application form for this document is available on the Internet on the US government Web site.

Social Security Guarantees

Many foreign governments require assurance that US personnel working in their countries have basic medical and Social Security costs covered. The proof of this may be in different forms as requested by the presenter. Occasionally a formal proof of Social Security and Worker's Compensation coverage will be required. Note that standard Worker's Compensation for US workers in the US does not automatically cover them for international work, which must be added at an extra premium.

US State Withholding Tax

A number of states in the US have instituted taxes on the fees paid to shows or artists from outside of the states (whether from other states in the US or from abroad) for performances within the states. Unlike the federal tax, which is standardized for the whole country, the details of these taxes vary state-by-state, but many of the issues are similar.

Conventional wisdom is that this practice grew from taxation on highly paid traveling athletes and later on megatours of large-scale pop music acts. As states' economies have been challenged through the early years of the twenty-first century, states have become increasingly aggressive in pursuing this tax, even on fees paid to low-paid artists and ensembles. Some states are having tax officials scan the media for announcements of concerts, plays, etc., and then calling the presenters to demand the engagement details and the tax.

Regardless of how it started, it has become an increasing burden on many smaller cultural attractions touring, creating unfair competition between in-state and out-of-state artists, and working to circumvent the very intention of the nonprofit laws of the United States as the tax laws in this area in many states make no allowance for whether the artist is a nonprofit entity or not. But for those involved in the touring business it cannot be ignored as it can represent a significant cost of touring.

How it Works

As a means of insuring collection, many of the states that are taxing are doing so in the form of *mandatory withholding* by the presenters—along the same lines as the federal requirement on foreign artists discussed above—with the states holding the presenters liable in the event of non-payment of the taxes. The states do not recognize any withholding agents other than the presenters.

Many states do provide an advance appeal process for the producer (or occasionally the presenter) to seek reduction or waiver, mostly based on the budgets and proof that large profits are not being made and no one individual is being paid a large amount. The individual income calculation is based on all earnings by that individual in that state in an entire year, so if there is more than one visit to the state they all need to be taken into account.

Questions to Ask

The questions that agents and producers must ask in each taxing state are routine, with the answers to each of these questions varying state-by-state:

- Does tax exempt status granted to a company incorporated in another state allow for exemption in the taxing state? (In some cases the answer is yes and in some cases no.)

- What is the starting taxation level—the percentage of the fee due in tax?

- What is the basis for the taxation? Is it on the fee only or on all remuneration and services provided to the artist—per diems, for instance, and royalty payments?

- Is there an advance petition process to seek waiver or reduction of the tax? How far in advance may the petition be submitted?

- Is there a minimum fee or per person salary earned in the state in a single year below which tax does not apply? If so, what?

Who to Ask

Most states have some information available on the Web sites of their tax authorities, though experience shows that they vary considerably in clarity and ease of use. Likewise there are information phone numbers to call, but experience again shows that it is often worthwhile to call twice to make sure you get the same advice both times since tax office employees are often confused on the details themselves!

Presenters are becoming increasingly well educated as to the processes in their states, and in fact some have organized to help both inform incoming artists and assist with an advance tax relief appeals process. The State of North Carolina through the *North Carolina Presenters Consortium*[5] is an excellent example.

At present there is no single source for research on the tax withholding policies and procedures for all the states in the US, but that will hopefully change soon.

Filing to do Business in States

A related issue is the requirement in some states for the contracting organization representing the visiting artist to file to do business in the state in question, which often involves a filing fee and a requirement to submit a tax filing at the end of the year.

In some states—New Jersey as an example—the state government is enforcing this requirement by forbidding any presenters receiving funding from the State of New Jersey to issue fee payments without receiving written proof that the recipients have filed to do business in the State. The State has made it quite simple to file to do business online and, for now at least, there is no charge for doing so.

By filing in a state, a producer thereby earns the right and sometimes the obligation to file a tax report at the end of the year, and potentially to receive some or all of the tax back if he can prove that little or no profit was made. For smaller artists or shows, this simply compiles the burdens of touring, now adding the filing fees and accountants costs to the tax.

For larger producers doing business regularly in another state, it pays to file to do business there and even to engage a payroll service within the host state to pay the producer's employees and withhold taxes as required.

US City Tax Withholding

There is a nascent effort by a few cities, notably in the state of Ohio, to join the bandwagon and also levy a withholding tax on fees payable to out-of-state artists. At the time of this writing, fortunately, there is little indication that this is gaining ground.

End Notes

1   This applies in both directions: US artists touring into foreign treaty countries and artists from those countries touring in the US.

2   Copies of the tax treaties are available online through the US Treasury (*www.ustreas .gov/offices/tax-policy/treaties.shtml*) and directly from the Internal Revenue Service (*www.irs .gov/businesses/international/article/0,,id=96739,00.html*). A comprehensive overview is available with the United States Department of the Treasury/IRS Form 901 (Revised May, 2004) titled "US Tax Treaties."

3   Internal Revenue Service Publication 597

4   See *www.irs.gov/businesses/small/international/article/0,,id=122559,00.html* for instructions.

5   *www.ncpresenters.org*

SECTION II

STRATEGY AND SPECIAL AREAS

CHAPTER 10

Strategy and Curation

Strategy is the approach one takes to achieving one's objectives. Obviously in our tour planning world, all participants—presenters, agents, producers, and artists—will or should have some sort of strategy guiding their activities. *Curation* is the process of making artistic choices ("curating").

Our focus, related to touring, will be on how our players think strategically about the productions they create, represent, or present, and on the influences behind programmatic choices.

Attendance Motivations

The ultimate determinants of what gets produced, survives, and tours are what people will pay money to go see, along with what donors and sponsors will subsidize. It is beyond the scope of this book to explore sponsorship motivations and we will focus on the area of public taste and ticket purchase motivations.

The issue of taste is far from simple, however; with the first hurdle being that people can't know that they want to experience something until they have already experienced it, leading to the obvious question of how to get them to experience it in the first place! So our field is simultaneously serving the paradoxical needs of *leading the public's taste* and *following the public's wishes*. It both chases after what the audience *thinks* it wants to see, based on what it has already seen, *and* introduces entirely new shows and ideas. Everything now old to each of us was once new to each of us!

I often think of booking agents and presenters as vacation travel agents with two types of client demands:

> "Send us back to that wonderful place where we have been many times before. We've always loved it and appreciate its familiarity, and we know we'll love it again."

"Send us somewhere new and exciting, where we can explore new things and have an adventure."

Is there a wrong or right between these two choices? Of course not. Yet they reflect the precise duality of going to the theater for the treasured and well-known classics versus going for the exciting unknown, and, for producers, agents, and presenters, the choice between producing, representing, or presenting a remake of a tried-and-true show or formula (following), or rolling the dice on something new (leading).

Over time it has been proven that both sides of this paradox *must* ultimately be addressed or the field becomes stale. Despite what may be reported on audience surveys, there is a point at which, being offered the same fare too often, the public will silently vote with its feet and simply not buy tickets to go back to the theater. The public will rarely demand to be shown totally new, challenging, and often-provocative theatrical ideas, and many will walk out when they are. Yet without just such new ideas brought into the theaters, the field would become a stagnant relic—a museum of historic ideas and tastes.

Producers Lead

If producers could follow a proven formula for shows and have a hit every time, many surely would and some try. But public taste and mood don't often work like that. And a show that follows a "proven" formula may well flop while an off-the-wall, crazy new idea may catch on and become an overnight sensation. This field is a lot like the "science" of economics, which is generally good at identifying the factors that affect the economy and at explaining why a historical event took place but weak on being able to realistically predict what will happen tomorrow.

Producers are a perverse and highly idiosyncratic lot, much like restaurateurs and fashion designers. The effective ones operate from some combination of head and heart that is unique. The *head*, of course, is the part that studies how other shows have done and makes an effort at "scientific" assessment of the producer's shows in comparison—essential in convincing people to invest money in the ventures. The *heart* part is the gut feeling that underlies each enterprise and brings the fire and passion to the process. The balance of both sides has proven over time to be essential to happy survival in the field; those who wish to operate only from *head* generally end up either working in the finance office or moving to other fields; those with only *heart* either become artists or are forced by financial losses to move to other fields!

Agents and Presenters Follow

What goes for producers who bring the works into existence in the first place, applies perhaps to a lesser degree for the agents who decide to bring them onto their rosters and for presenters who ultimately decide to bring them to their communities on tour. The strong advantage these two players have, of course, is that they generally are able to see the finished product before making their commitments. And good agents and presenters have their own head–heart interactions, each according to his or her own particular psychological makeup and risk tolerance.

Objectives of the Three Primary Players

With curatorial considerations in mind, we will review the objectives of each of our three primary protagonists. They vary, of course, and it is important that some people want to produce, some to present, and some to be in the middle to make the marriages. But to a large degree the objectives of all three arrive at the same place.

Producer

For the producer of a show, the objectives will include some combination of making money and sharing the show with as many audience members as possible. There is also an excitement about discovering and introducing a talented young performer, playwright, choreographer, director, etc., to the scene. And of course there is the intangible goal of contributing something lasting to the theatrical record—achieving a place in the pantheon inhabited by David Merrick, Martin Beck, Joseph Papp, and others who have significantly contributed to and transformed the industry through their producing.

A producer's initial business plan for a new show may not count on touring, but the prospect looms large in the background as the show comes into being. And of course for many producers, touring *is* central to their plans with an initial New York City run intended primarily to provide the imprimatur associated with running in that city.

Agent

For the agent, hopefully allied closely with the producer in setting goals and objectives, objectives will also be to maximize exposure and revenue for the production or artist he represents and "get it out there." He will look at markets—their size, geographic distance from each other, and relative importance in a nuanced hierarchy within the presenting world. He will be considering the right presenters and venues for each production in each market to be sure that the show is placed as strategically as possible in prominent venues, being handled by presenters best suited to marketing this type of show. He will be part of the producer's strategic team related to the life of the production. His place in history is defined by the artists he has represented and the deals he has made for them. His archetypal historic models might be William Morris, who is credited as the first booking agent, who fought for the interests of previously mistreated artists against the rapacious presenters (venue managers and cartels) in the late nineteenth century, and Sol Hurok, who is credited as the first impresario whose name attached to a production could sell out an unknown show and whose agency, Sol Hurok Presents, dominated the industry in the mid-twentieth century.

Presenter

For the presenter, the obvious immediate goals are selling out and maximizing income and impact. Short term, of course, the concern is to hit or exceed financial projections. Longer term, presenters build credibility with their audiences through each critical success, with an elusive but highly desirable goal being that the phrase *The XYZ Arts Center Presents* . . . will be sufficient for some people to buy tickets to an artist of whom they have never heard. The complex interplay of short-term and long-term goals is addressed elsewhere in this book and involves a classic money/art balance.

Strategies for achieving this are numerous and warrant a separate book on the art of presenting. One example is to build an ongoing pattern of repeat presentation with particular artists and to invest in creating a rapport between those artists and the local community to assure return and expanding audiences. A second is to balance mass appeal presentations that generate profits with the introduction of lesser-known artists, whose presentations may lose money to the community. Many arts centers operate as nonprofit institutions, seeking charitable support for operations and programming; others develop programming formulas that allow them to run commercially.

What Does Strategy Mean in this Context?

Remember that the producer can be anything from a single artist working up his/her routine in a studio, to an ensemble or institutional nonprofit organization such as a dance company, a touring theater company, or perhaps an opera company, to a pop music group or the company formed to produce a Broadway show. Experience suggests that most people involved in producing were first motivated, not by a quest to get rich—there are surely fields in which there is a more direct and easier route to that end—but because they were bitten by a love for the live-performance experience. Indeed many studies show that there is a strong correlation between youthful performing experience and a love of live performance. So strategies for shows and the motivations of the producers are inevitably linked.

Producers vary tremendously in style, and the strategy for each differs not only in ambition and scope but the level of formality. A self-producing solo artist may have an opportunity to put on a show with no strategy past those first performances, assuming that what happens after will be a matter of luck, how the press and audiences respond to the show, and who sees it and wants to take it somewhere.

At the opposite extreme, the general manager of a Broadway production company, with millions of dollars on the line from investors watching over his shoulder, will have been expected to present a highly developed and professional business plan for the show with targets for the initial run in New York, often (though not always) including the potential merchandizing, commercial tie-ins, and touring.

Regardless of the style, at a certain point, in order to have a life, the resulting production must serve two masters: it must have artistic appeal and entertainment value to at least a segment of the press and public *and* be able to survive financially through sheer ticket sales revenue, sponsorship, or a combination of the two.

Curatorial Process

What all three of our players—producers, agents, and presenters—are involved in is a process called *curation*. While the word historically means to oversee or protect,[1] the term in our field has evolved through use by the museum and visual art world to imply a more active role in making artistic choices.

Presenters Curate

From the original and evolved meanings of the word, *curation* affects the presenter's role on two levels:

1) Her broad curatorial role implies a responsibility to protect her community's relationship to the live performing arts, perhaps to be interpreted as the mission to serve as many community members as possible, which in turn hints of artistic choices with wide public appeal (what we term *following the public's wishes*).

2) An evolved definition of the term—to adjudicate and carefully select artists for a performance season—implies a responsibility to educate and expand the knowledge and/or experience of the audience members, which hints of moving beyond what the audience already knows and introducing the new (*leading the public's tastes*).

Agents Curate

In the same way that an agent is to a large degree defined by his roster, his *curated* selection of shows being offered for tour is also viewed from this paradoxical dual standard of popularity and exciting newness.

The Mix is Critical—A "Curatorial Mandate"

Regardless of what any one producer, agent, or presenter may choose, the *curatorial mandate* of the field as a whole must encompass both the established and the new. Without both, we risk on the one hand drowning in a soup of nostalgia with upward spiraling ticket prices to narrower audiences that will simply, at some point, stop coming, and on the other hand letting go of the reference links to our past and our daily lives by offering such consistently bold contemporary work as to risk alienating the majority of the theater-going public almost entirely.

In cities with the scale and range of cultural offerings of a New York, Boston, Chicago, or Los Angeles, one can assume that there are always people planning to go out to a show and a natural diversity of presenting tastes and values will provide a balance. The greater challenge exists in smaller communities with, perhaps, only one performing arts center under monolithic control, where the public's entire worldview of live performance is dictated by the tastes of the few in control of the arts center who are all too often most comfortable on the *follow the public's wishes* side of the equation.

Sadly, nearly universal concerns that young people are not coming to the theater bear this out. In the US in the early twenty-first century, anecdotal reports and audience surveys tell us that they simply don't see the traditional live theatrical experience in general, and most of the programming in particular, to be relevant to their lives. They do not see most performing arts venues to be a regular part of their routine migratory pattern, nor can they typically afford to pay anywhere near the real cost of tickets relative to what it takes to mount labor-intensive live shows. There is hardly a performing arts center, dance and opera company, or producer of live entertainment of any nature in the US not presently wrestling with how to tune their image, pricing, and programming to align with the tastes and lifestyles of young people.[2]

Endnotes

1   It is derived from the Latin *curare* meaning "to care for or attend to."

2   The trap here is in the perception of what is of value. Indeed, young people make up a large part of the enormous expenditure on tickets to certain pop music concerts each year, so a segment of that demographic *does* spend money on live entertainment, and the question of what can be afforded is clearly tied up with what is perceived to be of interest and value. This is not to say that there is not a next circle of potential audience members interested in attending cultural events who are held off by admission prices, but to tap a significantly larger social network, issues of both program choices and the image of the host venues can be of equal importance.

CHAPTER 11

The Life Cycles of Productions

There is a life cycle to every production from its earliest concep-
tion through *development*, sometimes called *workshopping*, to
performances. Once given life, the show might be a one-off tour of a
rock-and-roll show timed around a CD release or become an enduring classic, such as certain ballets, symphonies, and Broadway shows
that are remounted periodically over decades. The characteristics of
each show will have impact in its life's journey.

Significant Factors

Let's examine factors that have significance in the life cycles of almost
all shows.

Getting it Seen: Three Target Audiences

Early in the life of a production—and even before its life begins and
long before it gets to the public—there are three different targets to
be considered.

Investors or Donors

This is the money to pay for the show. Invited in early to see the
work in development, these folks will often expect to see a rough
reading in a studio and hopefully will be excited about being part
of a new theatrical enterprise. They do not expect all the bells and
whistles as they come in understanding that the producer is seeking
money early in the process—hopefully theirs—to get the show to
full production. That doesn't mean that the showcase can be sloppy
or casual. A good Broadway producer will work hard to assemble a
first rate team of performers, prepare them as best possible within
the amount of time allowed under Actors' Equity regulations, and
make sure the full creative team is on deck, with everyone cued for

a smooth presentation. A well run showing—which either formally or informally (depending on whether the tender offer has been filed with the Securities and Exchange Commission) is often referred to as a *backers' audition*—gives potential investors confidence that this team will be equally organized and efficient in mounting the whole show and spending their money.

Alternately, if it is a show that has been produced on a small scale Off-Broadway or regionally, seeking investors to *enhance* the show and move it to Broadway, the potential investors will see a full performance. But again, the lead producer and creative team will be on hand to explain what they will be doing to the show to bring it up to the larger scale of a Broadway venue, replacing the sparse low-budget set with a fancier setting, expanding the music, etc.

A nonprofit dance or theater company will be seeking to bond the prospective donors more to the organization as ongoing patrons beyond an individual production. So the approach might be in the context of a membership or ongoing support relationship, with this new production as an introduction to the company's work and process. Of course there are some funders who will support institutional nonprofit companies to create productions based on descriptions alone, before any work has been done. But showing these funders the works in progress or completed is still critical to maintaining credibility with these funders for future support.

Presenters

While some presenters will be interested in a new production in its early stages, most won't spend the time until they can see near finished performances—whether in showcase at a booking conference, a preview performance, or a public showing—with an eye to whether or not the show will fit in their venue and be right for their audiences. That doesn't mean one shouldn't keep presenters informed of development on new projects, but don't expect active responses until closer to completion.

Having said that, as noted elsewhere in this book, some presenters are able to actually take part in producing or developing new shows, and these (regrettably few) presenters might be invited to early studio showings in hopes that they will agree to help commission the new productions, or at least make early commitments to presenting them when finished. Indeed, certain conferences, such as the annual gathering of the International Society for the Performing Arts (ISPA) and the biannual Commerce International des Arts de la Scène (CINARS)—or, translated, International Exchange for the Performing Arts—now have sessions within their conferences in which new projects can be *pitched* to prospective cocommissioning presenters much as to a room of venture capitalists—in the case of ISPA, appropriately termed *pitch sessions*. Note that the participation of presenters in the creation of new work need not always involve only money, since many offer in-kind use of theaters, studios, and accommodations to host productions during rehearsals and early production development.

Critics

These are of course among the most critical (sorry) to the life of the show as their words become part of the production's permanent record, for better or worse, and are what will be read by funders, donors, presenters, and, of course, the theater-going public. For those funders, donors, and presenters considering the show without benefit of having seen it, the critiques (along with any video available and reference of fellow funders, donors, and present-ers) are all they have to go on.

The critics will expect to see a finished production ready for critical analysis. If funds are available, a producer will hire a press agent to work on a show, whose function it is to solicit, screen, monitor, cajole, inform, *spin*, and otherwise be the point of interaction between the show and the press. The job of the press agent is grist for an entire book of its own. But every press agent walks the terrifying lines between "Will the press come?" "Will they come too early in the show's development?" and of course "Will they love it or hate it?"

Getting it Seen: The Role of Showcases

Every production will have some key performances in its life that are vital *showcases* for people who can directly and significantly impact its future, nota-bly investors or donors, presenters, and critics. It is important for the pro-ducer to recognize and plan these performances according to the projected development of the work. They might be early studio showings of a work in progress, staged performances *in preview* if the length of the run allows for previews, "out of town tryout" performances if such can be arranged before the big New York or other significant opening, or postopening public per-formances in New York or in venues and locations that are deemed to be of significance.

Obviously funders and donors need to view the work as early as possible if their support is needed to create the production.

Good press is important at any time but most urgently needed early in the show's life to get the word out and the audiences in. Though it may help future touring, a great review does little good for immediate ticket sales if it appears after a show has closed!

Viewings by presenters are also good any time, but the booking cycle must be kept in mind. By around February or March (north of the equator), most presenters will have completed their programming for the following season, which means that a viewing then or later may result in faded memories by the time planning for the following season comes around. Fall presenter viewings are preferable for bookings the following season.

The subject of *conference showcases* is important and warrants special attention. As most presenters don't have the time and money to fly all over to see shows in regular performance but attend at least one of the major booking conferences, arranging a conference showcase of one's production can be an effective and efficient way to expose it to a large number of presenters. Additionally, the conference environment permits opportunity for the producer, agent, and/or artists to speak directly to the presenters and *spin* the production.

The biggest downside for many productions is that the spaces available for any reasonable amount of money are often hotel ballrooms or meeting rooms or nearby studios, not designed for much if any production refinement. A small music ensemble or a monologist, with the ability to set up quickly and perform anywhere, can do well. In a studio, a dance company can show the moves. But to the degree that the effect of the production depends on sophisticated lighting, sets, and a fly system over the stage, etc., *a showcase in limited conference conditions can actually do more harm than good to the perception of the show in the presenting field.*

The Role of New York City

The weightiest press will be in major cities, starting with New York. So the questions of if and when in its life cycle the show should be seen in New York are among the most important issues with which producers and artists will wrestle. And there is also the question of *how*. Bringing a show into New York City on one's own can be an extremely expensive and risky undertaking, and there are a limited number of presenters in New York, all besieged by programming proposals.

It is very rare that any show will or should open in New York City without being *tried out* elsewhere first to be as sure as possible that it is ready. Even New York–based dance companies, who will often want to offer the official world premiere of a new dance during their home season in New York to attract more press and satisfy funders, will arrange to preview the production on tour as far away from New York as they can to break it in and work out the bugs before hitting the glare of the Big Apple.

When a commercial show does get to New York, there is a press convention that, as long as the show is *in previews*, it will not be reviewed. But the trade off is that there *must* be an opening before it closes—that is, in agreeing not to review previews, the press must be offered at least one shot at reviewing the show. Well you might ask why a producer would preview a performance without wanting to open it. But keep in mind the devastating effect of bad New York press—far worse than no New York press at all! There have been shows that, after extensive tinkering during previews, have still not *jelled* or *found themselves*, and have literally opened and closed on the same night with the producer seeking as little press attention as possible.

Among the shows that *originate in New York City* without out-of-town try-outs are those from locally based nonprofit producers, such as the Manhattan Theatre Club, the Classical Theatre of Harlem, Atlantic Theater Company, and Second Stage Theatre, that will produce new plays, many with a solid subscription base to guarantee audiences for the first weeks of a run. With positive critical and public response, some of these productions will extend their runs or move to other venues without leaving the city. In fact, two of these organizations—MTC and Roundabout—have expanded operations to cover both sides of the Broadway border, operating and producing in both Off-Broadway and Broadway theaters.[1]

The archetype for this in recent history is the surprise hit musical *A Chorus Line*, developed by the nonprofit downtown New York Public Theater under the legendary Joseph Papp in the 1970s and moved for a long and profitable run to Broadway. In these instances, a) most critics understand the context of the production for reviewing and often will be gentler to a new production Off-Broadway than to a Broadway opening, and b) in most cases the Off-Broadway producer doesn't start off assuming (though perhaps hoping!) that the production will move to Broadway.

Advance Press versus Critiques

While critics coming to review a show will expect it to be finished and open for public consumption, press agents will also work hard to get advance press attention for the upcoming show to assist in creating buzz and to have tickets sold even before the show opens. This can take place during rehearsals or previews, which the press may observe as long as what they write does not constitute a review of the show.

The advance press might be a human-interest story about the lead actress who recovered from a near-fatal disease just in time to do the part, the Broadway director now directing his first opera, the difficulties in getting a British star clearance to perform in New York, or the unique puppets being created for the show. The young ingénue might show up in a fashion magazine, the set designer's fabulous home in an architectural magazine article, or the lead actor's culinary secrets on a popular cooking show.

Any way the press agent can get the show mentioned and to the attention of the audience—"top of mind"—is considered fair game. And of course conveying some insider feeling about the process of creating the show and the personalities behind it gives potential audience members some of the excitement the investors and production participants feel being part of the process early on.

The Role of Touring

Of central interest to this book is the role of touring in the life cycle of shows. Assuming a significant formal opening of the show is planned—perhaps in New York City—the objectives of touring before and after that event differ.

Preopening

As noted above, most producers want their show tested (*tried out*) in front of live audiences before the official opening. They also seek opportunities to work through the technical production issues without paying the high union stage labor rates often applicable in larger theaters in big cities.

In the popular music industry and for other one-night and very short-run shows, the careful press rules about not reviewing preview performances that apply to Broadway are less severely applied and viable. If such an act wants to polish before being seen in the city or on a big city tour, it needs to do so out of the limelight.

For many productions, preview touring can be arranged. Of course it is not as easy to sell an unknown show to presenters, and the nature of these deals will vary.[2]

Some presenters, often universities in smaller communities, with good venue facilities, low cost labor, and students interested in learning about the business, will offer trades: new shows can spend extra time in their theaters working out the lighting, sound, and other tech issues in exchange for some performances at low ticket prices to the campus and neighboring communities. The deals might involve dormitory space provided by the host, and perhaps relatively small fees to help offset actors' salaries and per diems. For a school wanting its students to experience first hand the process of developing a professional show, and for a producer seeking a *laboratory* to refine the production, this can be a win–win.

One hears the occasional story of the famous rock musician, who routinely, sells out large arenas, showing up virtually unannounced in a modest-sized theater in a small town to test new material in front of a responsive audience before all the production trappings get added—even announcing a false name to avoid the stampede!

Some presenters, such as the highly respected Massachusetts Museum of Contemporary Art (MASS MoCA) in the Berkshires—with an abundance of space but lean program funds—have built a reputation for hosting exciting new performing arts work early in its development based almost entirely on services provided in lieu of funds.

These preopening engagements, in addition to providing opportunities for the creative directors to tinker with the shows, also provide occasions for videotaping and photographing the show for later promotional use.

Postopening

This is of course the primary touring, wherein the shows that have opened in New York or elsewhere and begun to establish reputations now seek to head out on the Road. Not all shows can or will tour, of course. But most producers will at least give the matter serious consideration as a means of extending the lives of their shows, and generating revenue to help recoup the creation costs if still needed or of leveraging profits from the initial creation investment.

It is a rare production that can open and close in its home city with the costs of the production recouped and the participants satisfied that that is all the life the production should have.

Producers of most new shows don't really know whether their show will be suitable for touring until it is opened. Many report that touring is not factored into the original business plan for the show, though of course the option—and hope—exists for the show to have a great and profitable touring life.

Producers of restaged classics and importers of shows from other countries will often plan for a tour in conjunction with a featured engagement in New York and/or other major cities.

Tour Concepts and Expectations Vary by Genre

Within this broad outline, the nature of touring envisaged in producers' strategies can vary greatly.

- *For a pop musician*, the plan might be to go out for a grand tour that coincides with a new album release and then lay low for a year while working on new material and reconnecting with family, or, as crossover professional opportunities open up, work in other areas such as film, fashion, and video.

- *For a dance company*, runs in the home city often lose money and the company will look to touring to generate extra revenue and help recoup the costs of the new production. Also with dance, retaining a core of dancers experienced in the particular technique and familiar with the repertoire for as much of the year as possible is a high priority. As many dance companies have been around a while and built up followings in multiple cities, their tour stops will hopefully include some regular return locations as well as new ones.

- *For a production from a League of Regional Theatres (LORT) member*, there might be an invitation to appear at other LORT's for runs of four to six weeks, with a hope of recovering at least part of the initial production costs before the show is retired. These productions might also be appropriate for appearances internationally—especially at festivals where there is more money to bring in larger and more unusual productions—and of course might make it to New York for a commercial run. Unless the production can offer split weeks and single performances, which most LORT productions can't, there are regrettably few touring opportunities in the US for drama that does not carry the Broadway stamp.

- *For an opera*, the initial production is unlikely to tour as the initial cast is not available and the initial orchestra locally based and not a touring unit. But the initiating opera company may seek to rent out the set and costumes and license its production to other opera companies to produce, with the rental and licensing income helping to recoup the initial creation costs.

- *For a Broadway show*, touring is often an expected part of the show's life as will be analyzed in greater detail in chapter 14. The tour will either capitalize on the great success of the initial Broadway run or seek to recover from an initial Broadway failure.[3]

- *For an Off-Broadway show*, the producers might look at two models: sitting replications of the show down for extended runs in other cities even while the show continues to run in New York, with a good example being the successful *Blue Man Group*, or expanding (*enhancing*) the show for Broadway-style touring in larger venues. A combination of the two may also be possible as has been done very successfully with *Stomp*. Sadly, little Off-Broadway drama makes it out on tour with any consistency.

- *For classical musicians*, the degree of touring typically works inversely to size. Large orchestras do tour, but only very selectively and for limited periods of time as the costs of moving such large groups are so high and most orchestra musicians do not have lifestyles geared to long lives on the Road. Chamber orchestras will tend to tour more and small ensembles even more yet. Many solo artists, including conductors and guest virtuosi, practically live out of suitcases as they span the globe—language, of course, being no barrier to the offerings of a pianist or cellist.

- *Comedians and Circuses.* Here are two touring productions at opposite extremes of scale and flexibility. A successful comedian can jump on a plane, walk into a theater and perform, and be home the next morning. At the opposite extreme, a circus epitomizes one of the largest touring operations with the big ones equivalent to a military operation of convoys and personnel, carrying not only all the usual theatrical equipment, but often animals and its own venue as well! Of course they do tour, but rarely locating for less then some number of weeks and offering a much higher number of performances per week than any other genre.

Finding the Audience

There is a lot of talk among producers of letting or helping a show *find its audience.* This is of course more urgent with shows that are entirely new in concept and somehow *break the mold* or *push the envelope* of what has been done before, where it can be challenging to pigeonhole the audience by type or through comparison to other shows.

With any show, as any product being brought to market, the producer and marketers must start by comparing the characteristics of this show to other shows for shorthand reference, focusing on those that were successful. They look at the demographics of the audiences that enjoyed those other shows and work from the assumption that these same audiences will enjoy their show.

This may also involve test marketing by placing images in varying media with different demographic appeal to determine the characteristics of the most motivated buyers. Taken to the extreme, it can be a somewhat scary, Orwellian process, but the more demographic data the producer and agent can glean (*the people who like this show also love baseball,* etc.), the greater the probability of the show finding its audience and being financially successful.

Finding the audience means not only the core demographic appeal but, for tour planning, determining the show's appeal among regions and even nations and continents. Bollywood productions are wildly popular in India but have only scratched the surface in the US. A country music musical that was not embraced in New York City did well on national tour. Straight dramas seem to do better in London than in New York. The producer and agent will focus their tour booking attentions on those regions of the globe, and those presenters with audience demographics, that match the audience that has been determined to find the show most appealing.

There are no easy formulas or we'd all be rich. Like the "science" of economics, the producer makes the best plan possible for his show based on all available experience and good advice, and attempts to stay flexible to adjust the strategy if the planned course proves wrong.

Some Additional Considerations Related to Touring

As producers consider the viability, potential, and business model for touring their shows, following are some additional areas in the discussion and planning.

Replicating the Show

A show centered around one famous or highly specialized artist is just that. It can only be in one place at one time. And if the central artist is indisposed, the show gets cancelled. So a very important question in the early strategizing for the show is whether the performers can be replaced or replicated in a second production. And if a second, how about a third, fourth, etc.?

Obviously, from the standpoint of investors, the ability of the show to be replicated is very attractive. It means that if a show becomes a long-running hit in a center such as New York or London, it is possible to mount additional *sit down* shows in other major cities and/or send duplicate shows out on tour, expanding the revenue potential of the initial investment. From the standpoint of the producer and presenter, overdependence on one figure places great risk on the health of that individual and potential financial loss if he or she gets sick or injured.

This is not to minimize the importance of the world's great and irreplaceable artists—Yo-Yo Ma, Mikhail Baryshnikov, and James Taylor, for example—but raises a strategic question about the production, which must be evaluated. The success in recent years of a musical production involving unknown performers from England called *Stomp*, and since replicated a number of times, is overwhelming. The *Stomp* business model has resulted in huge profits for the investors and has awakened the field to the potential for leveraging of initial investment through replication.

Costs Adjusted for Touring

How many people really need to travel with the show, and be fed, paid, housed, and transported? Does the full light plot from the original home run of the show need to be duplicated at every tour stop? Is the show a full union production? These are important questions for the producer who wants the show to successfully tour and for the buyer deciding whether he can afford to bring the show in. This is not always a simple process as directors and creators are often loath to let go of cherished artistic elements for the show to tour, and the issue of union participation in touring shows and at what contract levels and salary scales, has significant cost impact.

International Touring Potential

Shows that rely on understanding dialogue for appreciation—especially language-intensive straight dramas—are a hard sell outside of countries for which the production's original language is native. This appears especially true of non-English-language productions touring the US, whose English-language audiences seem to be more resistant to enjoying shows in other languages with surtitles than their European, Asian, and South American counterparts.

However, as the percentage of the US population for which English is not the first language increases, there is an emerging market for productions in other languages geared to those immigrant populations—a business model through which Sol Hurok established his business in the 1920s to the immigrant Russian and other populations, primarily in New York City.[4]

Musicals have fared better, but are often recast in non-English countries with translated spoken script performed in the local language and only the music offered in English. Dance and music have, over time, been the most successful in moving across national boundaries as language is not a factor.

The Union Factor

The role of unions, and especially the salaries and related performer costs mandated in agreements with the Actors' Equity Association, is currently a subject of heated discussion, primarily in the world of Broadway touring but in other areas as well, and has tremendous bearing on the nature and economics of tours.

Having fought for a century for the protection, benefits, living wage, and respect lacking in the 1800s theater business, performers and their unions are now facing challenges born from their own success. In interviews for this book, it was clear that the issue is affecting every aspect of the industry and is not a simple matter. Producers, agents, and presenters, most of whom are conceptually in support of professional trade unions and the talented performers represented, are faced with the glaring reality of show costs that exceed revenue with increasing consistency and the risk of debilitating losses. While the salaries of the performers are not the only factor responsible—the increased cost of fuel for transport, costs and work rules of nonperformer unions such as stagehands, a growing price sensitivity on the ticket buying side, and the current dearth of blockbuster hit shows are examples of added contributors—nonetheless the alternative of working with non-Equity shows looms as an economically attractive alternative to bankruptcy for many producers, agents, and presenters.

As we write, the League of American Theaters and Producers is engaged with the Actors' Equity Association in protracted discussions to find mutually acceptable solutions. The latest contract[5] makes some effort to address the skyrocketing costs of touring and the negative impact on ticket prices and attendance (and therefore bookings). But the consensus seems to be that the challenges have not been fully overcome and the discussions must continue.

The other union with the most cost impact on show touring is the International Alliance of Theatrical Stage Employees (IATSE), which governs the stagehands where a show touring "on the yellow card" means that the touring crew are IATSE members and a locally provided crew is expected to be the same. Traditionally the management concerns with this union have centered less on basic rates of pay and more on work rules that are often designed with less than optimal employment and cost efficiency in the labor to set up and run shows. It is a reasonable bet that this relationship will also be forced into significant review if the financial pressures on touring continue.

These agreements are in a highly dynamic state and this will be an important issue for readers of this book to continue observing closely.

Revivals and the Role of Rights Holders

Our discussion has focused primarily on strategy for rolling out new shows in the best possible light, for giving them the opportunities to be seen, hopefully, on their way to becoming well-established hits.

For those productions which become classics and are returned periodically (often termed *revivals*), there are further strategy issues related to how often and where the productions should be remounted so as to keep up public awareness on the one hand but not oversaturate on the other.

Dramatic Works

In the case of dramatic and musical theater works, these decisions are made by the publishers or rights holders, such as Tams-Witmark and Samuel French, which keep track of when and where the productions are offered everywhere in the world and grant the permissions necessary for producers to remount the works. Some rights holders dedicated to preserving and promoting the work of one or a few creators, such as the Kurt Weil Foundation and the Rogers and Hammerstein Foundation, are renowned for their aggressive protection of not only when and where the productions can be mounted, but by what producers and under what directors. Such protection, while strict, is often responsible for keeping the productions alive in the public mind and insuring that exposure to new young audiences will always meet a minimum standard of quality.

Artist-Led Companies and Intellectual Property

In the case of repertory and ensemble companies, where the rights often reside with the companies or the primary creators (as in the case of many dance choreographers), these decisions are usually made within the companies. In instances where the rights have remained with the creating artists, there have been some highly publicized and regrettable battles over control after the death of the creators. These have risked damaging the public perception of these works. Such was the case with the death of Robert Joffrey, founder of The Joffrey Ballet. The company ultimately folded—over this and other reasons—and was recreated under his designated successor in Chicago, the work being lost to New York audiences. Likewise with the death of Martha Graham, where court battles over creative control after Ms. Graham's death forced the Martha Graham Dance Company to close and the work to go unseen anywhere for several years.

While not necessarily true in these cases, difficulties often stem from a lack of careful planning and written agreements on the issue of rights control and succession early in the relationships. Seeing these sad cases, younger artists are being more thorough in planning for the succession of ownership and creative control after their deaths—an extension of strategic planning for productions for, in some cases, years after the works were initially created. One never knows at the outset which new work will become a classic in perpetual demand and which a brief blip at the edge of the screen.

Endnotes

1   Broadway theaters comprise thirty nine 500 + seat theaters in midtown Manhattan. Off-Broadway theaters are those with 100 to 499 seats throughout Manhattan. This classification of theaters is governed by language in Actors' Equity Association contracts and by venue agreements with various unions, rather than by whether the theater has a Broadway address.

2   Some presenters have managed to develop an "I saw it first" motivated audience that gets excitement from seeing shows *before* they make it in the big time—adventurous travelers!

3   One must be careful with the concepts of *success* and *failure* here, remembering that a show can be a critical success and a financial failure or, occasionally, the reverse.

4   See Sol Hurok's book, *Impresario* (New York: Random House, 1946), for a look at early Hurok strategies.

5   See the Document Library on the Actors' Equity Web site: *www.actorsequity.org.*

CHAPTER 12

Special Issues for Institutional and Ensemble Companies

For ongoing institutional producers such as dance and opera companies, orchestras, and touring repertory theater companies, there are unique issues to be considered.

Establishing the Audiences

For an institutional producer such as a ballet company, opera, or orchestra, establishing an audience is quite a different process than for a one-off production. In one sense it is easier because it offers differing work each season, but the artistic genre doesn't change year to year. Also, the institution is a known entity in the community with ties that go beyond the performances. Traditionally these audiences have been loyal: the ballet audiences are known, identifiable, and it is reasonable to assume that many of the people who attended last year's ballet season are likely to attend this season. This may vary somewhat—a special ballet with a rock star singing might attract some new, younger audience members and, conversely, a disappointing series of programs last year might cause some to not return—but in general the ballet audience in a community is known and reachable and the attendance and revenue each season relatively predictable.

A greater challenge exists in trying to grow this audience, which means introducing young people to the experience at a faster rate than older people cease to attend. Sadly, for many institutions, this has proven to be a daunting task.

This all becomes relevant to touring in two ways:

1. Many institutional producers are exploring options for sending their productions out on tour as a means to a) generate revenue and b) help satisfy minimum employment periods

for performers. Challenges abound, as will be explored below, for those institutions used to producing for their home base and not set up for touring from the start.

2. Such institutions are also increasingly active as presenters. If a civic ballet company has availability of the good dance venue in town and a database of ballet attenders, it is a relatively small step for the company to invite a touring ballet company in for a guest appearance—again, hopefully, to earn revenue, keep subscribers happy, and satisfy financial obligations such as a commitment to use a certain number of days in the venue. A regional theater, already carrying the overhead of its staff and venue, may find it tempting to fill a hole in the season with a guest production.

Creation Cycle

For an institution dependent on touring and whose work revolves around the creative work of one or a limited number of artistic directors, the issue of the *creation cycle* distinguishes it from one-off productions. This is basically the average amount of time it takes the artistic directors to create new productions and the financial ability of the companies to support new creation.

For a regularly touring dance or theater company, since many of their tour stops are return engagements and the press pays little attention to repeat productions, the time it takes to gestate and produce a new work is important to the company's overall strategy. Presenters will usually expect new work to be part of return engagements and won't book the return without that assurance.

In the case of a repertory company that engages different directors or choreographers for each new production, this issue is more financial (raising the money to create each new work) than artistic. But for a company centered on the work of only one creator, the rate at which that creator can turn out new work can be a major factor in the multiyear objectives and strategy for the company.

Size of Active Repertoire

Related to the creation of new work is the size of the repertoire the company can keep active. This also addresses the issue of new work for repeat presenters, since their primary concern is that a return engagement of the company offers work that is new *to their community*, whether or not it is new overall. By maintaining a large enough active repertoire, a company can return to a community at least once with an entirely different program than the last visit without needing a new work. If the return cycle is every two years, it means the third engagement is five years since the first, the repeat of part of that original program—especially a part that was particularly well received—can be acceptable with that much time having passed and if accompanied by a new work. So a smaller active repertoire for an actively touring company seeking a high return-engagement rate necessitates a faster creation cycle; a larger active repertoire allows a high return rate even with a slower creation cycle.

Correlation of Creation Cycle and Active Repertoire

Since our book is about touring, and assuming that a high return-engagement rate is always desirable for an institutional producer, the formulas look like:

Fast Creation Cycle + Small Active Repertoire =
Higher Tour Engagement Return Rate Capability
Or
Slow Creation Cycle + Large Active Repertoire =
Higher Tour Engagement Return Rate Capability

Theoretically a company could have a fast creation cycle *and* a large active repertoire, but at some point it would end up with a backlog of new productions beyond what the touring market demands. This might be important for annual press attention at home but does not represent an optimal expenditure of resources from the tour business perspective.

Hit Rate

Carrying the manufacturing analogy one step further, as there are no guarantees that every new work will be a success, the question of the artistic director's *hit rate* is a third important factor. It is a simple fact that some creators demonstrate a more consistent rate of successful shows over time than others, whose work is more up and down.

Based on past experience, what percentage of new creations by this director or choreographer have been hits, and how does that calculation play into the optimal business model? One would have to create a measuring scale based on audience and critical response, apply it to the history of the choreographer's work, correct for outside factors (such as available funds and rehearsal time), and project forward. This represents a fun exercise for highly business-oriented board members who were trained in business school to disassociate from the specific product and refer to *widgets*.[1]

I fully recognize and respect the difference between widgets and theatrical productions. But institutional producers are businesses—albeit nonprofit dance or theater companies—and have obligations to their donors and themselves to operate in the most efficient manner in serving the visions of their artistic directors *and* delivering their output to the public. In this regard, the issue of hit rate is a critical factor that cannot be overlooked in constructing optimal long-term tour plans and objectives.

Major versus Minor Productions

Most institutional producers consider some pattern of producing *large productions*—perhaps defined by cast size, scale of set, and of course cost—and *small productions*, often alternating between the two. This can also be important to the tour planning, since the larger productions will be in demand for the larger venues in big cities—some requiring minimum full-week engagements to allow for transport and set up—while the smaller productions can allow the company to take dates in smaller venues, presumably in smaller markets.

Production Designed for Tour

Finally, the intention to tour a production is often more predictable by institutional producers than by producers of one-off new productions. Presumably a dance company with a regular touring history and pattern can more easily expect and plan for the new production to also tour than can the producer of a new Broadway show. This being the case, the dance company will typically plan in advance for issues such as the transportability of the set, scale of lighting, and size of touring company in creating the production, minimizing the later cost of retrofitting for tour.

Anticipating touring encourages the creation of a good promotional video while the show is originally running, rather than deciding after the close to tour the show and having no video to show.

Considering hot-button social issues such as subject matter and nudity in the production, if broad touring is wanted, is also important. What plays successfully in major coastal, urban centers may or may not always be acceptable in other parts of the country.

An Alternative to Touring: Second-Home Relationships

For institutional producers, not really geared for location-to-location touring but with unique productions to offer, an alternative model for leaving home is to build second-home relationships. These can be open ended or for a defined number of seasons. This approach to booking represents a potentially strong win–win for both presenters and ensemble or repertory production companies that offer new plays or ballets each season. When audience members learn to identify the individual performers in a ballet or theater company, they often develop a sense of rapport and are interested to see those performers in other works. A commitment by a presenter to bring the company back each year allows for strategic planning of programs to nurture and take advantage of this rapport. It allows both presenter and producer to plan ahead and for substantive community involvement by the artist. It also allows a community that is not ready to support its own permanent ballet or theater company to have the benefit of an ongoing institutional relationship with a good company from another community—a sort of "time share" approach.

Tour Agents in the Picture

For one-off productions, unless the producer has an ongoing affiliation with a particular booking agent, it is not common for an agent to be in the picture when the show is first produced. If the show is ultimately to tour, the choice of agent and the type of presenters may vary according to what the show turns out to be. And the producer may wish to hear proposals and ideas from various agents before selecting the one she feels is most suited to the production (see chapter 2, Producer/Agency Relationship).

Institutional producers that expect to tour routinely, such as dance companies, will typically be signed on a multiseason basis with a tour agency, which allows the agent to be involved early in the planning of new works to determine the timing of the fit into the company's touring cycle and develop early ideas of the markets in which the new production might have special appeal. It is not uncommon for a repeat presenter of a dance company to become involved financially in commissioning a new production, and the agent may well be involved in securing this commission commitment.

It is relatively rare for regional theaters to have ongoing relationships with booking agents since most do not see touring as a routine objective. A regional theater might produce a show in its home venue with only the vaguest idea that the show will go somewhere after its initial run. It can only determine after opening if the show has the public and press appeal for a commercial move to Broadway and/or for a touring life. If to Broadway, that deal is likely to be undertaken directly with interested Broadway producers, and touring thereafter through a commercially oriented agent chosen only after the show opens on Broadway. If the show is being sent to other regional theaters, this is often arranged directly through the relatively close-knit regional theater network without benefit of an agent at all.

Endnotes

1   Ironically this ubiquitous business word had an early start in theater! It first appeared in the 1924 comedic play *Beggar on Horseback* written by George S. Kaufman and Marc Connelly. The hero, a struggling composer, must choose creating music that stimulates his soul but earns no money or earning a soul-deadening living in a *widget* factory. *Widget* is never explained but represents a generic mechanical product without artistic or spiritual value.

CHAPTER 13

Attracting Presenters and Connecting to the Public

As with so much else to which show touring is connected, issues of positioning and marketing the product, both wholesale (to the presenters) and ultimately retail (to the ticket buyers), are the subjects of their own books. We will share some thoughts, which, if they don't provide detailed answers, are intended to at least help frame the discussion and provoke ideas.

Legitimizing Elements: Establishing Credentials

Audiences don't go to the theater in a vacuum. Citizens have many demands on their leisure time and money, and contemporary US culture involves attendance at live shows far less, for many people, than in previous generations. The strategy for all parties involved in producing and presenting live shows must consider the *legitimizing* and *hook* elements to which potential audience members can attach and feel positive about committing the resources of time, money, and effort necessary to attend shows. These can include, among other things:

- Press from other cities and nations

- Information provided in advance from trusted sources, including friends and competent press

- Testimonials from famous people

- Attractive imagery

- Famous star, director, or other creators associated with the show

- Topical associations with current societal issues

- Societal subset associations—that is, ethnic or religious groups, minorities, nationalities, etc.

- Respected producer or presenter

- A feeling of personal connection with the show

The show could be famous from Broadway, or unknown but with a famous star or director or playwright; in musical parallel: a famous work of music, or a famous orchestra or musician playing a lesser-known work.

The show could be coming "direct from New York" with quotable accolades from the New York press and perhaps famous actors or the same from London's West End.

In certain fields, notably classical music and ballet, where the performers change but the classic works being performed don't, receipt of awards and winning of international competitions carry much weight.

Appearance at certain bellwether festivals means much. To name a few: the Edinburgh International Festival and, in English-language drama, the Dublin Theatre Festival are highly regarded as showcases for significant work. Many major cities around the world host significant festivals, from Moscow to Athens, Hong Kong, Bogotá, Paris, and Vienna. In dance, Jacob's Pillow Dance Festival in Lee, Massachusetts, and the Lyons Biennale in France signal significance. Almost anything appearing on the Next Wave Festival at the Brooklyn Academy of Music or the Avignon Festival receives notice. Olympic cultural festivals and the European practice of designating two cities each year as cultural capitals provide enormous attention and legitimacy to productions and artists invited to appear.

Any and all of these add to the credentials that will collect around a production through its early life and give it *legs*.

Press

Articles in the paper, clips on the local news, and, even more impactful, appearance on national talk shows carry much weight, again because they provide authoritative testimony on the quality of the work, offer description of the show, signal heightened legitimacy based on the fact that the press paid attention to it, *and* bring the production into the broader ongoing community dialogue. The local info helps inform and serves as a potential social reference point—"Did you see that article about that new show that's opening?" The appearance on *The Tonight Show* to X million people, means a) "this must be a rising star whom I should know about," and b) "I can discuss this with my friend at work or my sister on the other coast because they always stay up and watch that television show."

Note that the press is not always simply on the show itself, but can be in response to manufactured press events—a tradition dating back before the Internet and even television. Obvious examples are highly attention-getting stunts by magicians before their theater shows, or amassing hundreds of trombonists for a parade before a special concert. Having the artist appear live in the central commuter train terminal during the morning rush hour with live feeds to the news or at lunchtime in a busy commercial plaza can do wonders for attracting press attention to an upcoming theatrical performance.

Live Exposure

As with the train terminal or commercial plaza appearances mentioned above, there is often little to beat an advance taste of the live theatrical experience or meeting the artist in person, if time, opportunity, and artist's energy are available.

Media Mix Updated

Studies have shown that awareness increases exponentially in people who hear about something from more than one source, which, hopefully, translates in our case into greater interest in attending our performance. In the late twentieth century, this concept was trumpeted by marketing experts as achievable through *media mix*: the idea that if a potential customer heard a product name on the radio and saw it in the morning newspaper, the combination would set up a purchase motivation that was greater than twice the impact of either ad placement on its own.

While this concept still holds validity, the latest thinking recognizes a couple of important factors:

Traditional Marketing Burnout

As the post-WWII baby boomers have aged, we have become increasingly suspicious of regular advertising channels, and the effectiveness of newspaper and radio ads is not as great as before. This has lead to the birth of an entire genre of promotion known as *guerrilla marketing*. The concept was explored in the 1984 book titled *Guerrilla Marketing*[1] by Jay Conrad Levinson, and a number of books by the same author since, as an approach to marketing characterized by low budget and unconventional approaches to the prospective buyers. Also referred to as *stealth marketing*, such promotions are sometimes designed so that the target audience is left unaware they have been marketed to or the originality of the approach breaks down resistance.

Word of Mouth Matters—a Lot!

Personal references from trusted friends and authorities have significant impact on purchase decisions. This issue was addressed very effectively in Malcolm Gladwell's book *The Tipping Point: How Little Things Can Make a Big Difference*[2] exploring how networks of friends and acquaintances can make or break the success of a new idea or product. The recommendation of friends is arguably the most effective, if elusive, determinant of ticket-purchase decisions.

Community Conversation Topics

Hearing about a show from friends has a further implication that is rarely explored. The importance is not only that your friends are telling you the show is good and you should go see it, but that they are *talking about it at all*! The implication is that if you go see it, it will be a subject you can discuss with your friends. Indeed, if more than a certain number of your friends have seen it and you haven't, you'll feel left out.

I contend that one of a number of reasons why watching television has replaced theater attendance for so many people (aside from obvious issues such as cost and convenience) is the sense that since so many more fellow citizens watch television than attend the theater, the experience is more likely to serve as grist for conversation later even if not shared socially at the time (and even that factor is slowly being overcome with large television screens set up in viewing rooms or minitheaters in homes). An obvious extreme example is major league sports as both television entertainment AND social connector and ice breaker: "Did you see that homer in the bottom of the eighth inning?" is far more likely to get a reaction from fellow office workers than "Wasn't that glissando amazing?!" Sad but true. So it is no surprise that a live artist is likely to sell more tickets (and therefore be more appealing to a presenter to bring in) if reference to an appearance on the *Tonight Show* or the Academy Awards is possible.

The Internet is Taking Over

In nearly every interview for this book with presenters, agents, and producers, the talk turned to the impact of the Internet in the sales process. The reduction in marketing costs related to the dramatic increase in use of the Internet to provide show information to potential buyers and to actually sell admissions is startling and highly welcomed by all at a time when budgets are universally under attack.

Audience Members as Former or Present (albeit Amateur) Performers

It has long been shown that active participation by children in the performing arts increases their receptivity to, and attendance at, performances later in life. The well-documented working paper *Critical Issues Facing the Arts in California*, undertaken by AEA Consulting on behalf of the James Irvine Foundation and published in September 2006,[3] reports:

> *Studies have (also) shown that exposure to the arts at the elementary and high school levels is a significant determinant of adults' subsequent participation in the arts. Involvement with artists and opportunities to learn different artistic disciplines while in school predisposes people to stay actively involved in the arts through adulthood and partake of cultural offerings of various kinds.*

A second issue of public participation reported in the working paper is perhaps more significant for thinking through the connections to audiences for our touring shows:

> *The number of serious amateurs actively engaged in making art is rising dramatically. The evidence of this growth can be seen in the escalating sales of various kinds of artistic equipment (pianos, guitars, cameras, film, and video editing machines) as well as rise in adult education courses in the arts at community schools, colleges, and nonprofit cultural organizations. The International Music Products Association, for example, estimates that guitar sales have tripled in the last ten years. Dramatic increases in people's interest in actively participating in the arts and pursuing personal creativity are occurring simultaneously with declines in their appetite for traditional forms of nonprofit arts presentation and interpretation. There are more people making art themselves and fewer buying season passes to theaters, ballets, symphonies and museums.*

The paper goes on to suggest a historic context for this with alarming implications for professional artist touring:

> *Some argue that the late 20th century mode of art creation and consumption was, in fact, an exception, and that we are returning to an earlier, more populist way of experiencing*

culture that was common in 18th- and 19th-century America. For most of history, people's cultural experiences were live and often participatory, such as playing music in the home or performing in a community theater production. With the advent of recording and other technologies that facilitated mass distribution, cultural products created elsewhere by professionals became readily available everywhere and gradually eclipsed local and amateur producers. The explosion in the number of nonprofit arts organizations in the late 20th century continued the trend toward the institutionalization and professionalization of art consumption.

While this does not suggest that audiences will stop appreciating the performances of professional artists all together, in the spirit of popular empowerment reflected in the Internet explosion, the public is demanding to reframe its relationship with the artist and to expect more participation in the creative environment. The boomers are no longer willing to limit their roles to passive adoring fans.

This would all validate the global trend toward increased workshops and audience interaction opportunities with artists in the plans and business models of presenting organizations.

Transmission Options Beyond the Live Stage

While most obvious in the music field with the distribution of CDs, and a significant precedent in radio broadcast of live music performances, options for distribution of artistic product in other venues such as music videos, pod casting, etc., are expanding. This can relate directly to live touring as it broadens public exposure to the artist and creates an additional revenue stream to help the overall show operation.

What has proven effective for television transmission in relationship to live ticket sales is not the complete production being offered on the screen, which might tempt audience members to stay home and view it on television and not go to the theater. Rather what are very effective are documentaries about the artists, their lives, work habits, creative processes, etc., with snippets of performance—enough to whet audiences' appetites to then go to theaters and experience the final results.

That being said, experimentation is under way to broadcast performances live for paying audiences at movie theaters equipped for digital projection to reach an audience outside of the opera house. The Metropolitan Opera is leading this exploration, transmitting live performances of popular productions such as Julie Taymor's *The Magic Flute*, with very positive initial results reported. As with much in this book, this is a snapshot of experimentation at the time of writing to which the reader will be able to add over time.

While much needs to be done to align the interests, attitudes, and facilities of transmission with those of live performance, it is clear that there is a potential for relationships that has only begun to be explored.

Impact on Touring

You may well ask, important as these issues are to the retail sale of tickets, how do they affect our booking process and the purchase decision of a show by a presenter? Remember that as an agent pitches a show to a potential buyer, he is also pitching ideas for how the buyer will end up marketing the show to her audiences and working to convince the buyer that her audiences will really want and enjoy this show. The agent is selling through the buyer all the time. And if the marketing response patterns of the American buying public are changing, then so too must the marketing message conveyed by the agent to the buyer.

Endnotes

1   Jay Conrad Levinson, *Guerrilla Marketing* (New York: Houghton Mifflin Company, 1984).

2   Malcolm Gladwell, *The Tipping Point* (New York: Little, Brown and Company, 2000).

3   *www.irvine.org/assets/pdf/pubs/arts/Critical_Issues_Arts.pdf*

CHAPTER 14

Broadway Touring

In the 2005–06 performance season, the last season reported as of this writing, gross revenue from the sale of tickets to Broadway shows in New York was $862 million and on tour was $915 million.[1] While this was still small compared to the $3.1 billion estimated gross from all major North American popular music concerts in 2005,[2] as a percentage of the approximate gross of $12.7 billion for attendance at all live ticketed theater and concert events in the same period,[3] it is a significant share.

Beyond the numbers, "Broadway" is one of the most instantly and universally recognized *brands* of live performance throughout the US and the world. The scale, significance to the overall touring field, and unique characteristics of Broadway touring warrant a closer look.

Broadway in a State of Change

It should be noted that as with all touring areas, Broadway is in a state of change and flux and this book, by necessity, explores a series of historic and present-day snapshots with an imperfect view into the future. The reader will hopefully be motivated to track developments in some of these areas as the history of Broadway continues to unfold.

For a first snapshot: measured in gross ticket dollars spent, tickets sold, and playing weeks, Broadway touring enjoyed an uninterrupted growth through the 1980s and 1990s, then plummeted in the 1999–2000 season. All three indicators have grown steadily since, though 2005–06 shows a slight downturn from 2004–05. A minor adjustment or the beginning of a down pattern?

Classes of Touring

There are multiple tiers or classes of touring, defined in part by size, cost, and union affiliation.

Class A or First National Tours

A new Broadway show going out on the Road for the first time after (or during) its initial Broadway run is normally called a *Class A Tour* or *First National Tour*. As one might expect, at this level the tour production is created to replicate the original Broadway show as closely as possible and normally plays only in the largest cities for multiple weeks each. If not the original cast, then a highly experienced team travels, often including some *name* actors.

The operations of such a tour can be enormous, with guaranteed fees often well in excess of three hundred thousand dollars a week. Depending on how many weeks are booked in each city, the First National Tour of a show may extend past one season in order to accommodate the full demand. While traditionally shows have gone out on their First National Tours *after* closing on Broadway, there have been exceptions for shows that continued to run so long in New York with such solid international tickets sales that the producers felt confident that duplicate productions out on tour would not undercut New York sales.

Second-Class or Bus-and-Truck Tours

Following the First National Tour are the *Bus-and-Truck* or *Second-Class Tours*. Characterized by lower salaries, these tours will often include *singles* (single performances) and *splits* (a week shared between two cities) in addition to full week engagements, and will play in smaller markets that could not afford the First National Tours. These tours will sometimes engage non-union performers, though the technical personnel (the road crew on tour as well as stagehands to be engaged in the local venues) are still generally in the International Alliance of Theatrical Stage Employees (IATSE).

Broadway as a Brand

Several years back, the League of American Theatre and Producers, which holds the trademark for "Live Broadway," made a conscious effort to enhance the branding of Broadway outside of New York City as synonymous with high-quality, compelling entertainment coming from the Great White Way[4] (any of the New York City theaters designated by the League as Broadway theaters, even if it's address is not on the street named Broadway). This was in coordination with a growing trend among major presenters to offer series of major productions under the heading of "Broadway," borrowing from the cachet and association with large-scale productions with wide popular appeal. While primarily involving musicals, from time to time a straight theatrical production makes it out on tour under the Broadway banner as well.

Definition of Broadway

The precise definition of what constitutes a Broadway show varies according to whom you talk to:

- *Actors' Equity Association* attempts to define it as a show having appeared on Broadway with performers who have also appeared on Broadway.

- *Most agents and presenters* are willing to accept that it is a show that has appeared in one of the thirty-nine theaters designated by the League as Broadway theaters, whether the touring cast has performed there or not. (It is not uncommon for a show that the producer predicts will not have the audience demand for a long run on Broadway to offer a limited run[5] in order to garner the Broadway credential and then move out on tour.)

- *Less scrupulous agents and presenters* are willing to stretch the definition to almost any show that has been a hit in New York City, regardless of the venue in which it appeared.

- *At the bottom of the scruples pile, if being presented as Broadway shows,* are shows produced for the Road with titles such as "The Best of Broadway," which are compilations of numbers from Broadway shows but that themselves have not appeared in New York City.

Interviews with various agents and presenters on this issue for this book found a range of integrity around two issues:

- Whether every show billed as a "Broadway show" had to have actually appeared in one of New York's Broadway theaters, and

- Whether or not all productions handled or presented involve Equity (unionized) casts.

As the costs of large-scale Broadway touring have risen in advance of viable ticket prices and Broadway does not always have enough *product* to fill the demand in any given season, boundaries have softened. The highly successful Off-Broadway show, *Stomp*, was able to remount a large-venue version that has appeared on tour on many presented series labeled "Broadway" without ever having actually appeared in a Broadway theater. The same is true for the occasional production that will come on tour in the US from London's West End and other international suppliers without actually hitting the Broadway boards. Note that this is not true for all presenters of Broadway series, many of whom—the purists—only include shows that have actually appeared in Broadway houses.

On the Equity front, several tour producers have mounted productions with nonunion casts, creating a furor within the industry. The debates continue, but the need to balance the economics of touring is a real and continuing issue. The union status of the performers and their salary and work rule costs are often brought into the spotlight by this issue.

Roles and Relationships

In contrast to the basic relationship described above, producer-agent-presenter, there are some new players in the Broadway mix:

Tour Producers

It is not uncommon that the original producer of a Broadway show in New York will not be the producer of the show for tour. Rather the show will be licensed to a producer who will specifically create the touring production—a different definition of *tour producer* from that in the taxation chapter. The original producer receives a royalty based in part on how long the show ran on Broadway.

Publishers

Unlike ballets, the rights to productions that are either music- or text-based (or both, in the case of musicals) are held by publishers. While most do publish the music or words, their other function is to hold and negotiate permissions for the rights to produce the shows or use the material in any manner.

In the music world, names such as Schirmer's and Boosey & Hawkes are well-known. In the Broadway world, names to know include Tams-Witmark, Music Theatre International (MTI), and the Rogers & Hammerstein Organization. These are significant players with their catalogues available to be reviewed online.

A new show coming from Broadway may tour initially under the rights agreement worked out with the initial producer if that producer chose to include an option for touring in the negotiations and exercised that option within the allowable time. Once a show has completed its First Class touring, the rights revert to the publisher and must be applied for by a producer wishing to send it out again.

Investors

One thinks of investors as the all-important suppliers of the funds to produce shows, most with the hope of financial return on their investment as well as the fun of being involved in a Broadway show from its inception.

There are also what might be considered *strategic investors* that put money into a show with an additional motivation of controlling some aspect of the show's future. This could be a booking agency that invests in exchange for the rights to represent the show on tour. The list of producer credits for the oft-discussed hit *Stomp* (technically Off-Broadway and not Broadway, but a good example nonetheless!) includes Columbia Artists Management Inc., which is now also the booking agency for the show.

Other strategic investments might include an individual performing arts center seeking to obtain first rights to the show when it comes to its community over the competition across the street. Along the same lines, but on a multicity scale, a conglomerate, such as Live Nation, with control of venues in more than forty cities, will invest in shows with the same motivation for its circuit.

Conglomerates Historically

There has been much attention paid to the role of the company presently titled Live Nation, which was formerly the theatrical division of Clear Channel, before that SFX, and originally Pace Theatricals. In the tradition of aggressive commercial entities with national vision, Live Nation has created the brand *Broadway Across America*,[6] the largest unified theatrical subscription marketing program in the country, and established Broadway programming control over major venues in more than forty cities throughout the US and Canada. In each venue, working with a local partner or promoting firm, it has created a Broadway series with a significant subscriber base. The combination of exclusive access to the venues and ticket-buying power allows it tremendous clout in acquiring touring rights to shows—currently the largest single buyer in the country. Adding to this, its ability to secure options for its venues by investing in the original productions and its partial ownership in one of the major tour booking agencies, Live Nation optimizes its own profitability and holds leverage over its competitors.

Given its size and clout in the field, Live Nation has drawn criticism and even law suits as its annual reports attest.[7] But in its favor, Live Nation does not do business in a number of the largest cities in the US, controls only one venue in New York City, and, as it points out, is able to deliver high-quality Broadway entertainment to a number of smaller cities that might not otherwise be so entertained.

And as this book is readied for printing, Live Nation has announced an intention to divest itself of much of its theatrical business interests and focus increased attention on the music business—a next iteration in this saga appears set to unfold. According to the 2006 Fourth Quarter and Full Year 2006 Financial Results Statement from Live Nation:

> *As part of our strategy we have launched a process to divest the majority of our North American theatrical business assets. The assets we anticipate including in this divestiture include (i) our Broadway Across America business—the largest subscription series in the United States for touring theatrical performances, (ii) 13 theatrical venues which we own, operate or have an equity interest in located in the seven major North American markets of Chicago, Boston, Baltimore, Minneapolis, Toronto, Washington D.C. and Philadelphia and (iii) our remaining 50.1 percent interest in a production of the* Phantom of the Opera *at The Venetian Resort Hotel & Casino in Las Vegas. Our United Kingdom theatrical assets as well as the [Broadway] New York Hilton [Theatre] and the Boston Opera House will not be included in the divestiture process due to certain tax restrictions associated with our spin-off from Clear Channel Communications.*

Regardless of the name or the ownership, the role played by Live Nation in the Broadway touring field is by no means new and is far less market dominating than its forbears. As entertaining as any best-selling beach novel is the story of the rise in the late nineteenth century of the most powerful theatrical conglomerate in the history of American theater. On August 31, 1896, six men gathered at the Holland House Hotel, then at 30th and Fifth Avenue in New York City, to plan the creation of what would be named *The Theatrical Syndicate*. Abraham Lincoln Erlanger, Charles Frohman, Al Hayman, Marc Klaw, Samuel Nixon, and Fred Zimmerman pooled their resources—theaters nationwide that they owned or leased, and booked—to create what they contended were more "rational" trips for theater troupes on the Road. Rationality and efficiency, of course, also brought considerable power and wealth to the owners at the expense of the performers and the competition. At its peak in the early twentieth century, the Syndicate controlled approximately seven hundred theaters nationwide, making Live Nation—measured, at least, by venue count—small by comparison.

Antitrust Challenge

An antitrust legal challenge was brought in 1907 by the State of New York against the Theatrical Syndicate for "criminal conspiracy in restraint of trade" but was dismissed with the statement by Judge Otto Rosalsky that,

> *In light of the lexicographer's definition of trade, commerce, play,*
> *entertainment, and theatre, ... it seems to me that plays and*
> *entertainments of the stage are not articles of useful commodities*
> *of common use, and the business of owning theatres, and pro-*
> *ducing plays therein, is not trade, and that, therefore, the defen-*
> *dants did not commit acts injurious to trade or commerce.*[8]

Nearly a half century later, another court took a different view of another conglomerate.

Rise of the Shuberts

Aside from giving rise to performer unions in an effort to counter the Syndicate's control of performers' livelihoods, the organization also spawned a competitor with a name better known to us today, begun by two brothers with the family name of *Shubert*. The scrappy young Shuberts began their own chain of theaters that, by some accounts, ended up as controlling as the Syndicate, though never with as many theaters. A significant Shubert contribution was the erection of new theaters, forced by the refusal by the Syndicate to sell them any of theirs. The rise of the Shuberts and decline of the Syndicate was prompted in part by the death of one of the Syndicate's leaders, Charles Frohman, in the sinking of the Lusitania in 1915.[9]

It is also worth noting that, whereas the Syndicate had been constructed around the performance content and episodic structure known as Vaudeville,[10] the Shuberts were more involved early in the daring concept of shows that had story lines—both dramas and musicals—which would evolve into the Broadway model common today. As a result, while both organizations were severely impacted by the advent of talking pictures in the early 1930s, Vaudeville was more directly decimated by talking pictures and ultimately television, with many Vaudeville artists transferring to those media. The Shuberts' program format was better positioned to survive the evolution of taste in theatergoing.

According to a history of the Shuberts' enterprises available online:[11]

> *By the fall of 1910 the Shuberts owned 73 theaters outright,*
> *held booking contracts with many more, and possessed at least*
> *50 dramatic and musical companies. They were fully as des-*
> *potic as the [Theatrical] Syndicate and banned a number of*
> *critics from their premises for less than enthusiastic reviews. . . .*
> *The Shuberts were, in their heyday, heartily despised for their*
> *hammerlock on the American theater. Shrewd dealmakers,*
> *contentious litigators, tight-fisted producers, they raised*
> *intimidation to an art form and, despite acts of charity, kept*
> *their benevolent impulses as private as possible.*

In a midcentury wave of antitrust activity, the story continues:

> *In 1948 the Shuberts still owned 16 theaters in New York City and 21 elsewhere—about half of all the legitimate theaters in the United States—including all the Philadelphia theaters and all the Boston theaters but one. Through their United Booking Office, they were able to make producers book their shows exclusively in Shubert theaters around the country as a condition of renting a Shubert theater on Broadway.*

In stark contradiction to the ruling of Judge Rosalsky in favor of the Theatrical Syndicate nearly a half century prior, the Shuberts faced a different judgment: In a 1955 US Supreme Court decision, the Shubert interests were found to be in violation of antitrust laws. As a result, in a 1956 consent agreement it was required to sell about a dozen theaters in six cities, including four in New York, and the United Booking Office was dissolved.

From this turbulent history, of course, the Shubert Organization has survived and today is one of the most respected in the industry, with a reputation for excellent care of its historic theaters and generous support to new artists and productions through the charitable Shubert Foundation.

A Third Conglomerate

Reading Trav S. D.'s informative book on the history of Vaudeville titled *No Applause Please—Just Throw Money*, one also reads of the near monopoly in that theatrical genre by the Keith-Albee chain, which, at the turn of the nineteenth century, owned or controlled the majority of first class Vaudeville theaters in the US as well as operated its own booking agency. While not ultimately involved with Broadway productions, the story sheds light on the times.

Without unions or any but fledgling agencies representing the interests of performers, Keith-Albee held complete dictatorial sway over the careers of many major Vaudeville artists. The driving force was Edward Franklin Albee (1857–1930), a vaudeville impresario and the adoptive grandfather of Edward Franklin Albee III, the playwright. He had toured with P. T. Barnum as a ticket collector and in 1885 partnered with Benjamin Franklin Keith to operate the Boston Bijou Theatre. From that beginning they created the Keith-Albee circuit of vaudeville theaters. They are credited as being the first to introduce moving pictures in the US.

Albee was president of the United Bookings Office from its formation, later controlled by the Shuberts. It charged acts a 5 percent commission for bookings. Acts Albee disliked were not booked, and when performers tried to form a union, he set up National Vaudeville Artists and made membership in it a requirement for booking through his company. His partner, Keith, died in 1914. Albee made several misjudgments in the 1920s, notably building lavish new theaters and producing extravagant shows at a time when movies were becoming a popular low-cost alternative. The Keith-Albee-Orpheum (KAO) Corporation was formed in 1928. Joseph P. Kennedy partnered with Albee, then took full control of the company and the newly formed RKO, and turned the Orpheum vaudeville circuit into a chain of movie houses.

Conglomerate Impact Today

The lineage does not change the enormous impact of conglomerates today in the Broadway touring world, but it provides historical perspective. And despite their power in contrast to their forebears, conglomerates today are faced with both independent agents and performer unions, as well as a degree of organization among independent producers, presenters, and venue operators unheard of a century ago. But the conglomerates are the *elephants in the room*, and a thumbs down from Live Nation on a production can well mean that an insufficient volume of touring is available from competitors to make a tour financially viable and the show won't go out. Conversely, because the options are so limited, a thumbs up is no guarantee that the producer will receive the terms sought as Live Nation is in a strong position to establish price.

Competitor to Live Nation

The closest competitor to Live Nation for Broadway touring in the US is a membership organization of independent presenters called the Independent Producer's Network (IPN). An affiliation of theaters and performing arts centers in one hundred plus cities in North America and Japan, the collective is able to act as a *strategic investor* (see above) in new productions en route to Broadway, leveraging access to the shows for its members. While decentralized and operating in an entirely different fashion than Live Nation, IPN offers an active and viable alternative to that commercial enterprise for the touring of Broadway shows.

Through discussion with various agents representing touring Broadway shows, it appears that Live Nation can represent approximately thirty-seven weeks of touring for a strong show and IPN approximately twenty-seven weeks. The same discussions suggest that an average of about thirty to forty weeks is needed to assure the financial viability of an average Broadway show on tour. So Live Nation can, by itself, make a tour happen, while IPN, without additional presenters, is on the edge.

Not merely one industry, but civilization, itself,
is concerned, for the morals and education of the public are directly
influenced by the stage. Every one who takes a pride in the art
of his country must regret a monopoly of the theatre, for that
means "business" and not art.
—William Dean Howells (1897)[12]

The Importance of Blockbusters and the Structures of the Deals

Regardless of who controls the theaters, the true lions in this jungle are the occasional blockbuster hit shows—the *Phantom of the Opera, Lion King*, or, most recently, *Wicked*—that are the must-see touring productions driving all the rest. These are members of what is now being referred to as the "million dollar club," being those productions that have consistently experienced over $1 million in ticket sales per week. And the selling power of these shows allows their producers to dictate the structure of the deals.

Most Broadway shows tour on a guaranteed-fee basis, in which the risk of loss is being taken by a tour producer or promoter who guarantees the fee and expenses to the producer, whether this be Live Nation, regional promoters, or local presenters. But the producers of blockbusters, in confidence that their shows will sell out, can insist on *four-wall* deals in which they effectively rent the theaters and present the shows themselves, assuming all the risk. Of course the motivation for this is that the producers thereby take all the profit as well and cut out tour producers, promoters, and local presenters.

Live Nation, regional promoters, and local presenters will still welcome the blockbusters onto their series as their presence will help drive subscription sales for all the rest, and to have the shows at competing theaters would be very damaging. The local theater operators, of course, are pleased at receiving the rent plus revenues from ticket fees, parking, concessions, contributions to marketing costs from the shows' producers, and the increasingly ubiquitous *theater maintenance* or *restoration* charge added onto the cost of tickets; though they are less happy if large show profits are carted out of town.

Timing and Communication

Two factors that are noteworthy about the Broadway tour booking process are a) the relatively insular nature of the industry, where most players are well-known to the others, and b) the need for Broadway shows to be booked before presenters will consider most other booking.

There are not more than a half dozen agencies booking the vast majority of Broadway shows, and presenters who routinely present Broadway productions are relatively limited in number and well-known. Most if not all are members of The League of American Theatres and Producers (currently contemplating a name change). It does not mean that there is no negotiation around costs and dates, but it takes place within a fairly restricted framework.

Because Broadway shows will, in the case of larger-scale presenters, take up full and sometimes multiple weeks in the theaters and they do not want to run the risk of losing out on dates for desirable productions by having booked single night events, Broadway presenters will often not make final commitments to other types of presentation until the Broadway show dates have been firmed up. Given the costs involved in moving a Broadway show around, the tight routing and scheduling of the tours is also critical. If the Broadway booking system is delayed for any reason, it is not uncommon for tours of hundreds of other artists to be delayed in confirmation until the Broadway plans are resolved.

Union Relations and Impact

Issues of union labor invariably raise passions on all sides. Certainly the more one learns about the treatment of performers—as with much labor in the US—in the late nineteenth century and the unwillingness of the producers of the day to improve pay and conditions, one has to appreciate the role that collective bargaining has played in insuring fair treatment to workers.

And as a cost/income squeeze continues in a field with a fixed number of seats available and a nonexpanding audience, it is inevitable that producers will look to cut costs and questions of fairness in the cost cutting will arise.

Actors' Equity Association

The first focus in almost any union discussion related to Broadway touring shows is on the actors' union.

Growth in Nonunion Productions

In the last few years, under pressure from presenters—and indirectly, the ticket buying public—to reduce costs, an increasing number of touring productions have been mounted with non-Equity actors. This would have been unthinkable not that long ago, and not surprisingly the Actors' Equity Association is flexing its muscle in response by refusing to allow any of its members to perform in shows created by those producers.

The actions by these producers, however, have awoken the field to three important effects, none of which strengthens Equity's hand:

- As the productions have often received generally favorable press and public response, it has disproved the long-held assumption that union actors as a whole are of significantly higher quality than nonunion actors.

- While the Society of Stage Directors and Choreographers (SSDC) boycotted the producers of non-Equity productions in sympathy with AEA, other unions more critical to the immediate delivery of shows into stages—notably the stagehands' union and the teamsters—did not.

- The costs of touring have been lowered as a result of paying the performers less, which has translated into lower ticket prices and greater public accessibility.

Equity "Lite"

Citing a drop of over 50 percent in overall Road employment by Equity actors over the previous five years, the Equity membership in 2004 voted to ratify a three-year contract, being referred to informally as "Equity lite," that includes an experimental set of terms intended to reduce payroll costs on a complex and variable basis.[13] The jury is still out on its long-term impact on Broadway touring, but in a field that—like any major trade industry—favors peaceful conduct of business over turbulence, an effort is being made on both sides of the table to work with the new contract to the degree possible. As with much in this book, this is necessarily a snapshot in time of a complex and evolving matter to which the reader will no doubt be able to add.

Emotions Run High

It is important to note that in interviews for this book, the emotions over this issue ran high and were not simple to categorize. A regular producer of non-Equity productions indicated that she was developing a plan that she hoped would allow her to shift to Equity productions in the next few years—not, apparently, out of fear of or pressure from the union, but because she felt it would increase her stature as a producer. Another, who is passionately in support of unions in principal and presently working on a production to open in London, decried the costs and labyrinthine work rules of doing business in the US. He indicated that while he would not consider producing a non-Equity production, he also might not bring his production to the US at all!

International Equity Issues

An area in which there continues to be friction with the union concerns non-American actors being permitted to perform in the US. As you will recall from our discussion of visas, the current regulations call for a "no objection" letter from the relevant guild or union to accompany a petition for a working visa for a non-American to work in the country. This hands the key to entry of non-American actors to the Actors' Equity Association, which has been using this power liberally to thwart efforts by producers to bring productions that it views as inimical to its members' interests—especially from the UK—into the US. Traditionally there has been an exchange agreement between the US and the UK that allows British actors to perform in the US provided that an equal number of American actors are offered an equal amount of work in the UK, but the agreement has also placed a cap on the number of weeks any actor might appear in the other country. Reports are that the exchange relationship is starting to break down in part due to limited opportunities for American actors in the UK, that this cap is proving to severely impede recouping the costs of moving shows across the Atlantic, and that a new round of negotiation and debate on this issue can be expected in the near future between producers and the union.

Other Unions Involved

There certainly are other unions involved in Broadway productions, and their employment costs, rights, and claims are not insignificant in relationship to touring.

Creator's Royalty Claims

An issue of significant current debate has to do with claims by the original creators involved in productions, many represented by unions such as the Society of Stage Directors and Choreographers (SSDC), for royalties on their work if the productions are remounted without engaging their services. As with anything that increases production costs in this sensitive economic time, the matter is being contested by producers and may well find itself into contract negations, the courts, or both in coming years.

Stagehands and Teamsters

Two other unions with very strong influence on Broadway touring are the stagehands and the truck drivers. Traditionally these unions have supported each other much more than they have any of the other unions. Union stagehands will often refuse to unload or load trucks not driven by union drivers, and conversely a union driver may be unwilling to open his truck to a nonunion stage crew. And in the case of the stagehands, there are usually some members of IATSE traveling with and contracted by the show, and many more provided locally in each city under work rules negotiated with the presenting or hosting theater. The national network is strong, and the cross connect between the touring and local union members means that if at any point along the way nonunion crew were brought in either with the show or locally, the trucks would stop, the corresponding touring or local crew would refuse to work with the nonunion crew, and the tour would not continue.

That being said, as stagehands tend to operate in their own backstage world, it is not always easy to track precise body counts and work hours and there are whispers of featherbedding and other tactics to illegally drive up costs among stagehands on tour. While there is little chance that there will be significant changes in the terms of stagehands' union contracts, nor will we see shows going into major theaters with nonunion crews, it is not unthinkable that a scrutiny of work practices will be undertaken in the foreseeable future as financial pressures continue to mount.

Unlike the stagehands and drivers, the traveling actors and musicians have no such sympathetic support from fellow unions and have only their own membership to back them. And actors need to work!

Las Vegas and Broadway

A not insignificant new set of players in the Broadway touring game is the program directors for the large entertainment complexes in Las Vegas. With enormous capital to expend and an insatiable demand for name brand product to entertain their customers, these buyers have turned their attention to one of the most famous entertainment brands, Broadway. Recently, a Las Vegas producer severely affected the touring of *Avenue Q* by buying the rights to the show even as it was still running on Broadway, exempting it from any touring at all!

While the deal for this production was rescinded after nine months and the touring rights sold back to the producers, it is not the last we can expect to see of involvement by Las Vegas in the Broadway touring dynamic. Recognizing that the eight-performance week and the two-plus hour running time of most Broadway shows are not compatible with the need for more audience turnover in Las Vegas as the producers want the customers to get back to their gambling, the newest approach is to offer ten performances per week of Broadway shows in versions cut down in length to ninety minutes without intermission. This is again a snapshot in time and the reader is invited to research the latest on this trend.

The Commercial Theater Institute

While focused on producing commercially, and only incidentally involved in touring, a word must be said for the Commercial Theater Institute and its annual intensive workshop in New York City, founded by the late Frederic B. Vogel. For those seeking expert and in-depth immersion into this complex process, the Institute is highly recommended. For more information visit *www.commercialtheaterinstitute.com.*

Endnotes

1 The League of American Theatres and Producers, Inc. report.

2 Pollstar report.

3 National Endowment for the Arts, Office of Research Analysis, Note 91 report dated August, 2006 (*www.nea.gov/pub/Notes/91.pdf*).

4 Following the installation of electricity and the erection of the Times Building, and the resulting creation of Times Square in New York City in 1904, the area was christened the "Great White Way" in response to the dramatic increase in illumination.

5 A distinction is made for shows on Broadway between what are termed "open-ended runs," which means that the shows can continue to stay in the theaters as long as the box office revenues are above an agreed-upon percentage of gross potential, and "limited runs," which are runs usually defined by a number of weeks with a definite end date. Theater owners often seek the latter to fill windows of time after one show has moved out and another is preparing to move in.

6 *http://broadwayacrossamerica.com/BAA.Public.Web/index.aspx*

7 *http://phx.corporate-ir.net/phoenix.zhtml?c=194146&p = irol-reports*

8 From Abby Manzella, *The Syndicate and the Shuberts* (American Studies at the University of Virginia, December 2000).

9 See more detail at The Lusitania Resource (*http://web.rmslusitania.info:81/pages/saloon_ class/frohman_charles.html*).

10 *Vaudeville* refers to a style of program that involved a wide variety of different acts on one bill but also—and perhaps more importantly—a network of theaters throughout North America that brought the acts to audiences and that dominated American entertainment from the late 1800s until its demise in the face of moving pictures as the new, low-cost popular entertainment in the early 1930s.

11 *www.answers.com/topic/the-shubert-organization-inc#after_ad1*

12 From Norman Hapgood, *The Stage in America, 1897–1900* (New York: The Macmillan Co., 1901).

13 See "Equity Okays Production Pact: Tiered Touring, Increase in Wages, Health" (*Backstage*, September 10, 2004).

CHAPTER 15

Notes on Popular Music Touring

Our chapter on this gargantuan topic is intentionally described as *Notes*. The subject is so vast and complex as to warrant not only a book but an entire series on the subject!

Defining the Genre

We'll begin by identifying some of the challenges to addressing this topic.

What is "Pop Music?" If we loosely accept that pop music is all music that is not classical, it can include as vast a range of music as the human race has devised. Everything from country and western to Indian ragas to hip hop to reggae to rock and roll fit in this big tent and literally hundreds if not thousands of genres besides. Even within the most common American genres, one must include soul, gospel, R&B, hip hop, jazz, fusion, disco, folk, Latin, new age, rock, rap, country, and traditional pop. We will arguably offend a number of purists in many genres by even including their styles under the generic word *pop*. This represents a lot of different audience tastes to be artificially squeezed under one title! It ends up as virtually all music that is not Western, classically based, or played on Western classical instruments.

How is the Field Structured? Unlike almost any other performing art genre, pop music filters through an extremely complex set of participants in the creation and delivery system. In one conversation during the preparation of this book, the field was described as *the last of the Wild West* in terms of how business is often conducted, involving a set of formal and informal interrelationships that are very difficult to pin down and codify.

Much like the world of solo or ensemble classical music, pop music often revolves completely around the individual performer or band and its reputation. So Yo-Yo Ma and Sting might be compared, or the Tokyo String Quartet and The Rolling Stones. But the comparison largely ends there, as the impact of the near-mythic status of successful pop musicians is far more comparable to that of famous film actors or sports stars than anyone else appearing routinely in live performance.

Range of Venues and Media Relationships

The ability of pop music to attain a level of social influence while still involving live performances has two components:

1. Venues

The upper end of venue scale to which pop musicians can aspire involves the largest arenas in the world with seating in the tens of thousands. The revenues from a large-scale rock tour can compete with those of a Hollywood feature film and are so far beyond what any other tour in any other genre can achieve as to be in a separate conversation entirely.

It is interesting to note, for instance, that in the oft-referenced Rand Corporation's thorough study of entertainment consumption patterns in the US (*The Performing Arts in a New Era*, 2001), itself relying in large measure on many prior studies, even in its most detailed analysis of audience patterns among various genres, and including exposure to movies and television, it makes no mention of attendance at pop music concerts. Yet from the figures reported at the beginning of the previous chapter, we glean that in 2005, gross admission dollars spent attending just the major pop music concerts in North America represented roughly a quarter of all dollars spent attending all live performances—a significant factor in live-entertainment audience patterns.

Adding together the grosses for all forms of distribution of pop music, including recordings, music videos, and world tours, the sum dwarfs all money spent or earned in a given year by Hollywood studios. And on a personal level, there are many among us who will report that our earliest teenage live-performance experiences were at pop music concerts, a trend which—if my teenage daughter is any indicator—continues today.

2. Relationship to Alternate Distribution Avenues

The second component, of course, is the ability for music in general to be distributed through increasingly high-quality reproduction means. Recently this was the sale of CDs, but as we write the field is undergoing a revolution in distribution through Internet downloading. And the popularity of music videos continues to grow as an alternate means of distribution involving visual as well as audio transmission.

As large as the ticket expenditure is for attendance at live concerts, it is a small fraction of the layout on consumption of pop music as a whole when purchases of recorded music are added in. In fact, live-performance tours are often timed with the issuance of new recordings and are undertaken as much for promotion of the highly profitable recordings as for the value of the tours themselves.

Touring Structure

To bring this vast field into the context of the tour booking structure risks as many exceptions as rules. Some of our players introduced in other chapters remain as well as at least one that is new:

Producers

In general, since the decisions for an artist to tour and the timing are often made by a combination of the artist, his manager, and his record label, the role of the producer here is less that of decision maker and progenitor, and more that of the expert who is brought in to coordinate the elements of a tour coming together. In fact, the significant—sometimes legendary—producers in this field are not the tour producers but the recording producers, whose work in some cases is memorialized for the ages.

Agents

Agents continue to play a very strong role in this field, with a few agencies tending to dominate the large-scale pop music field. As popular musicians tend to retain the loyalty of their audiences and to be able to return to markets successfully on a regular basis throughout their careers, many agency relationships with artists are stable and longstanding.

Managers

Pop artist managers tend to be gatekeepers and guides to a complex professional career of which live-performance touring is often only one part. Music careers in some cases now cross over to film acting and fashion modeling to the point that one sometimes forgets where a new face was first seen! To be effective these managers must become conversant with a variety of fields.

If the musicians are also composers, they will build up a library of their work that may have a life beyond them as their songs are *covered* (played by other musicians) on a licensed basis, and sometimes licensed for use on television commercials and in films.

A successful artist may have several different agents representing her interests in various areas, all coordinated on behalf of the artist by her manager. These managers may operate within large management companies or be private depending on the wishes and comfort levels of the artists. Successful artist–manager relationships can last for entire careers, that between Elvis Presley and Colonel Tom Parker being a famous example. Obviously, the reverse can be true, as with the much-publicized firing of managers by Michael Jackson.

Presenters

The role of local presenters remains highly important, but is often quite different in the pop music relationship structure than the typical guaranteed-fee presenting deal. This is often influenced by the involvement of two additional players, which, in some instances, are one and the same: regional promoters and conglomerates.

Regional Promoters

This is a role that is somewhat distinct to the pop music industry. It is in effect a type of tour producer who, when an artist announces availability to tour, will bid on the artist for a specific region—often a state or set of contiguous states. He will guarantee X number of performances over one or several weeks' time, usually with a guarantee of $Y, taking much or all of the risk and handling all the logistics. The advantage to the artist and agent, of course, is a cohesive tour block with a guaranteed income (perhaps with a percentage of overall tour profit offered in addition), working through one presumably experienced and qualified regional promoter. The promoter, in turn, while taking the ultimate financial risk if he doesn't sell enough tickets, is able to spread his risk among a set of markets so that if he loses money in one city he might more than make it up in another. He can also bulk negotiate for intercity transportation for the artist, for publishing of promotional materials and perhaps ad buys in regional media, and he might even secure an accommodations sponsor for a hotel chain active in the region.

Conglomerates

Far more than in the Broadway field, the company now known as Live Nation has emerged as a strong national and international player in popular music, controlling venues, managing artists, and producing significant national tours, and has purchased many of the former regional promoting companies to form a national circuit. It continued its acquisition policy in 2006 with the purchase of its former competitor, the House of Blues. In that year Live Nation's music business was worth upward of $3 billion.

The Deal Structures

Pop music touring deals tend to be structured along much the same lines as Broadway. The popularity of the artist works much like the salability of a blockbuster hit show in determining the amount of control—and retained profits—that will be held by the show's producer.

Large-Scale Shows

A large-scale show with proven appeal such as The Rolling Stones, much like a *Phantom of the Opera* or *Wicked*, will often go out on a four-wall basis, in which the show's producer is effectively renting the venue, paying all marketing and production expenses, and keeping all or most of the revenues (depending on his arrangement with the show and the venues). The difference, of course, is that the Stones are playing huge arenas with tens of thousands of seats and *Phantom* and *Wicked* are playing venues of between 2000 and 3000 seats. The precise relationship of the tour producer to the artist herself in this may vary, but, presumably, whether the producer is hired by the artist or the artist by the producer, each will have a share of the profits. In this case we can reasonably assume that a regional promoter is not involved and that the relationship is between the show's producer and the venue management.

Midsized Shows

A midsized show playing PACs[1] will tend to come in on either a four-wall deal through a promoter, a full guaranteed basis by the local presenter, or a copresentation agreement (a *co-pro*) that shares risk between the promoter and local presenter.

Ancillary Income Streams

In the pop music world, the live tour performances are often only the centerpiece of a network of ancillary income streams that can generate far more profit than the performances themselves. The venue may be content with the significant revenue from concessions, fees from ticket sales, parking fees, and a percentage of merchandise even if it keeps little or none of the box office. The artist may make so much money on the sale of CDs (and music videos, a clothing line, etc.) as to be okay sharing a significant part of the live-performance profit with the tour producer. The potential for corporate sponsorship of such tours as well as broadcast and video rights also offer additional potential revenue. Like so much else, the scale of ancillary revenue streams in pop music outdoes that of any other live-performance genre, even Broadway with its healthy sales of baseball caps and cast albums.

Pop Music Trends

Acknowledging again that this chapter makes no attempt at a complete overview of this complex field, there are several trends worth noting and continuing to observe.

Artist Entry into the Field

The astounding public success of the television show *American Idol* has brought to a peak a trend of using the mass-television medium to confer instant stardom on some of its contestants, and the genre of choice for the production is pop music. While the idea in some form has existed for many years, back to *American Bandstand* in the early 1950s, *Idol* has struck at a time when the convergence of mass marketing and entertainment interests provide a delivery structure into which contestants who demonstrate strong public approbation can move, almost overnight, into a limelight of unprecedented brightness through a marketing and entertainment machine of remarkable synergy and effectiveness. Of interest to our study of the tour booking process, of course, is the potential, with the addition of a bit of stage polish and production elements, for an *Idol* winner to move out on national tour within weeks of winning on national television. The contestants are already showing up as freshly minted movie stars, and the first big winner, Kelly Clarkson, since her appearance in 2002, has become a well-established singer whose Web site announces a significant tour of large arenas among her many activities.

What is significant in the *Idol* model, compared to the traditional growth of an artist's reputation—from performances in clubs and a first successful album, to getting radio play, a move to PACs, and, potentially, ultimately arenas, and the consistent build of a solid fan base over a period of time—is that this entire process has been short-circuited. Mass marketers have found a way to cut development time by moving a performer from total anonymity to stardom overnight, and to systematically feed a voracious star system. What the future holds as more and more instant stars are made, and whether there will be a point of oversaturation, is yet to be seen. For now, one can only regret that young artists with comparatively little experience or depth to their artistry are moving so quickly into the places of industry leadership while many highly talented artists with great depth and experience, but perhaps less telegenic charm, continue to struggle.

Payola

One of the determinants of who gets famous in the music business is of course whose music gets played on the radio. And for years, through a system called *payola*,[2] in which industry executives have paid off radio disk jockeys to play their clients' songs, the blessings of air play have been bestowed on those artists with contracts with big management and recording companies able to make the pay offs. In the process, of course, many very talented musicians have had their music kept off the air.

At the time of this writing, the new government leadership of New York State has been making a concerted effort—and is gaining some courthouse wins—in fighting payola and securing a place for the work of more artists on the air. One can only hope that over time this will open the doors to heightened public awareness and demand for a greater variety of music.

Ethics

The imagery of the Wild West referred to earlier continues to permeate the live music industry. Many of the ethical niceties outlined in our ethics chapter are routinely ignored in the high-dollar, cutthroat business of pop music touring. Anecdotal presenter reports of musicians showing up and demanding increased fees before performing, with the presenters facing alienated, sold-out houses if they don't, are very disturbing. Likewise, agents' empty promises that "the contract is in the mail," keeping one buyer on the hook while shopping elsewhere for a better deal, are all too common.

It is a business that often involves significant cash transactions, and one that might be considered more business than art as it often seems the art exists only to serve the business.

All this being said, like the rest of the live-entertainment touring business, the pop music field is heavily reliant on personal connections and reputations, and a black mark can take a great effort to overcome. And there are honest and effective people working in all aspects of the pop music field. A young person considering entering this field—and it does hold great attraction for young would-be entrepreneurs for obvious reasons—should do so with caution and a keen grounding of his own personal integrity.

As with the Broadway blockbusters, but focused on iconographic artists rather than productions, it is a field that ultimately revolves around the elusive qualities of fame and public adoration for those artists who remain in good health and "on the charts." And one significant constraint is that, unlike most theatrical productions, if you don't take into account "tribute" lookalike acts, pop artists can't be cloned—yet!

Closing Thoughts

In considering this topic for this book, I found myself questioning how far to attempt to go in opening the Pandora's box of how these artists get to the stages on which we hear them perform (if we can obtain tickets!). And of course, at its simplest, it works like all the rest: a presenter calls an agent to request an artist or an agent calls a presenter to advise of an availability, a negotiation takes place, a contract is issued, the artist travels to the community and performs, and memories are made for those who attend.

Overhead, above this simple process, roars a hugely complex alignment and realignment of marketing forces and big business, feeding frenzies involving many millions and even billions of dollars, and levels of rapaciousness virtually unimaginable from the ground. Past a certain point, musicians become brands that are marketed and traded into every corner of our lives and of the globe. Just think of where and when you have recently heard all or portions of a song by The Beatles and you'll obtain a glimpse of how interconnected these industries are around a band that hasn't existed for years. Elvis Presley remains one of the highest grossing names in the music industry long after his passing!

And at the center of this maelstrom, thanks to popular demand to occasionally get a glimpse of the human artists behind the machine—coupled perhaps with the artists' love of adoring crowds—even the great ones perform live and on tour. And then, in all the high-powered wheeler-dealing, our tour booking process matters.

Endnotes

1   The term "PAC" refers to *performing arts center*, and tends to be used as a generic reference for traditional single theaters with capacities of up to about 7,000 seats and multiple-venue theater complexes, often owned by nonprofit organizations, municipalities, or academic institutions.

2   From Wikipedia: *The term gets its name as a take-off of the names of some early record-playing machines, such as Victrola. (These names in their turn stem from pianola, c.1896, the trademark name of a player piano, the ending perhaps abstracted from viola and meant as a diminutive suffix.)*

SECTION III
CONTEXT

CHAPTER 16

Ethics

The man of character, sensitive to the meaning of what he is doing, will know how to discover the ethical paths in the maze of possible behavior.
—Earl Warren, Chief Justice,
US Supreme Court[1]

Ethics are a set of moral principles and values that guide one's behavior. In order to respect the ethics of our profession, we must recognize the line between fighting hard for the interests of our agency, production, artist, or arts center, and lying, by omission or commission, or otherwise acting without integrity to achieve our goals.

With the advent of the Internet, high-speed travel, and international conferences, the already tight-knit world of touring arts has become even more connected, and an active agent, enterprising presenter, and quality artist quickly make many contacts and establish reputations in the field. With those reputations comes a tag related to ethical conduct. There is no danger in having a reputation of being a tough negotiator or, for an artist, even a bit of a diva, as long as it is balanced by professionalism, quality, and delivery. But woe to he or she with a rep for unethical practices!

This can apply to an artist who doesn't show up and deliver the contracted performance; an agent who changes the deal at the last minute after the contract is signed, promises the contract is in the mail when it is not, or provides misleading information about the production being delivered; or a presenter who holds up a scheduled payment without justification, cancels at the last minute, or doesn't deliver on other contracted obligations.

Institutional Guidelines

Various professional organizations have outlined what they consider ethical behavior for their constituencies, examples being the "Statement of Values and Code of Ethics" from the Association of Performing Arts Presenters,[2] "Guidelines for Ethical Behavior" from the North American Performing Arts Managers and Agents (NAPAMA),[3] and the "Code of Professional Standards for Agents and Managers Representing AGMA Artists" from the American Guild of Musical Artists,[4] the latter having as much to do with AGMA's proposed standards for the terms of business relationships between artists and managers/agents as what we are defining as ethical conduct. There is a fine and perhaps unimportant line between guidelines to fair business practice (e.g., the correct amount of commission for an agent) and rules of ethical conduct (e.g., don't demand more money than was contracted at the last minute when the presenter has a sold-out house and is vulnerable to such demands).

As Justice Warren's quote above suggests, efforts to write out codes of ethics will never accommodate all circumstances that might arise, and, hopefully being "of character," we will find the correct ethical course of action in a given situation by our internal senses of what is right and fair.

Ethical Issues Related to Tour Booking

Without attempting formal codification, we will examine some issues specific to our topic based on experience and the internal, ethical sense of this writer.

Money

Not surprisingly, we will start with a list of money issues related to ethics; suggesting practices that will not only be ethical but will hopefully leave one's negotiating partner willing to conduct repeat business.

- Clarity of terms and payment schedules, captured in writing in the contracts, including both agent's commissions and performance fees

- Respect for the deal after agreement is reached

- On time, full payments as agreed, without surprise hold backs

- Rapid transfer of agencies commission (if through artist to agent) or fee share (if through agent to artist)

- Respect for the payment currency agreed upon (For international engagements, if an American producer agreed to accept a fee in euros without a specified conversion formula, he cannot be surprised if the amount of dollars delivered varies from his projections as the exchange rate may have changed since the time of contract signing and the time of payment.)

- Payment of wiring fees by payer unless otherwise agreed

- Precise, detailed, and transparent accounting of expenses and gross and net ticket revenue on deals when such information is to be shared, especially where box office splits are a factor

- Access to books where sharing of such information is included in the arrangement (This includes producer's access to the manager's books where gross income goes through the manager or agent's access to the presenter's books where revenue [net or gross] is to be shared.)

- Notification of local mandatory tax withholding (and any other factors that will affect the full payment of fees) up front, before the contract is signed

Honesty about Identity and Capability

In a world not unused to braggadocio and obfuscation as to roles, rights, and representation, clarity and veil-piercing are golden.

- Agents, be clear about productions being offered (first class, bus-and-truck, second company, amateur, etc.), status of star guarantee, and genuine article versus knockoff.

- Presenters, don't mislead others about your presenting history, financial ability to bear risk, capacity of venue, and overall ability to handle the presentation.

- Agents, don't promise the moon and the stars to an artist to get him or her on the roster.

- Producers, don't promise productions you can't deliver.

Confidentiality and Information Approval and Release

Protect privacy and respect rights.

- Agents, managers, producers, and presenters, never release an artist's private contact information unless specifically authorized to do so by the artist.

- When on tour, neither agent nor presenter should reveal the hotel of an artist unless specifically authorized to do so.

- No party should announce an engagement publicly until a contract has been signed *and* the presenter has approved the announcement date (sometimes the announcements have big publicity value for presenters and it is generally within their right to control—including announcements on the artist's or producer's Web sites).

- Respective parties should all approve descriptive copy and images before public release (e.g., the title of the presenter and venue on the artist's Web site, image and description of the show in the presenter's press release, promotion, and program).

Clarity on Engagement Status Prior to Contract

Don't say the contract is in the mail if it's not!

- A request for a hold by a presenter in a show's calendar, while not binding, implies serious interest or intent.

- Presenters should call back to release holds if not intending to proceed. Also, calendar holds should have agreed-upon deadlines for automatic release if not confirmed.

- Calling for a contract implies readiness to commit to an engagement.

- Delaying and promising that the engagement is proceeding while shopping for a better deal by either the agent or presenter (the old "the contract is in the mail") is a real no-no.

Honor Agreements

Your word, both oral and written, is a critical part of your ethical image. Honor it.

- Artists, show up and do the dates and deliver the full show you are contracted for, regardless of whether it is Podunk or Broadway.

- Agents and presenters, don't try to renegotiate at the last minute, especially when the other party would be harmed in cancellation and is therefore more vulnerable.

- Details count. Tech requirements in the rider need to be provided; artist agreements to offer press interviews to help sell tickets are important. Deliver what you've promised.

Terminate (if you must) with Sensitivity and Respect

Cancellations happen. They are rare but inevitable. How you conduct yourself at this often-traumatic time matters and is remembered.

- Whether an engagement is cancelled or a producer and agent part ways, assuming there is integrity in the process and legitimate reasons for terminating, the parties should not then badmouth each other in the field.

- If producer and agent are parting ways, the producer still needs to honor the engagements contracted through the ex-agent and pay the ex-agent the commissions. This applies to multiyear deals for the show to return to the same presenters even though the producer–agent relationship may have been long terminated by the time the engagements take place.

- If presenter or artist is voluntarily canceling due to a better deal, the canceling party needs to be prepared to pay.

Honor Territories

- Agents, do not actively impinge on territories in which you know the artist is exclusively represented by another agent.

- Respond clearly and sensitively to an unsolicited booking inquiry from a presenter in a territory not your own. There is no harm in taking an offer to the artist and agent representing that territory as long as it was not actively solicited by you. Expect to split the commission, and be prepared to accept the possibility of a decline from the artist or agent if the engagement conflicts with other plans they may have in the territory.

Other Ethical Issues Observed along the Way

Following are some additional insights regarding questionable ethics observed over the years.

Booking Shows Not on Your Roster

In the same spirit as the agency situation above, an agent with a special relationship to a presenter may be asked by the presenter to seek a show not formally represented by the agent. As long as the agent has not falsely promoted representation of that show to presenters, there is no harm in the agent approaching the authorized agent for the show in question, informing him of the interest, and proposing a split-commission relationship on the engagement. This situation appears commonly in the US with certain agencies that act as middlemen for presenters with limited booking staffs, and with presenters from foreign countries who get to know and trust one particular agency and who may ask that agent to serve in a booking capacity beyond the agent's own roster. Most agents, when approached by another agent with a proposition for one of their shows, which means revenue, even on a shared-commission basis, that they would not otherwise have obtained, will not object to such an arrangement occasionally.

Reengagement and "Presenter of Record"

- If a presenter introduces a show or artist to his market and does a credible job, he has the implied right of first refusal to bring that artist back to the community the next time, exceptions being an opportunity for the show to move to Broadway or a significantly larger venue with a much larger fee. In the latter case, if the ability for the artist to move up in scale results in part from the introductory efforts of the initial presenter, some consideration should be extended for that presenter to either participate in the new presentation or receive a courtesy commission or residual.

- If an agent brought a show and presenter together for a successful engagement, and there is a return engagement in a reasonably short time—suggested maximum two seasons from the first engagement—the initiating agent should receive at least a partial courtesy commission even if the agent and show have separated in the interim.

- If a presenter does not exercise the implied option to make a competitive offer for a return engagement within a reasonable period of time, she needs to let go and not cause problems if the agent pursues another presenter in the market. She had her chance and the artist needs to work!

Respect for Intellectual Property

There are a lot of claimants to intellectual property associated with the public presentation of shows. Know who they are and make every effort to respect those that are legitimate.

- Just because there are increased avenues for distribution of an artist's sounds and/or images, such as through TV, Internet, cell phones, and PDAs, doesn't mean a presenter or agent has the right to distribute those images without the artist's permission. Be responsible to check who holds the rights and make sure you have the necessary permission—whether agent, presenter, OR artist using the work of another artist. Presentation of a show from another country should be treated the same.

- Photographers have rights, too. Presenters, use only photos approved for publicity use, and don't reuse publicity images provided by an artist for purposes *other* than show publicity without express approval in advance. Credit the photographers in print or online in connection with use.

- Don't portray a show or artist to presenters (agent) or to the public (presenter) with sounds, images, or descriptions other than what the producer has approved—it's her show! (Discuss and push for more, better shots or other materials if needed, by all means, but don't abuse.)

- A live-performance contract means no televising, broadcasting, sponsor affiliation, production and sale of artist-related merchandise, or other exploitation by presenter that is not preapproved and, if appropriate, additional terms should be negotiated with producer in advance.

Conflicts of Interest

These little devils can show up in many forms.

- Be honest in revealing conflicts that would be harmful to the other party, especially around geographic exclusivity—agents, don't sell the same artist to two different theaters in the same community in the same season without telling them you're doing it!

- Producers, in exploring a relationship with a new agent, be clear about lingering relationships with other agents or with bookings that may affect your new relationship.

- Presenters, if you're really holding off commitment until knowing if an alternate, preferred show is available on a date you are asking this show to hold, tell this agent the situation and provide an honest probability of booking this artist so he can plan his show's tour accordingly.

- Presenters, don't be overly greedy in establishing geographic exclusivity. Be realistic about how far your audience will travel.

Don't "Steal" Artists

This goes for both agents and presenters.

- An agent calling a show or producer currently on the roster of another agent and inviting the producer to change agents is unethical. If the producer reaches out to a new agent and initiates the contact, however, directly or through intermediaries expressing interest in changing agencies, that show is "in play." Proceed with sensitivity and discretion.

- Presenter A, seeking to woo a show that already has a successful history with presenter B, can certainly put in an offer. It is up to the artist and agent to decide, but be wary of unrealistic overbidding. If presenter B is not returning the show or artist to the community in a reasonable amount of time, or if the agent calls presenter A first if the producer is dissatisfied with presenter B, proceed with sensitivity and discretion. There is a fine line here between free market competition and unethical behavior.

Conference Decorum

As booking conferences are a big part of the booking process and primary opportunities for direct interaction between agents and presenters, some basic rules and ethics apply:

- An agent must not move into another agent's booth space or seek to distract a presenter while he/she is talking with another agent.

- Agent's booth setups should not block views to neighboring booths.

- An agent should not allow sounds from his booth to disturb activity in neighboring booths and should not allow his activity to extend out into the aisles.

Sharing my Experience

Having spent half of my career steeped in the nonprofit business ethos and the other half in a more entrepreneurial framework, and half as a presenter and half as agent, I am often torn between rules or guidelines to modify and constrain behavior and a desire to see open market capitalism given free rein. I try to err on the latter side on the assumption that I and all with whom I will conduct business are, to use Justice Warren's term, *people of character*.

A wise person with a solid ethical compass will always seek to temper his aggression with clarity and integrity in communications and business dealings with others. This doesn't mean give away the store or that all of one's cards have to be on view all of the time. It doesn't mean that you have to be Mr. or Ms. Jolly all the time, either.

I don't believe one can go far wrong following these precepts:

- Honor your word as if it were a written contract. Your personal integrity is ultimately the most important thing you carry through your business life.

- Transparency! Reveal all that should be revealed about an artist, your venue, a deal, etc., so that your negotiating counterpart is able to respond in a fully informed manner. Don't try to win your deals by lying, even by omission.

- Make careful notes of what you quote or hear quoted through the negotiation process to avoid later confusion.

- Confirm agreements in writing.

- Be clear and forthright about money—whether payable or receivable.

- Remember that any one deal is not going to make or break your existence. Be prepared to walk away from negotiations or to let the deal not close if it becomes clear that it is not going to work or that the engagement is set up for failure.

- Remember that it is likely that you will be doing business with the same people again in the future, and their willingness to do business with you will be based more on your integrity than whether you're a nice person.

- Remember that in this business, the entire planet is a surprisingly "small town" and the junior-level staffer you might brush off today could be running a major presenting or agency operation tomorrow!

PROCESS AND RESULTS

This business is a lot about process. At the same time, we are mostly judged on results. Learn to enjoy the process *and* achieve results!

Endnotes

1 Earl Warren, *Christian Science Monitor*, 21 May 1964 (from an editorial on moral codes).

2 See the Association of Performing Arts Presenters (APAP) "Statement of Values and Code of Ethics" (*www.artspresenters.org/about/codeethics.pdf*).

3 See the North American Performing Arts Managers and Agents (NAPAMA) "Guidelines for Ethical Behavior" (*www.napama.org/guidelines.php?m=about*).

4 *www.musicalartists.org/Agreements/ManagersCode.htm*

CHAPTER 17

Technology and Media

When discussing arts and *technology*, one most commonly thinks of a) how artists use technology in their productions and b) how presenters are using technology to communicate with, track, and otherwise relate to their audiences. We will attempt to look at trends and implications of technology in the tour booking process.

To do this, it is important to recall the premise stated in the introduction to this book that almost the entire activity of agents and presenters in the booking process boils down to *communicating* and *transmitting data*. We don't actually *make* anything. The *services* that are provided by the producer to the presenter and by the presenter to the ticket buyers are after the booking process is complete. The booking process itself is one of selling, negotiating, conveying technical information back and forth, and various other areas of communication, all of which lend themselves particularly well to advances in technology.

The relationship of live performance to *media* and its impact on tour booking is complex and, to some degree, varies according to the artistic genre being offered for tour.

Rate of Change

Though most readers of this book will have grown up with the Internet, computers, and digitized data, and find it difficult to imagine a world without them, there was such a world and not that long ago. There was even a world before faxes! Contact information was kept on Rolodex cards. Communication was by telephone and mail or courier. There were no cell phones. The sales process was a laborious reprinting and sending of photographs and color slides, and cutting and pasting press reviews for black-and-white photocopying at the copy shop. Press releases were typed on typewriters and sent in printed form. Courier services did not have tracking and shipments got lost. Printed heralds and posters were standard coin of the business, involving color printing as much as it could be afforded! Before videotape, promotional clips of performances were transmitted on film reels. And before that . . . the mind boggles!

It is easy to see how the advent of computer databases, Web sites, digital images and transmission, wireless communication, and file downloading has changed all this. As we write, VHS video—not that long ago the hot new technology—is considered passé, fax machines are being replaced by Internet transmission of documents, and the new online file sharing lead by Google is making it possible for remote agents to share information on artist availability. File sharing offers further possibilities for the tour booking process as well. Soon, for instance, it is likely that the negotiators to a contract will view the same document simultaneously on a shared file and sort out final wording in an entirely new and highly efficient process.

No doubt in the nine months it will take for the printing process to bring this book to readers, entire revolutions in the digital world will have taken place!

Three Phases of the Tour Booking Process

We'll examine technological influences on three phases of the tour booking process: 1) Pitch, 2) Negotiations, and 3) Formalization.

- *Pitch.* Communication of appealing aspects of shows by agents in an effort to obtain bookings via mail, Internet, telephone, and personal communication during booking conferences and visits. A pitch may occur via *audio, video, image, and text, as well as voice communication.*

- *Negotiation.* Data sharing about dates, terms, technical needs, accommodations requirements, etc., passed on as *text, data files,* and *voice.*

- *Formalization.* Transmission of formal contract documents as *text.*

This will seem obvious, of course, and it is. But looked at this way it is easy to see why the communication revolution led by opening the Internet to private and commercial use and subsequent related developments has dramatically changed the tour booking process. It has also placed a new level of demand on all parties to operate at a level of technological sophistication, including Web sites and digitized materials, unthinkable even a decade ago by most in this field.

Pitch

Various facets of the early sales phase of the booking process are affected by advancements in technology and media. From a world in which, due to time, distance, and lack of recording and media options, pitching a production to a presenter was focused mostly on previous press reviews in other cities and recommendations of trusted authorities, presenters can now expect to see/hear high-quality video and/or audio recordings of the production, providing a basis for more personal judgment by the prospective buyer. An EPK (electronic press kit) can include anything from interviews with the actors and audience members to what may soon be a direct, live or recently recorded transmission from a performance in another city, perhaps custom broadcast to prospective presenters via the Internet.

While producers of more complex visual productions, such as dance companies, often decry the poor quality of the recordings or editing, and feel that an on-screen presentation is far from the effectiveness of the live experience—and in many cases they're not wrong—nonetheless it opens up an essential sales tool. The reality today is that while the video or audio may not be ideal, it is often not possible to book a show at all without at least *some* recording for preview by the buyer.

Rather than waiting a couple of days for courier delivery of promotional materials, a presenter urgently considering a production can expect to receive materials instantly via the Internet. And if a courier service *must* be used, electronic tracking allows the sender to know the moment it arrives. Also, the move from VHS video to DVD disks has sped up and lowered the costs of such mailings, especially internationally where packages often now go through as quickly as documents instead of packages, and these innovations often speed up the customs approval process.

When the artists can't be there to showcase, a digital replication can. This is often a poor substitute for the live show, to be sure, but in most cases still advantageous over only still photos and written words. Can we envision a showcase at a conference with holographic projections of the entire production?

Negotiation

Obviously the exchange of e-mail as a means of negotiation is now the norm, leaving a reference trail as the parties near agreement. Multiple parties can be included in the exchanges. Technical directors can electronically exchange stage and production schematics from AutoCAD systems, equipment lists, load-in schedules. Quotations on freight can be obtained from multiple bidders in far less time than previously and airline flight costs determined without speaking to a human.

Formalization

With the one outstanding question of the validity of a digital signature, the contract finalization process can also be done via Internet transmission. Digital signatures are becoming commonly accepted, with a more leisurely follow-up exchange of originals by mail if needed.

Contact Management Software

The use of contact management programs such as ACT![1] and Goldmine[2] by salespeople to maintain databases of buyer contacts and track the ongoing relationships is by now old technology, though still surprisingly new in a field that has tended to hold on to old-fashioned practices far longer than others.

Elements unique to the tour booking field have spawned development of some exciting niche software such as Artifax Agent[3] from the UK, which puts contact management into a larger picture. These tend to recognize that the agent's clients include both the shows and the presenters, and that the ultimate *product* being sold is both a show and a date on which that show is available. Technology allows the system to be approached as an interaction between the two client databases connected to a calendar or set of performance dates with greater efficiency and multiagent access than an analog calendar and Rolodex ever could.

Computerizing Complexity

One can easily see how the interaction of a dynamic time line and an agent's *audience* lists (productions and presenters) results in a highly robust system, far better suited to complex computer programs than to hard copy data systems.

Is the pattern any different than that which existed in the pretechnology era? Not really. But the technology allows the process to be formally tracked to a far more refined degree, speeds the process of updating, makes sharing the data easier, and increases the effectiveness and customer focus of a single agent many times over.

Data Sharing

The issue of data sharing crops up at various points on the tour booking map. As with the pitch process, at present the most immediate benefits tend to be on the agency side, with the presenters at the receiving end of those benefits (there are also tremendous benefits of technology to presenters' relationships to their ticket buying public, which is the subject of a separate book!). However, as noted above, Google has focused its considerable development attentions on the process of file sharing via the Internet, where the shared files are saved on Google's servers. Given the often far flung geographic nature of tour booking, this development promises interesting opportunities for the field as yet not fully explored.

Within Agencies

For an agency with more than one agent, all needing real time access to shows' calendars as they discuss availabilities with prospective presenters, file sharing is golden. It has the potential to replace the regular calendar meetings within the agencies and speed up agents' response times to the presenters. With remote server access and portable PDAs, of course, that is also available as agents' travel on presenter visits or to conferences.

As in other fields, there is a small but persistent trend for agents to move away from urban centers such as New York City and Los Angeles to set up shop in more rural—and lower cost—environments, with individual agents often working from virtual offices at home and while traveling. Additionally, several agencies have reported successful networking of agents located in different parts of the country and even internationally, linked by Internet technology.

With Prospective Presenters

There are three particularly important areas of file sharing by agents with presenters:

Show Availability Schedule. Technology offers an opportunity for presenters to look into a production's tour schedule and see available dates and even request holds without calling the agent! A pioneer in this in the public speaking field is a company called eSpeakers,[4] which offers, among other products, a software and service called eVENTPRO, a complete shared-file tracking system of *holds* and *solds* for professional speakers. The shared files can interface directly with, and appear through the Web sites of, speaker's bureaus (agents for speakers) that subscribe to the eVENTPRO service.[5] This capability has not yet been applied to any significant degree in the live-entertainment field but is a likely future development.

Marketing Materials. As discussed under "Pitching" above, traditionally, one of the most expensive and time-consuming aspects of the sales process was reproducing promotional materials and mailing them out to prospective presenters. This process is all but eliminated by the availability of digitized equipment online and is made vastly simpler and faster by transmission via the Internet.

The ability for artists and producers, working closely with their agents, to make marketing materials available for download off their Web sites has had a tremendous affect in reducing shipping costs (especially for international tour booking) and the time needed to deliver materials. As Internet access speed and volume expands around the world promotional video clips are becoming downloadable as well.

A concern, of course, is the unauthorized use of images for purposes beyond the routine marketing needs of presenters. One solution to control this is to make low-resolution images and brief low-resolution video clips available that are okay for viewing but not usable for commercial reuse. Once a booking is contracted, higher-resolution images approved for promotional use can be made available through issuance of passwords.

Technical Information Exchange. Along with marketing materials, there is the routine need for the production offices of the show and presenter to exchange data on the requirements of the show and the resources and design specs of the venue. These can often be sizeable files, with documents running to many pages, plus computer-aided design (CAD) drawings. Transmission by attachment to e-mails or through File Transfer Protocol (FTP),[6] or available for download off of Web sites, are all increasingly common on both sides. This has dramatically sped up the process, increased efficiency, and lowered costs of duplication and shipping.

Regional Service Organizations Get Involved

In the US, regional service organizations and state arts agencies have entered the act by providing searchable databases of artists living in their regions for access by presenters. Examples are:

- *SouthernArtistry.org.* Developed by the Southern Arts Federation,[7] this is a free, adjudicated, online registry showcasing the diverse artistic community of the Southeastern region.

- *MatchBook.org.* Launched by the New England Foundation for the Arts[8] with the Massachusetts Cultural Council and state arts agencies of Vermont, New Hampshire, Rhode Island, Connecticut, and Maine, this is an online cultural marketplace designed to bring together New England's performing artists and the people and organizations wishing to present them.

Basic Web Sites

In our enthusiasm for the latest technologies, let's not forget the basic Web site as perhaps the most useful core tool for agents to learn about the booking patterns of presenters—the type and scale of productions offered, number of performances, day preferences, ticket pricing, etc.—and for presenters to learn about the roster offerings of agents. As video becomes standard on sites, allowing tours of the venues and promotional clips of the artists, the sites become more valuable to the tour booking process.

Note that for presenters seeking additional information on artists and shows beyond what is offered by the agents, there are often various Web sites that will collectively offer a multidimensional picture of the artist, the work, and the responses it has received. And while actual performance video is still a rarity both legally and free on the Internet, one unique source for primarily music artists is the Millennium Stage Performance Archive of the John F. Kennedy Center for the Performing Arts in Washington, DC.[9]

Artist–Public Connection

The Internet and expansion of broadband access are opening up direct communication and exposure of artists to the public without efforts by theaters, presenters, and agents. Presently dominating the field are YouTube and Google Video, allowing artists to post promotional videos on the Web for convenient, free viewing. Given their popularity we can expect fast followers.

The Internet has also facilitated the development of artist fan clubs around the world. Fan clubs can have direct bearing on booking negotiations if agents can assure prospective presenters of significant early ticket buying from these groups.

The impact on the booking process from both of these is the increased pressure on the middlemen (the presenters) from their ticket-buying constituencies to bring the artists/productions to local theaters. The free and easily accessible video clips also provide agents with an easy, low-cost reference for prospective presenters to view videos without the costs of either storing the video on commercial servers or shipping disks to the presenters.

Internet Telephone

The dramatic reduction in telephone costs globally through VOIP (Voice Over Internet Protocol) is having the paradoxical counter-technological effect of making it more cost effective for presenters and agents to work through issues in person that were previously limited to telex, fax, and e-mail—all positive in this intense people business. Various commercial VOIP providers, plus the groundbreaking free service offered by Skype[10] for global Internet telephone communication, are becoming standard operating tools for many involved in international tour booking.

Context Trends

There is an increasing trend toward placing the presentation of live performances in a broader context in which the ideas and/or skills generated and presented in the performances can be grist for community sharing and public discussion.

The contextualization of live performances within an Internet-based framework for follow-up reactions and interactions by and between audience members is adding meaningful social relevance to live performance. This can be as specific as joining the social discourse in response to the late poet Sekou Sundiata's view of post 9/11 America in his production *51st Dream State*, becoming active in V-Day[11] after viewing Eve Ensler's play *Vagina Monologues*, or seeking greater understanding of the AIDS virus after experiencing Tony Kushner's *Angels in America*. It can be sharing an aesthetic response to a work of art, or it can be as practical as a young ballet student communicating with a touring *prima ballerina* for career advice.

Internet blogs and some production-specific Web sites have opened up avenues for public interaction with productions and artists, and ideas generated by their work, which add significant dimension to one-time live-performance experiences.

While at first glance these developments may seem to more directly affect the public presentation of the arts rather than the booking process, it most definitely affects the shape and tone of the early agent/presenter discussions of engagements and of the overall *product* being sold. The Internet has allowed the discussions to move, in many cases, from being narrowly focused considerations of a number of public performances, terms, and tech to a broader focus on engaging the presenter's community in a process of exploration and discussion generated around and catalyzed by the artist with potential impact long after the show has left town, all with the performances at the core.

Media Sharing of Performances

As we write, the Metropolitan Opera Company has for the first time arranged live, digital-video broadcasts of selected performances to a set of digitally enabled movie theaters around the country, and first reports on ticket sales are very positive. Other venues, not able or willing to go this far, nonetheless are opening their walls to public view along the lines of live Internet sharing of backstage interviews. The trend is to use the relative ease of transmitting a digital-video signal beyond the bounds of the live-performance venue, involving, in some cases, the actual performances (the Met Opera transmitted to paying audiences in movie theaters, the Kennedy Center's Millennium Stage to the Internet for free), and in others, context-setting nonperformance activity such as artist interviews.

Noting that anything involving video cameras in unionized theaters normally raises a high level of concern, an increased demand for agreements that allow for some degree of live transmission can be expected over the next decade as such transmissions appear to be contributing to public attention and a sense of access to the live performing arts.

Direct Connectedness

The net benefits of technology to the tour booking process, both directly and indirectly, include the following:

- Electronic tracking of contacts and relationship histories among presenters, agents, and shows

- Ability to share the booking calendar among agents within an agency, and potentially with presenters

- Increased cost and time efficiency in all communication and data transmission involved in the booking process

- More sophisticated curation of shows by presenters as a result of more information more easily available

- More targeted sales approaches by agents to presenters based on improved advance knowledge of their presenting profiles

- Greater efficiency in transmission of technical needs and resources between show and presenter, including transmission of large CAD files

- Greater salability of shows that have technological enhancements such as high-quality EPK's, fan databases, and audience context-enhancement opportunities such as blogs

- Lower costs of communication between agents and presenters, including increased telephone access over longer distances.

- Media transmission of live shows (nascent) to off-site viewers

This list can undoubtedly be expanded upon by the reader.

Endnotes

1 ACT! by Sage software (*www.act.com*).

2 *www.goldmine.com/micro.aspx?id=4398*

3 *www.artifax.net/*

4 *www.espeakers.com/index.php*

5 Note that unlike live-entertainment touring, speakers are not always signed with one exclusive agent and a speaker may be offered on a nonexclusive basis by multiple bureaus or agencies. By allowing all bureaus as well as prospective buyers to see the identical real-time availabilities of the speaker, eSpeakers adds value to this circumstance with coordination of holds and solds controlled by the speaker's manager in response to requests for holds and confirmations from the various bureaus.

6 FTP or File Transfer Protocol is used to transfer data from one computer to another over the Internet, or through a network. It differs from attaching files to emails as FTP can handle considerably larger amounts of data. See *http://en.wikipedia.org/wiki/File_Transfer_Protocol* for a more detailed description.

7 *www.southarts.org*

8 *www.nefa.org*

9 *www.kennedy-center.org/programs/millennium*

10 *www.skype.com*

11 *www.vday.org/main.html*

CHAPTER 18

Investing, Commissioning, and Sponsoring

The means by which new productions are financed is subject for one or more books unto itself and mostly outside of our scope here. But there are areas in which the investors or donors to the creation cost of productions can impact the tour booking process, and these are worthy of note.

Investing versus *Commissioning*

These terms refer to funds provided both to create new or revived productions, or to expand (*enhance*) a smaller production for staging in larger venues. The funds generally have the same purpose and effect: to pay the costs of the creative design and construction of production elements, rehearsal salaries, development of marketing materials and related needs, and often some of the initial presentation expenses until shows are on their feet.

The difference is in what is expected in return by the provider of the funds, and these financial models often sort into the for-profit and not-for-profit sides of the industry.

Investing

Investing is just what it sounds like: money put in early in hope that the show will be a financial success and the investor will *recoup* (make his investment back) and earn a profit from the production. The initial investor may or may not have participation in touring rights, though if not he often has a first option to invest in a tour if it takes place and if he so chooses. By definition, investing must be in a for-profit entity since it is forbidden under the laws governing nonprofits in the US for these types of companies to sell shares or receive invested funds.[1]

The corporate vehicle for theatrical investment has traditionally almost exclusively been a *limited partnership*, which involves general partners who put the whole thing together and are the lead (decision-making) producers, and limited partners who put up the money. The *limited* in the designation refers to the limitation on the limited partners' control over the artistic product and business decisions—presumably they are trusting the general partners and the artistic team (as well as the general manager normally involved) to make wise business decisions and deliver a good show—and to a limitation on their potential loss only to the amount they invested in the first place and no more.

Limited Liability Companies

In recent years the form of *limited liability company*, used extensively in film production, has been used increasingly for live-entertainment productions. It works somewhat the same as a limited partnership, except that there is greater flexibility in defining what the investors own and what they might get back, and it is much easier to set up in the first place.

Investors in an LLC are members and not shareholders. An LLC combines aspects of partnerships and corporations, and an LLC is therefore less formal and more flexible than a typical corporation, yet offers protection as well as certain advantages to investors that are much the same. For example, members cannot be found personally liable for company debts and their assets are separate from the assets of the LLC so they cannot be seized.

Another advantage of an LLC is that taxation is based on the partnership model. Flow-through taxation is advantageous since members are only required to pay taxes on their earnings once instead of paying both corporate and individual taxes.

On the more restrictive side, while in corporations shareholders may transfer stock or their interest in ownership, members of an LLC cannot. Transferring one's interest in the company may be dependent on the approval of other members.

There are pros and cons between LPs and LLCs, and one should study the implications of both before deciding what form is best for a particular production or theatrical enterprise.

Commissioning

The alternative, *commissioning*, also involves the provision of funds and other resources to support the creation of new work, but generally does not contemplate a financial return on the investment *per se*.

If provided by a philanthropist or foundation, it is often motivated by a nonprofit mission to support the creation of new work that would otherwise not likely receive the support needed.

If provided by a corporation, the company may seek the public relations benefit of being associated with creation of new art.

Commissioners often prefer to provide their funds in the form of gifts to nonprofit organizations so they can take advantage of deducting the value of their gifts from their taxable income.

How Can Each Affect Tour Booking?

While the investing/commissioning process normally takes place very early on in the life of a production and a touring agent may not even be on the horizon, there are ways in which investing and commissioning can affect the later tour booking process.

Investors' Impact on Tour Booking

In the world of Broadway especially, it is not at all uncommon for large presenting organizations, regional promoters, and conglomerates controlling venues to invest in new productions. They do so, in addition to hoping to see a return on their investment, with caveats that control certain aspects of the touring life of the production.

- Presenters who invest will insist on first options to bring the resulting productions to their venues and not let them go to the competition down the street.

- Regional promoters and conglomerates that invest will require an exclusive first option to bring the productions to their territories.

Obviously the good news about such investors is that a) they provide needed funds, and b) their involvement increases the probability that the show will tour. The bad news, of course, is that benefits that might spring from competitive bidding by different presenters in a market may be lost.

Commissioners' Impact on Tour Booking

Commissioning organizations will generally be nonprofit presenting arts centers, festivals, regional theater companies, or other producers, many with expectations of first performances of the resulting shows, and some with further claim on credit and or residuals from further performances.

Arts centers and festivals that are not themselves producers will more typically commission existing producers—whether independents or institutional dance or theater companies—to create new works with restrictions that often include the world premieres taking place at the commissioning institution's arts center or festival. Their primary motivation may be to obtain the shows for their venues and to receive the perceptual benefit of being sources of new productions with the associated respect, excitement, and press attention. These institutions will usually not place significant restrictions on future touring of the productions as long as it does not overshadow the press and public attention to them at the premieres. They will expect to receive appropriate program credit in future performances for having commissioned the productions, and some may seek royalty payments for future performances if the productions move into commercial realms. If the show is a seasonal favorite, they may retain regular return rights to the show as part of the deal.

Producing entities will commission new work for the same reasons they produce shows. If commercial, the goal is to make money. Commercial producers will, in all likelihood, be planning for Broadway or Off-Broadway from the start and will pursue some variation of the route to Broadway and, if appropriate, subsequent touring. Nonprofit institutions such as LORTs will honor their missions to produce new plays of a certain artistic standard, presumably within financial parameters but rarely with the expectation of profit. Resident theaters will be more concerned with successful runs at home and perhaps arranging guest runs at other LORT theaters, but are less likely to offer their shows on tour through agents. Having said that, of course, if recent works from La Jolla Playhouse are an example, there is precedent for productions—more often musicals than plays—from LORT theaters going to Broadway and, if successful there, heading out on tour as *Jersey Boys* is in the process of doing now. Sadly some of the finest produced drama in the US is not seen outside of one or a few cities as it is not designed to tour nor are the producing institutions geared in that direction, and drama can rarely command significant audiences at the level of musicals.

Producers may also retain ownership of the physical production elements and charge rental fees for future use by other producers wishing to mount the work.

Dance companies, by contrast, are almost entirely geared to touring, and the most popular tour some months out of every year.

Commissioning is Not Only Cash

Not all commissioning relationships involve money only. Arts centers and universities are often able to host creative residencies allowing the cast and creative team time and venues to work on the new productions, and those with production shops can offer to build sets and costumes in lieu of cash.

Agents as Matchmakers

Some agents play an expanded role beyond basic tour booking, put together often complex cocommissioning networks, and consider themselves as much producers as agents. This is a logical outgrowth of their ongoing relationships with presenters around the world as some of the latter move beyond passive presenting and become involved in supporting creation.

Sponsorship

Sponsorship differs from commissioning or investing in that sponsorship is generally associated with the presentation of existing productions and not often involved with the creation of new work. Sponsorship is the provision of funds or other services often with a promotional motivation; by association with selected productions a sponsor seeks to raise awareness of its product or service among a target audience.

Not all sponsorship is targeted to the ticket-buying public. There are *business-to-business* sponsors whose interest in a production will be to be able to bring select business clients to the show and who don't really care about the public impact of their support except as window dressing for the client schmooze.

Sponsors more Conservative

Sponsors tend to be more conservative than commissioners in choosing their beneficiaries, either by insisting on the presence of a star director and/or performers that, as much as it is possible, guarantee the popular success of the project, or by waiting to see a production prove its audience appeal before getting involved.

Another difference is that sponsors often support a presentation context involving multiple productions—typically a presenter's entire season or a festival—rather than becoming associated with an individual production. This allows the sponsor to receive credit for the big picture (season or festival) while establishing some distance and deniability from any individual production that may be at all artistically or socially controversial.

Presentation versus Tour Sponsoring

Typically, sponsorships related to touring productions fall in two categories:

- *Presentation*: sponsorship through the presenter of the local presentation of the show or a full season

- *Tour*: sponsorship through the producer of this production in multiple markets

Depending on who has secured the sponsorship—the presenter or the producer—one or the other party becomes responsible for honoring the terms of the sponsorship and insuring that what was promised to the sponsor is delivered. This in turn can impact on the producer/presenter relationship quite substantially.

Producer-Generated Marketing Materials

Larger productions with national-tour sponsors will often print their own posters and create television and radio ads for use by tour presenters as vehicles for insuring that the national-tour sponsors' credits appear as have been negotiated. The offsetting of what would otherwise be a marketing expense to the presenters helps soften their acceptance of such crediting to an outside sponsor from whose funds the presenters do not directly benefit.

Product Placement

Taking a page from television and films, there is a growing trend for sponsorship tied to actual product placement within productions. The use of a particular brand of sports shoe in a dance performance was an early example. The next time you watch a Broadway show, see if you can spot the use of name brand products in the show—a particular cereal served at breakfast, a soda consumed, or a poster decorating the set. It is quite possible that the manufacturers of those products are sponsors of the show. A looming hurdle is the actual mention by actors of certain products in the scripts of the shows themselves. How far will this go?

Other Sponsor Issues

A number of more specific sponsorship issues can arise, which are addressed in greater detail in appendix I. Such issues include:

- *Product or service exclusives.* These may be required by a sponsor as a condition of their involvement.

- *Approval of sponsor by other party.* Since the producer and presenter each rightfully claim some responsibility for the attractiveness of the presentation to a sponsor, and since each may have its own concerns and potential conflicts with a sponsorship brought in by the other, each will often seek approval authority over any sponsorships associated with the presentation.

- *Limitations of crediting and relationship of sponsor to artist.* Producers, and artists in particular, will be concerned about the fine line between sponsors supporting the presentation and what might be viewed as the artists actively endorsing the sponsors' products or services. This is an area often fraught with considerable sensitivity on the part of artists and requires careful sorting out in the presentation agreement.

Money is Important

Obviously, whether the producers and presenters are commercial or nonprofit, money is essential to professional performing arts and entertainment and the creation of new productions. Whether early in the creative process through investments and commissions or later through presentation and tour sponsorships, the participation of the individuals, foundations, government agencies, and corporations who provide these funds is vital.

Much is being written about shifts in funding patterns, referenced by almost every one of the studies on trends in this industry in the US. Many indicate that, as described in *The Performing Arts in a New Era* (Rand Corporation, 2001), the US national interest in privatization and market-oriented approaches for much of society is affecting the orientation of financing of the arts and entertainment.

This in turn opens broad concerns about a funding shift toward supporting proven audience-pleasing shows at the expense of early risk-taking creative development. But as our focus here is on the touring of shows that, by defi-nition, must already be in existence and available to hit the road, we have attempted to limit ourselves to the distinctions between investing, commissioning, and sponsoring as they potentially impact the tour booking process.

Endnotes

1 Note that nonprofit companies with certain restrictions may invest and own shares or membership in for-profit companies, but not the reverse.

CHAPTER 19

Nonprofits and For-Profits: The Rise and Decline of the High Arts in America

Viewing our field through the last century, the rise, and subsequent relinquishment, of cultural-entertainment leadership by nonprofits in the arts in the latter half of the twentieth century parallels a larger picture of America's sense of itself in the world. The motivation for American society's support of the "high arts" after World War II is reported in various studies as a desire for the newly international and economically dominant country in the world to throw off its cowboy image and show that it too could have cultural *class*. This motivated the formation of the National Endowments for the Arts and Humanities and the State Arts Agencies, and the increased focus of foundations and philanthropists on funding the construction of temples of culture (performing arts centers and museums), funding arts schools so America could raise its own performers and not always have to import, and disseminating culture to the populace through expanded touring support. The expansion of arts in the schools was also prompted by a belief that a well-rounded, civilized person in a great society has a knowledge and appreciation of the arts. Not only was this promotion of culture directed within the US but, at one time, the US State Department maintained an office of culture that specifically subsidized American artists to tour to strategic parts of the world as cultural ambassadors.

Depending on what yardstick is used, this flowering of the arts in America peaked somewhere in the last three decades of the twentieth century. More recent analyses, however, indicate a clear shift away from this vision to the more market-driven sponsorship model indicated in the Rand study.[1] At the clear risk of losing some of our finest performers in the high arts of dance and theater and in opera companies and symphony orchestras, as well as the risk of arts schools shutting down, of arts temples being "sold off" to mass programming (or to churches or malls, or torn down altogether), and of our smaller communities being deprived of professional, higher-arts experiences, our society seems to be saying, "That's OK. We don't need that now."

But if the cycle that began post-WWII was driven by America's vision of itself in the world, can it be that this new trend should be viewed similarly? If Americans are in essence saying, "We don't care if we measure up to the rest of the developed world in the high-culture game," is that because we don't care what the world thinks of us anymore or that traditional definitions of culture have gone underground while mass entertainment strides the continent? Recent events would suggest that there are those involved in guiding our nation's foreign policies who feel that the respect of other continents for America's culture no longer matters and that the pursuit of higher American arts is not worthwhile and out of synch with the times. I would contend that for many Americans these *do* matter, a lot, and the pendulum will swing yet again. The question, of course, is, by the time it does, how deep will the damage to America's cultural consciousness and to the training of its artists be as a generation is raised with little cultural exposure, artists retire, and cultural institutions succumb to bottom-line thinking.

Alternately, is the change we are experiencing more domestically focused; is our new model for a civilized person in a great society more geared around mass entertainment? Is what is being said, "We are satisfied with the culture offered to us via television and the Internet"?

Having offered the world jazz music and contemporary dance and been at the peak as a global creative force, are we *really*, as a society, prepared to settle down for a constant meal of such mind-numbing fare for ourselves and to so completely capitulate abroad? Whether for our place in the world, or for our own experience and that of our children, are we satisfied to let Coca-Cola, MacDonald's, and *American Idol* represent our entire culture abroad while we recycle British percussionists, Irish dancers, Chinese acrobats, King Tut's paraphernalia, and *Wicked* through our domestic temples?

"Build it and They will Come"

Regardless of the condition of and trends in the industry, Americans continue to construct or renovate theaters. A belief in the power of arts centers to drive urban renewal often appears to operate outside of any realities of attendance and operating costs, based on sheer optimism that if they are built, artists and audiences will fill them.

Once a theater or performing arts center has been built or restored, there is a compelling drive to have shows in it, and presumably at least part of the motivation to bring the venues on line in the first place is a belief that it is good for a community to experience live arts and entertainment. How and why theaters get built, and how this has changed over the past century and a half, is material for an interesting study of its own.

Certainly most of the Vaudeville and early movie palaces, some of which have been saved and successfully converted to performing arts venues, were built with the same motivation movie theaters are today: to make money. Later, during the Great Depression, the Works Progress Administration had theaters constructed across the US in part to keep Americans employed building and performing in the theaters under the New Deal.[2]

In the second half of the twentieth century, the motivation changed again. Many venues, such as New York's Lincoln Center begun in the 1960s, the newer New Jersey Performing Arts Center in Newark, NJ, or the recent Mesa Contemporary Arts Center in Arizona, were built to catalyze revitalization of decaying downtown areas. The same goes for restoring historic theaters from the vaudeville and movie palace eras, which were built in old urban cores—one only has to view the beautiful theaters in Atlanta, Pittsburgh, Columbus, Rockford, and elsewhere to appreciate the glory of these venues and understand the drive to restore them.[3] Academic institutions build performance venues for what is often a combination of serving their performing arts academic departments, providing entertainment as a lure for would-be students to apply, and building bridges with their surrounding communities.

But regardless of how the venues came to be built, the venues' owners inevitably wrestle with defining their roles as risk-taking presenters versus no-risk rental house operators. Before decisions are made to build or restore venues, extensive feasibility studies are conducted and almost invariably include a search for appropriate producing institutions that will rent and use the venues on a regular basis. This normally involves some combination of local civic institutions, such as ballet, opera, and theater companies, and commercial promoters who can be counted on for a certain number of use days. Academic institutions planning the design and construction of performing venues generally also take into account projections of internal use by student productions and performances.

With a trend toward separation of ownership and programming responsibility, actual presenting by venue owners, if any, is often left to fill schedule and programming gaps not served by others. Lincoln Center in New York is an excellent example of an organization that designed venues for resident, self-presenting institutions—the New York State Theater for George Balanchine's New York City Ballet, the Metropolitan Opera House for the Metropolitan Opera, and Avery Fisher Hall for the New York Philharmonic. There are drama theaters now operated by the Lincoln Center Theater Company and, most recently, new facilities operated and programmed by Jazz at Lincoln Center. Lincoln Center, Inc. itself managed to keep its own presentations to a relatively modest level until reductions in resident-artist seasons left the Lincoln Center campus largely inactive in the summer. With New York City's pattern of presenting international, contemporary programming in festival format having been well established by Lincoln Center's own small-scale Serious Fun Festival and the larger Next Wave Festival at the Brooklyn Academy of Music, Lincoln Center initiated the large-scale, summer Lincoln Center Festival in the 1990s to draw new and adventure-seeking audiences, some three decades after the institution's founding.

The Nonprofit Revolution

As much of the pursuit of higher arts in the US has operated within the context of nonprofit organizations, a review of the evolution and current state of the nonprofit business model as it pertains to the live arts is warranted. In the days before the Great Depression, before the benefit of tax deductibility of private contributions to nonprofit institutions was extended to corporations (1936), and before television and film became such low-cost entertainment forces (also 1930s), commercially produced live performances ruled. Impresarios such as the visionary Sol Hurok brought the world's great artists on tour in the US and made profits, and the entertainment structure and style called vaudeville employed thousands nationwide. It was a time when a far larger percentage of the average populace enjoyed going out to live entertainment than is the case today. Labor costs and admission prices were low with theatrical unions not yet in full swing, a livelihood in the entertainment industry was possible for thousands, and great fame and relative wealth was to be had from the industry by a select few.

While the laws in the US providing incentive for contributors to donate to charities were available to individuals in 1917 and extended to companies in the 1930s, the application of this structure to the arts didn't gain momentum until the 1950s under the leadership of the Ford Foundation.[4] For the next thirty years, an entire generation of artists and art managers grew up with nonprofit structures and the expectation of financial subsidy. Coupled with a rise in labor costs, those enterprises that remained in the for-profit live-entertainment field and didn't shift to film and television pursued only the most profitable genres, which we know to be Broadway musicals and what can loosely be termed pop music. Indeed, for the remainder of the twentieth century, a sizeable rift grew between the *mission-driven* nonprofit world, operating with a commitment to high art as good for society and worthy of production and presentation whether well attended or not, and the *profit-driven* world, which aspired only to entertainment that would allow all involved to profit. Each side viewed the other with an increasing degree of skepticism and mistrust.

Social and economic change in recent years, along with a realization that each side of this divide has something of potential benefit to the other, has caused cracks to form in the barriers and definitions to loosen up. Some commercial producers are recognizing the nonprofit arts world as a source of *outside-of-the-box*, new creativity to feed the commercial entertainment machine, which increasingly integrates Broadway, film, and television, and merchandise tie-ins, and that is hungry for new creative ideas. Walt Disney Theatrical Production's engagement of the bold innovator Julie Taymor to direct the stage production of *The Lion King* on Broadway was a watershed event in the late 1990s in this regard, though whether an isolated blip or the beginning of a pattern is yet to be seen.

While sensitive to *selling out* artistic ideals, many in the nonprofit arts have come to recognize that the occasional offering across the nonprofit/commercial divide can generate much needed revenue to subsidize theatrical experimentation and less-saleable work. The Alvin Ailey American Dance Theater has benefited greatly from the popularity of the work *Revelations*, which has brought significant new audiences to dance and ticket revenue to the company. Institutional, nonprofit New York producers such as the Manhattan Theatre Club and the Roundabout Theatre Company, formerly producing exclusively for Off-Broadway with an occasional move to Broadway, now own, operate, and routinely produce for Broadway theaters. At least one nonprofit regional theater company, the highly successful La Jolla Playhouse, has systematized its transfer of appropriate shows to Broadway with a club of wealthy investors standing by to support the moves.

In recent years, as financial support for the arts has declined, concerns for attendance and box office revenue have taken on increasing importance, sometimes over aesthetic goals, among subsidized nonprofit presenters. With turmoil in the field comes great need and opportunity for creative thinkers to help shift the paradigm and evolve new business models that address the art/money balance.

In numerous conversations with me, mainland Chinese producers and government arts officials involved in expanding their country's influence around the world and in bringing the world's arts to China have been very clear in the distinctions they make between "commercial" projects (those in which the performers are expected to be paid—if poorly—and profits to be made) and "cultural" projects (those in which it is assumed that the artists will accept no pay or that US corporate sponsors will subsidize). This is difficult to accept in light of the enormous imbalance of trade in China's favor and its vast accumulation of international currency. Efforts to discuss with my Chinese colleagues the matter of salaries to the performers are often met with shrugs suggesting incomprehension as to why I should be such a Philistine as to impede the exchange of cultural understanding between our great nations over the trifling matter of paying artists!

Likewise (as we observe the billions of dollars being spent by certain Arab nations to construct elaborate entertainment centers), in my first call recently from a hiring agent for a Dubai theater, I was clearly advised at the outset that the theater "cannot lose money" and told that the artists must expect to receive less than they might normally in order to protect the presenters from risk of loss.

These are not only difficult conversations to have for one representing the interests of artists and productions and used to negotiating agreements that are fair to both sides, but they point to the fact that, while the commercial and cultural worlds in the US might be in the early stages of reaching across the **great divide**, other parts of the world have a long way to go!

"Profit Driven" versus "Mission Driven"

Digging more deeply into the worlds of nonprofit and for-profit institutions, the distinction between them is often defined by what is considered to be *profit motivation* by the commercial, wherein the financial bottom line ultimately dictates decisions, and *mission motivation* in the nonprofit, wherein the institution is established to achieve a social mission with funds secured in support.

Applied to the live arts and entertainment, clearest are the commercial presenters—be they owners, managers, exclusive bookers of the venues, or outside promoters—who simply do not undertake presentations without the expectation that they will result in profits: salability ultimately trumps artistic considerations or efforts to lead audiences to new experiences.

The nonprofit institutions on the other hand, speak a language that often feels duplicitous, resulting from their need to serve two masters: art *and* money. Founded on a mission-driven basis to provide culture to their communities, they often speak of their roles as cultural leaders and their goals of bringing the most dynamic new arts to all segments of their communities. But from far too many such institutions around the country what is actually offered on their stages makes a lie of these noble words. In a scramble to not lose money in presenting, all too often only well-known artists with proven audience appeal are presented, some repeatedly, and billed as fresh and new. Recent increased support for educational programming should help, but with such support still severely limited, this too often means presentation of banal programs to audiences of school-age children with little access to live performances.

An informal, yearly survey of the season brochures of presenting organizations from around the country reveals very few that actually offer the truly high-quality, bold, new artistic images and ideas to their audiences so often promised. A confluence of factors is keeping institutions from "walking the walk." These factors include a) short term economic pressure, b) a lack of historic effort to develop new audiences and accustom patrons to seek new artistic adventures, c) rapidly changing demographic bases, and d) institutional structures inherently geared to serve white, middle-class audiences that celebrate stability over adaptability and that find real institutional change to be next to impossible.

The economic realities are obvious: as subsidies for bold, new arts and efforts to reach new audiences dry up and shift to market-driven corporate sponsorship, presenters receive pressure from both sponsors and fiscal monitors to get more "bodies in seats" to increase both sponsor impact and ticket revenue at a risk to the artistic vision side of the mission.

Our demographic changes are being trumpeted daily in the national news. As John Kreidler's report[5] states, in the rapid rise of nonprofits in the latter half of the twentieth century, the sad fact is that, during all that time with all those charitable dollars, the expansion of cultural delivery primarily impacted only the relatively affluent Caucasian population of the US. This fact is crashing home in the new millennium as this demographic is becoming the minority in many cities and an influx of immigrants from all over the world are arriving with their own cultural histories and expectations and finding a cultural infrastructure in the US ill-equipped to respond. One only has to read the recent working paper *Critical Issues Facing the Arts in California*,[6] quoted in chapter 13, to see that the disconnect between the traditional culture and culture-delivery systems and the evolving California demographics and lifestyles is vast and expanding. The paper reports that 26 percent of the State's population is foreign borne and 20 percent of California residents speak English "less than well" at home, and the percentages are expected to increase. While we are seeing some valiant efforts to multiculturalize some of these institutions, we have a long way to go. Presenters of the live arts are now paying the price for the lack of new audience investment during the better financial times and are forced into short-term measures to chase dwindling historic audiences.

Successful new models for nonprofit institutional management that will allow both innovative art and healthy bottom lines have yet to emerge. The leaders of arts centers, many built and still operated at board- and senior-staff levels by whites, are having enormous difficulty seeing the trees outside of their diminishing forests, and finding the evolved meaning of cultural leadership in this changed world and the avenues to effectively populate their proud buildings.

And none of this really addresses the *generational* disconnect as young people do not find an appeal in the traditional structures.

Short-Term Solutions

The quickest short-term response is to program only shows that the presenter can be reasonably assured existing ticket buyers already know and will pay money to come and see—effectively the same programming philosophy as most commercial presenters. The deeper commitment to new art and new audiences is the first thing often jettisoned when the going gets rough financially, and the hardest to get back once short-term, bottom-line thinking takes over.

Operating from a short-time horizon, this logic is unimpeachable and existing audiences are kept reasonably satisfied. But of course it postpones the deeper challenges to the long-term viability of these nonprofit cultural organizations and could be viewed as rearranging deckchairs—and perhaps putting on a show—on board the Titanic as the entire experience of live performance slips lower and lower on the social and personal agenda of much of the nation. It is not surprising that we are seeing a disturbing number of presenting organizations cease to operate altogether, former presenters of adventurous new shows now chasing formulaic programming, and performing arts centers being turned over to commercial entertainment conglomerates for nonentertainment uses, if not closing their doors altogether.

The issue is often compounded in the case of arts centers owned by municipalities and academic institutions. While both are often proud to own such facilities, they are obsessed with the prospect of the arts centers losing money and requiring financial subsidy, and they end up back in the short-term, bottom-line thinking that leads to such mediocrity in programming.

Nonprofit Structures in Question

As the programming philosophies of commercial and nonprofit organizations converge, there are some who question whether the nonprofit structure itself in its current form continues to serve the best interests of culture in our society. The problems often stem from the fact that nonprofit organizations by law are controlled by committees (boards of directors or trustees), which are unwilling or unable to maintain the true vision leadership so badly needed. These committees are typically made up of the wealthiest and most politically influential businesspeople to be found in hope that they will contribute money and "open doors." They often have relatively little connection to the arts or to the community beyond their social and business circles, and have little sense of their roles as board members beyond raising money, attending events, and keeping an eye on the books. What they often contribute is the same bottom-line thinking that they apply to their own businesses, sidestepping those parts of the arts centers' missions to undertake cultural leadership and community audience development that by their natures must operate with time horizons far beyond the end of the present fiscal year. These missions include reaching out to and serving ethnic and low-income demographics often outside the ken of these business leaders and historically alienated by such arts centers.

The professed missions of many arts centers require generational visions of programming and public relationships equivalent to the decades planned in the construction of most of these buildings. Design and implementation of such missions is a very difficult task to undertake and sustain, and involves a relationship among board members, staff, and the community quite different from what is common today. The cogent and provocative book *Governance as Leadership: Reframing the Work of Nonprofit Boards*,[7] by management experts Richard P. Chait, William P. Ryan, and Barbara E. Taylor, defines three types of board governance: *fiduciary*, which is essentially protective, *strategic*, which is proactive, but only to the extent of supporting the organization to reach its objectives, and *generative*, which is actively involved in the generation of the institution's vision from which the objectives derive. The writers conclude that most nonprofit boards are heavily rooted in the first, occasionally get involved with the second, but are largely not structured to capably address the third. This goes a long way to explaining why the mission claims of such seemingly well-protected and established institutions often ring so hollow.

And, yes, lest you think that I have taken us too far afield of the tour booking process, this issue is having a tremendous impact on the shows being offered for tour, and whether and how they are being presented to what segments of the public.

Artists and Nonprofit Producers Share Responsibility

In fairness to the nonprofit presenters, on the other side of the equation the artists and nonprofit producers themselves share responsibility for the evolving challenge of audience alienation.

During the heyday of the 1970s and early 1980s, when the National Endowment for the Arts and other foundations were funding open development in artistic expression and subsidizing presenters both directly and through state arts agencies, many artists and nonprofit producing institutions lost sight of accountability for their work to *entertain*[8] or even be understood by the majority of audience members. In fact, in the late 1970s, if an artist created a work that appealed to the public, in certain circles it was viewed as an artistic failure, with the artist accused of having "sold out" his integrity.

An artist's or presenter's choice to move onto a more esoteric artistic plane, thereby disconnecting with broader audiences, is fine as long as the subsidy is there to pay for this. This is much the same as free research in the scientific community: subsidized research not tied to any proscribed result. But as funding has shifted in recent years toward a demand for greater accountability in *deliverables*, both in creative output and donor exposure, and as governmental agencies have placed limitations on the freedom of artistic expression *and* had artists' funding cut at the same time, artists are forced to a *free-artistic-expression-versus-eat* choice as never before. And many of these artists—and nonprofit administrators—are of a generation better trained to fundraise among now disinterested donors than to please mass audiences.

High Art Rarely Equates with Profit

Finally, lest you think me so naive as to believe that with better boards and more audience development, innovative new artistic concepts can be expected to sell out on tour, let me assure you I have no such illusions.

While it may be true that my Italian, peasant ancestors sang opera while picking olives on the hillside, and that there was a time before television when going out to live entertainment was an accepted part of weekly or monthly life for many, there is little documentation that even in the best of times the higher arts were ever so accepted in the US as to be commercially viable. And the economics of such productions, even for those organizations that do sell a high percentage of their available seats at robust ticket prices, such as the Metropolitan Opera, require significant subsidies regardless.

As Trav S. D. reports in his history of vaudeville,[9] the savvy commercial producer Martin Beck (1867–1940), whose name adorns a Broadway theater to this day, had at the turn of the twentieth century an odd passion:

One of the best bookers in the business, the owl-like, multi-lingual Beck also stubbornly insisted on booking opera singers, classical musicians, and ballet dancers, even if sometimes he was the only one in the audience who appreciated them. He considered it his responsibility to educate the audience.

Does this sound like the mission of any nonprofit arts centers we know? And Beck had this notion before the Ford Foundation or the National Endowment for the Arts existed! But the concession that such work will not consistently sell out theaters does not in any way mitigate the need to operate with business models that involve the constant development of new audiences for new artistic expression as norms instead of exceptions.

Agents and Presenters at the Nexus

This all leads directly back to the subject of this book: the tour booking process, since agents and presenters are at the crux of the show engagement process, linked to producers, artists, managers and the many support roles involved.

When we stand and talk in booths at booking conferences, we are on the front lines of the debate about mission versus bottom line in performing arts presenting, and of the debate about which artists and audience members are declining and which are ascendant. Yes, the presenters have venues and series they must fill and can be expected to book shows. But if they can't get audiences to pay money to see them and don't have sufficient underwriting for the resulting empty seats, sooner or later the piper must be paid or the dance stops. And how will great art get to the populace if the presenters have gone out of business? At the same time, it is essential to society's well-being that artists be supported to freely express and create, and that they are provided opportunities for their work to be exposed to public view.

There are many bright, visionary people in the lead chairs at presenting organizations fighting this battle every day, and with every decision and every negotiation they undertake to bring high-quality, dynamic, and sometimes edgy shows into their theaters *and* have healthy audiences *and* not lose their shirts.

Endnotes

1 *The Performing Arts in a New Era* (2001).

2 See "The WPA Federal Theatre Project, 1935–39" at *http://memory.loc.gov/ammem/fedtp/ftwpa.html.*

3 For further research, contact the National League of Historic Theatres, with headquarters in Baltimore, MD (*www.lhat.org*).

4   John Kreidler, "Leverage Lost: The Nonprofit Arts in the Post-Ford Era" (*In Motion* online magazine, February 16, 1996, *www.inmotionmagazine.com/lost.html*), provides exceptional insight into what Kreidler defines as the *Pre-Ford Era* (Industrial Revolution to 1957), the *Ford Era* (1957–1990; "Leverage Gained"), and *The Post-Ford Era* (1990 to Present; "Leverage Lost").

5   "Leverage Lost: The Nonprofit Arts in the Post-Ford Era" (1996).

6   The James Irvine Foundation, *Critical Issues Facing the Arts in California: A Working Paper* (September 2006). http://www.irvine.org/assets/pdf/pubs/arts/Critical_Issues_Arts.pdf.

7   Richard P. Chait, William P. Ryan, Barbara E. Taylor, *Governance as Leadership: Reframing the Work of Nonprofit Boards* (Hoboken, New Jersey: John Wiley & Sons, Inc. for BoardSource, 2005).

8   From the French, *entre tenir*, this word literally means "to hold between." I prefer to consider the word with this root interpretation as the expectation of art to hold the attention of viewers and not merely to amuse. It provides a point of congruence between the best of the highest and most vulgar or plebian of forms.

9   Trav S. D., *No Applause Please—Just Throw Money: The Book that Made Vaudeville Famous* (New York: Faber and Faber, 2005).

CONCLUSION

I have attempted to overview the tour booking process from a multifaceted perspective, highlighting those elements that have proved over time to be relatively fixed as well as those that are changing and will change even before the print is dry on this book. The process of researching and writing the book has been eye opening. It has forced me to review my own three-decade history in the field and many of my own assumptions. And it has provided an opportunity to talk, from an interviewer's viewpoint, with highly experienced colleagues who represent vastly different perspectives and to read books and reports reflecting on the field's past, present, and future.

Three Themes

From all of this, three themes recur throughout:

It Has Happened Before

Despite all the hullabaloo about new technologies, there is little happening today within this field that has not, in one form or another, happened before. The development of the iPod, high-definition television, and plasma screens probably all have had less revolutionary impact on entertainment consumption patterns than the first *crystal sets* (early radios) that appeared in living rooms almost a century ago and magically brought the outside world into people's homes through the air for the first time. My mother's descriptions of hearing the first radio broadcast as a child in the 1920s are far more ecstatic and wonder-filled than my teenage daughter's delight with the latest digital goodie today.

When it comes to the role of conglomerates—so significant to the conduct of our business—Live Nation, with all its influence, doesn't hold a candle to the business tactics of The Syndicate and the early Shubert operation at the turn of the last century.

Waves of immigrants have arrived in America before, become assimilated, and influenced theatrical entertainment in the US for two centuries. And if the advent of talking pictures in any form—celluloid or digital—was going to shut down live entertainment entirely, based on the severity of the shock it had on the live-performance world of the early 1930s, it probably would have done so before now.

Knowing this, of course, does not make today's challenges any easier. And the solutions found to challenges in earlier times are not always the ones we would prefer to see repeated. But a knowledge of our field's history, while perhaps taking some of the fun out of the idea that we are facing a certain problem for the very first time, does provide comfort in the knowledge that we are inheritors of a long line of people bitten by the theater bug, who yelled and whispered, pounded and pushed our ideas into the general fray, who reflected the spirit and ethos of their times, and who hopefully added some value and had and shared some good times along the way!

Change is Hard

The second realization is just how difficult change is. And by change, I mean both institutional change and personal acceptance of bold, new artistic ideas.

I recall taking over the helm of the City Center Theater institution in New York City in the mid-1980s and being amazed at both the advanced age of many of the employees and the myopically set attitudes and job routines. Coming from being the general manager of the start-up, nonprofit, historic Flynn Theatre in Burlington, Vermont, where I was able to work from a clean slate and every idea was new and (generally) enthusiastically welcomed, I naively thought that I could get the dour ushers to actually smile at our customers and welcome them to City Center, that the matrons in the ladies room would stop hoarding and selling our paper towels to our customers to dry their hands, that the general management would see venue renters as our friends and welcome clients instead of adversaries out to break rules. I thought that the stagehands would actually join us in discussing how to lower production costs for dance companies facing increasing financial hardship so that they could continue and even expand their annual seasons.

While some headway was made, much wasn't. But I did end up with a sign on my office wall listing explanations I was given for why change was not possible and from which I would sometimes invite people to choose their answer:

- We can't change that because we tried it once and it didn't work.

- We can't change that because it will cost too much.

- We can't change that because the unions won't like it.

- We can't change that because the artistic tenants won't like it.

- We can't change that because we don't do that sort of thing here.

On an aesthetic level, I am well aware of the fear of change and new ideas among potential audience members, including ourselves. We shut out many incredible theatrical opportunities because we haven't already heard about them from the right people and don't know or trust that the experience will be worth our time, effort, and money. This brings up the seeming paradox for those of us in the business of, in one of my favorite phrases, both *guiding public tastes* while also *following the public's wishes*.

A relevant quote appeared in the *New York Times* by the newly announced General Director of the New York City Opera, the provocative Gerard Mortier, in which he says, "there is a big difference between what is popular and what is populist, and I don't want to be populist."[1] The writer proceeds to report, "[Mortier] believes in devising operatic programs and then selling them to the public, he explained. He will not tailor programs in advance to some populist notion of what the people want." Here at least are one man and one organization preparing to make a full-throated commitment to leading the public's tastes—or not—who are deserving of high praise (and, hopefully, funding) for trying.

The Endurance of the Road

A third realization is the intrepid nature of shows touring America. Reading of the efforts of nineteenth century divas to reach the American hinterlands by stagecoach to perform for the often poorly educated pioneers makes one appreciate that the urge for artists, producers, and shows to get out and find audiences—whether motivated by pride, financial gain, or simply the quest for new frontiers—is a proud and storied enterprise of longstanding and is well worth respect and study.

To the Next Generation

As I hope this book may make some contribution toward the education and edification of a new generation coming into the field, I will take the liberty of sharing the following thoughts:

Find your passion in the work, and the niche that excites you. You may not arrive there in a completely linear fashion and that is okay. Listen to your heart for the place you want to be in the astounding global enterprise of live arts and entertainment, and always seek enjoyment in what you are doing even as you advance in stature and scope of responsibility.

Don't be afraid to seek reasonable remuneration for your work balanced by whatever altruistic feelings you may have about supporting the arts. It is a field that will take everything you have to offer and, though giving much back, will rarely, on its own volition, assure your financial comfort or income and health benefits in old age. My generation lived through the mission-driven myopia that to give all, selflessly, in support of the arts, was the highest, best use of our lives. We now watch the leadership of major arts organizations turned over to corporate CEOs with little arts knowledge or experience, but what boards hope will be access to corporate contributions. If I've learned anything it's love the arts *and* know your worth and respect yourself. Your soul is probably a lot harder to sell than you think!

If you really want to be on stage, go for it and don't enter arts management as a poor second choice. The drive to perform is unique and needs to be addressed on its own terms. The satisfactions to be had from being a presenter, agent, producer, stagehand, box office treasurer, or any one of the many behind the scenes roles are entirely different. Deal with this early and clearly for yourself and your future happiness.

Your personal reputation is everything. This is an entirely people business. With every interaction you have in this business, remember that how you conduct yourself now will matter later, to yourself even if to no one else. It's a surprisingly small world and once you are active and known in the field, it is hard to hide. So play hard *and* keep your integrity compass firmly in hand.

And smile!

Endnotes

1 Anthony Tommasini, "Which Is the People's Opera? Let the Fireworks Begin," *New York Times*, March 11, 2007.

Contract Checklist

Following is a list of subject areas, together with notes, that should at least be considered for inclusion in engagement contracts. Not all items appear in all contracts, the most common reason for not including an item being that it does not apply. If there is no back-end percentage, for instance, then there is no point in including a section on sharing box office. If the engagement is not international, currency conversion is not relevant.

A second reason parties may leave out an item is that they simply can't agree about it but don't anticipate that the issue is likely to come up. A contract should anticipate all contingencies as comprehensively as possible, and obviously it is not desirable to consciously avoid issues. But if the parties simply can't agree on one point and they don't consider it an essential point, why jeopardize the entire agreement over something that is not likely to be a factor? The implication here is that if you leave it out and it *does* become an issue, you'll battle it out if and when it comes up.

The important point is that if you leave out an item in a contract, be sure you are leaving it out intentionally and not out of forgetfulness.

DISCLAIMER

It is important for me to state clearly that I am not a lawyer, and what follows is nonprofessional opinion, based solely on my experience over the years as presenter, agent, producer, and manager. It should not be taken as legal advice and I will accept no responsibility for the results of actions taken on the basis of this writing. My intention is to provide a framework to assist the reader in thinking through what subjects should be considered in touring contracts and providing some context from both the buying and selling sides. This is not intended to in any way replace the advice of expert legal counsel as contracts are being written or critical issues arise.

Identity of the Contract Elements

Contracts invariably begin with a definition of the essential contract elements, first and foremost the contracting people or institutions, which are referred to as the *parties* to the contract. It is not unusual to identify three parties at the opening of the contract: the provider of the show (the producer), the buyer of the show (the presenter), and the agent involved in the process (the agent).

The entities are normally defined by their full corporate names and office addresses, and assigned a one-word shorthand moniker. Specifically, after identifying the producer's corporate name, address, etc., it is customary to say in parenthesis, *hereinafter referred to as "Producer."* The same will apply to the "Presenter" and the "Agent." A similar application of one-word monikers may take place later in the contract related to other items that will be referred to repeatedly throughout the document such as the "Engagement" and the "Production." This provides convenient shorthand so that once fully identified the full names need not be repeated.

Additional details on this first page might include:

- The name, telephone, and e-mail of the primary contacts for quick reference later.

- Assuming delivery services such as messengers or FedEx are to be used for formal notification, it is important to have street addresses for the contracting parties, not post office boxes. This is also important for serving notices and tracking down the other party if need arises.

- Further identifying details about corporate status and location often appear, for example, ". . . a nonprofit company incorporated in the state of Delaware."

- For further identification, either here or on the signature page, a Tax Identification Number should be included, especially for the party receiving money.

- When working with an individual artist, it is not uncommon for her to sign as a private individual and not a corporate entity in which case her Social Security number replaces the Tax Identification Number. Note also that if the artist tours often and no one collects her mail, she might opt to have her address listed as that of her manager or agent.

The Producer

This is the entity that is providing the show to be performed, be it a solo artist who created his own show, an institutional dance company, or a Broadway show with its own limited liability company or limited partnership. This might be defined in the contract as "Producer," "Artist" (in the case of a self-producing artist), or "Company" (in the case of a touring dance or theater company).

The Presenter

This is the legal name of the individual or company taking the presenting responsibility. This party is rarely an individual since the degree of legal risk being taken by the presenter provides an incentive to have the protection of a corporate structure of some nature.

This organization may or may not be the same as the venue in which the performance is to take place.

If a department of a university, municipality, or other larger organization, it is important to clarify whether the department itself has legal authority to bind the parent organization or whether it is in fact the larger organization that is contracting on behalf of its department. If it is the ABC Arts Center at DEF University, is the arts center either independently incorporated or else authorized by the parent university to execute presenting contracts, or is the contract really with the University?

This entity might be defined as *Presenter, Promoter, Festival,* or, occasionally, *Licensee.*

The Agent

This is most relevant for identification and inclusion in the contract if the agent is authorized to sign on behalf of the producer and/or if some or all of the funds due to the producer from the presenter are to be sent to the agent by the presenter. If the agent is neither a formal signatory to the contract nor receiving funds directly from the presenter, it is not always necessary to identify the agent in the contract.[1] If the booking agency is identified, it is often following the definition of the producer, leading in with "represented for the purposes of this engagement by _____ ('Agent')."

The Licensee/Licensor

Occasionally the entity we are defining as the producer is referred to as the *Licensor* and the presenter as the *Licensee.* This is seen in contracts in which the hosting organization is in essence producing the show and licensing permission to do so from the show's original producer, even if in so licensing the host is bringing in most of the production from the outside and effectively presenting. The occasions for this are complex and generally outside of the scope of this book.

As an example, we recently experienced a show that was already corporately structured with and in the control of a limited liability company for a Broadway engagement being booked for a pre-Broadway engagement outside of New York. The terms of the LLC forbade the show to be performed in *presented* form before it appeared on Broadway, though the members of the LLC wanted the pre-Broadway run opportunity. To resolve this conflict it was agreed that the out-of-town host would, instead of *presenting* the show, *license* the show and engage the cast and other elements separately. The contract structure was somewhat more complex as a result, but the final outcome was the same as if the show had been presented.

Another example is the instance of a production such as an opera having been initially produced by one opera company and now offered for re-production by another, where so much of the production (orchestra, singers, and chorus) is to be engaged locally by the presenter that it cannot be considered a packaged show for touring. In this case, the sets and costumes might be rented from the original producer and the show licensed for restaging by the local entity—more accurately referred to as *Licensee* than *Presenter*.

The Production

Early on in the contract, the production to be presented is identified. Of course this includes the title but may also include certain star names or characteristics that differentiate it from other productions. This might be the first national touring company of a Broadway show as distinct from any later touring productions, or the first company of a dance company that might also have a second and even third company. Remember distinctions such as between a fully staged production of a musical versus a concert version, or an appearance of a musician solo versus in the context of a quartet, band, orchestra, etc. With some musicians and comedians, the definition of Production will include the minimum number of minutes the artist is to perform on the stage.

This paragraph often starts off with a lead-in to the effect that "the production to be presented under the terms of this contract is _____." Once clearly identified, the contract may assign a moniker by saying *(hereinafter referred to as the "Production")*, and from this point forward in the contract, the one word is sufficient to identify the show with all its qualifiers.

The Engagement

The Engagement is the broader context in which the Production is being presented. This will include the dates and times of performances, the venue(s) in which the performances will take place including seating capacities, the number of performances, and the related activities that may be offered to the public such as lecture demonstrations, talks, and book or CD signings.

Consider adding the specification "live performance" to differentiate from a broadcast or recording, and the genre of show such as "dance," "music concert," or "musical theater production." List all related activities covered under this contract with as much detail as is known at the time of contract issuance—workshops, lectures, promotional appearances, etc. Put in all information available at the time of the contract execution, with the number, schedule, and location of the live performances being paramount. If you know that a workshop is to be offered, for instance, but are not sure of the time and place at the time the contract is being executed, you should list it, noting that time and location are to be determined (TBD) by mutual agreement of the parties (or at the discretion of one or the other of the parties if that is the case).

This paragraph often starts off with a lead-in to the effect that "the Presenter hereby wishes to engage a production offered by Producer, and Producer agrees to such engagement, under the following terms and conditions." Once the engagement has been defined, the moniker of *Engagement* may be assigned to be used for all future reference in the contract.

Engagement Section Format

This section might be written out in prose form and also include a schedule of activity.

If the Engagement is at all complex or spans multiple days or weeks, it is normal to attach the detailed schedule as an addendum rather than taking space in the main body of the contract, in which case the definition of Engagement on the first page will stipulate that it is *per addendum (#) attached.*

If this is for a multiweek run of a production, and the weekly schedules are all the same, the start and end dates can be identified, with show times listed as, "Tuesdays through Sundays at 8 PM and Saturdays and Sundays at 2 PM."

If the production will take a day or more to load in before the day of opening performance, it is a good idea to show the schedule including the production days—even though a more detailed production schedule will undoubtedly appear in the technical rider—to insure that the correct number of days are being held in the venue and both parties know when on-site work on this Engagement is to begin.

If a dress rehearsal to which an audience will be invited (an *invited dress*) or preview performance has been agreed to, be sure to show it in the schedule and within the definition of Engagement.

The Venues

It is important to identify the venues of all activities—classes and performances especially—and the seating capacity of the theater in which the public performances are to take place. This is generally done in the context of defining Engagement.

In the case of classes, many artists and art forms are quite particular in choice of venues vis-à-vis floor condition, size, temperature, security, dimensions, and other factors.

In the case of performances the seating capacity is important because a) the financial terms of the agreement will have been based in part on gross potential and reasonable expectation of ticketing income, which is affected by the seating capacity, and b) the producer's agreement to send the show may be affected in part by the technical parameters of a particular venue.

Exchange of Value

A contract is between two (or more) parties, and in order to be valid there has to be an *exchange of value* between the parties. So after detailing who the contracting parties are, a typical contract structure next addresses what each side is providing for the other.

To Be Provided by Producer

In this section of the contact, you can refer to the *Production* and the scope of services defined within *Engagement* above, and clarify those elements being provided by the producer as his part in delivering the show. This normally includes personnel (cast and support people such as stage manager, company manager, lighting designer, etc.); costumes, set, and props; marketing materials, program copy, and reasonable press activity; and rights to perform the work including all permissions needed from holders of rights related to the production (unless royalties are being paid directly by the presenter to the rights holder).

It is important to stipulate in writing that the producer is paying all salaries, payroll taxes, and requisite Social Security and other benefits to protect the presenter from any potential liability in those areas. This becomes particularly important with certain non-US countries that require that any nonresident person conducting business in the country have benefits provided, if not by the producer then by the presenter.

To Be Provided by Presenter

This tends to be a much longer section than that for the producer with a number of sections. Included here may be some or all of the following, depending on what the parties have agreed to.

Terms

This, of course, is a significant section and usually appears on the front page of the contract for easy reference. It describes the amount of guarantee the presenter is agreeing to pay, qualifies that such guarantee is payable net of tax and without deductions,[2] and specifies any percentage agreements in addition to or in lieu of the guarantee. This section should also be quite specific as to the payment schedule and how the funds are to be handed over—"by corporate check payable to the producer's representative on site," "by wire transfer," etc. If an international contract, the currency of payment must be designated.

Travel

Intercity Travel. How many people are traveling? The class of travel? Clarify who will book it and pay for it. If the producer is advancing the funds to purchase the airline tickets, what is the expected reimbursement time from the presenter? If flights are booked early for an orchestra or large ballet company, this can be a tremendous cash flow challenge to whomever is paying up front.

It is not unusual for the producer to require that flights be on an IATA carrier—an airline that is a member of the International Air Transportation Association—to be assured of the safety and maintenance standards required of IATA members. This includes almost all major airlines in the world but not all of the private charter companies.

Airport Transfers at the Show's Home Base, Both Out and Back. If it is a symphony orchestra with every member paying fifty dollars each way to get to and from the local airport, this can add up to a considerable sum. Who pays, and is it included in the fee or reimbursed separately? If this engagement is part of a tour over which the initial and final airport transfers can be amortized, it may make life easier for all concerned for the producer to include an allocation for this expense in the budget underlying the fee and not attempt to tabulate and seek reimbursement on this item.

Local Transportation in Presenter's Community. This can include transportation between airport, hotel, theater, and engagement-related activities, such as press conferences. Specify type of transport and if public transportation is acceptable—remember that in many cities, public transport does not run late at night after the dinners following the performances. Some artists require limos or private cars. Note that if the accommodations and theater are within a reasonable distance, the personnel may be asked to walk. But a precise definition of *reasonable distance* may be important, and factors such as bad weather, the risk of walking late at night, and the age and physical condition of the individuals involved should be taken into account.

Freight

Intercity Freight. Clarify if this includes pick up and return to home warehouse, carnet, and insurance. If mode of transport is known—that is, by truck, air freight, sea, or as excess baggage, etc.—spell it out as there is often a significant difference in cost between surface and air freight transport. Clarify who will book the freight and pay for it. If the producer is paying the freight charge initially, clarify the agreed-upon reimbursement time from the presenter and what is required to trigger reimbursement (e.g., presentation of receipt). Additionally:

- Be sure to obtain competitive freight quotes. This is primarily the responsibility of the producer and sometimes the agent, but for productions with significant freight, presenters often wish to seek their own quotes for comparison.

- Globalization of shipping means that unlike booking airline tickets, where purchasing in the country of origin often (though not always) obtains the best price, this is not always or even often true of international freight. Seek bids internationally.

- When seeking quotes, be sure a written, detailed set of specifications ("spec") is provided to all bidders including not only the size and weight statistics needed, but whether or not ground transportation at origin and destination are required, carnet, customs importation, and insurance (state value) are included. Be sure that all bidders receive the same written specs so the bids are comparative (apples-to-apples).

- Be sure to ask for any unavoidable taxation that will apply—new security procedures in various ports have forced taxation or special charges on all goods arriving or departing regardless of the carnet and temporary importation.

- Freight costs in a contract are often stipulated with a cap or "not to exceed" figure. To determine this, clarify first whether the quotes being provided by the freight *forwarders*[3] are being guaranteed by them, or whether a shift in the international cost of fuel or other factors might cause an adjustment. This is critical for whichever side of the deal is responsible for the freight costs. If the presenter is paying for freight but insisting that the producer lock in an amount or cap on freight cost liability, and if the freight forwarder is not guaranteeing the quote, then a reasonable contingency (perhaps 10 to 20 percent) to cover unexpected cost fluctuation should be added in before establishing the cap.

Local Freight. Since most freight that is not traveling with the show can be expected to be delivered and picked up directly at the stage door of the theater, local freight as a separate item generally applies only when the freight is traveling with the show, notably as excess baggage or accompanying freight by air. The presenter would be reasonably expected to provide a truck or van plus loading personnel at the airport to greet the freight on arrival, bring it to the theater, and to return it to the airport at the end.

Per Diems

Per diems are typically included within the fees for artists touring in their home country, but payable separately by presenters in foreign countries. For such international travel, per diems are normally payable in cash on arrival in local currency. For US artists touring abroad, the rates are often established based on a US dollar equivalent.

- *Establishing the rate can be a challenge.* For domestic touring, rates are often established by the relevant unions or artist contracts with the producers. For international touring many producers refer to the rates established by the US Department of State for government employees as a guideline, available on the Web site of the US Department of State,[4] though those tend to be maximum rates and on the high side for what the performing arts field can and will pay. Some countries, such as France, have negotiated a touring per diem rate for French artists touring within their own country and French presenters will typically refer to that as the benchmark for what they will offer visiting performers. Festivals, some of which bring in a great many artists in a relatively short period of time, will often establish a rate for all artists and are unwilling to negotiate. The government of Hong Kong, which is responsible for most international touring artist presentations in that city, has a standard rate it will not exceed.

- *Rate conflict.* It is not unusual that, after good-faith negotiation, the rate a presenter is willing to pay is less than the rate a producer is obligated to pay under its contract with its performers. This means the per diem provided by the presenter must be augmented by the producer. The agent and artist must be aware of this early in the negotiation so as to include this added cost within the budget that underlies the fee negotiated.

- *Kitchen facilities provided.* In the event of extended runs, some artist/producer agreements allow that if the accommodations provided include kitchen facilities, the artists are prepared to accept a lower per diem rate on the grounds that they can save some money by doing some home cooking instead of eating at restaurants for every meal. Since presenters can often find apartment-style accommodations for multiple days or weeks at lower rates than hotels are willing to match, this can end up a win–win situation.

PER DIEMS IN ADDITION TO ACCOMMODATIONS

Note that we are referring to per diems in addition to accommodations being provided. Under the terms of some artist/producer contracts, the producer provides a larger per diem that covers accommodations as well as food, and the performers are on their own to accommodate themselves. Most producers—and presenters—prefer to have the touring troupe housed in one location for safety, ease of local transport, and because with group purchase more favorable housing rates are often obtainable. So producers and presenters often would rather offer the troupe members accommodations separate from a per diem, which is primarily intended to cover food.

Accommodations

Be sure to agree on the allocation of single and double rooms, and suites if required, and of course the total number of nights. Many contracts simply state a number of *room nights*, but if you know the precise arrival and departure dates, put them in. Also specify the quality level of hotel (sometimes defined by the number of stars) and the proximity to the theater (see "Local Transportation" above). Experience in international touring suggests that factors such as no smoking rooms, the size of beds, the presence of safes, high-speed Internet access and fax, and sometimes twenty-four-hour room service, if important to the artists, should be stipulated in the contract. If the artists will be driving themselves, parking is also important. Clarify if breakfast is included and whether it will be a full "American" breakfast or a limited "Continental" breakfast.

While most presenters expect to provide accommodations in addition to fee and other costs, some US presenters insist that the fee be inclusive of accommodations paid by the producer. While in theory, if the fee is increased sufficiently to cover this cost, who books the rooms shouldn't matter. But in the US, there is a potential tax implication to watch out for. Most hotels will exempt the reservations from federal, state, and local tax if the organization booking is nonprofit and incorporated in the same state in which the hotel is located. But for producers or artists incorporated and granted tax-exempt status in another state, while the hotel might waive the federal tax, the benefit of waiving state and local tax on the hotel rooms is lost if not paid for by the local presenter. In some states, the state and local tax rates can be significant.

VARYING HOTEL RATES

Anecdotal evidence shows that, all else being equal, if an agency or producer from New York City calls to a local hotel for room bookings without introduction from the local arts center, the hotel will often quote its higher, *out-of-state* rate compared to what it will quote to a local organization. And calls from Europe or Asia to book hotels in the US get even higher quotes! Unless forced to by time constraints or limited room availability, never take the first quote as gospel. Obviously in foliage season in New England, festival time in Edinburgh or Avignon, Marathon weekend in New York City, etc., little or no negotiation will be possible for *anyone*.

Visas and Work Permits

It is not uncommon for artists/agents to also stipulate that other costs associated with travel, notably incremental insurance mandated for foreign travel by the artist and the cost of inoculations, should be reimbursed by the presenter. Keep in mind the visa pick-up fees at the consulates in the producer's home country in addition to whatever the visa petition costs are in the host country. It is important for the parties to agree early on who is paying what for what so as to avoid confusion and potential conflict later.

Visa Fees Waived by Governmental Presenters. Some presenters, which are operated directly or indirectly by national governments—notably major government-supported festivals—have the power to obtain waivers or reductions in visa charges for entry into their countries. The agent should be sure to inquire about this information as part of the negotiations since it may not be automatically volunteered by the presenter.

Advance Planning Visit. Digital exchange of sophisticated schematics for performing venues, and even including virtual video tours of the venues via the Internet, have made advance technical planning between producer and presenter somewhat easier and more efficient. But for certain productions, an advance-planning visit is still required and can save money in the long run. The primary focus is usually on technical stage details and decisions, but this visit can also involve aspects such as review and approval of accommodations by the producer and early press interviews with the production's director, if he is on the advance. If this is important, be sure to include it in the contract and define who pays the trip costs.

Often the technical-planning visit is best undertaken as early as possible and prior to final contract execution. In this situation, it can be covered by a separate letter of agreement stipulating that the presenter will cover these costs, which are nonreimbursable in the event that for any reason the engagement does not take place. In such cases, it is our practice to leave this section in the final contract and to add next to it a notation indicating that this obligation has already been addressed—sometimes just the word "done" is sufficient.

Translators

For international touring, this is obvious but important to include none-theless. For backstage work, especially for a more complex production, it is important to stipulate that the translator be experienced and versed in technical theater language and practices. Be careful with the word *professional* in association with translators since in some countries that means a licensed person who often will charge much higher rates and, trained to provide service to corporate clients, often doesn't have a grasp of backstage process and terminology. A translator learning technical terms on the job can slow down the setup and cause cost overruns and risk the show not being ready in time.

If the artist is to do press interviews requiring a translator at the same time that tech preparation is taking place on stage, two translators may be required.

Royalties

As with the fee, the important issues here are:

- *How is the amount of the royalty determined?* Royalty is generally calculated as a percentage of gross box office revenue (or perhaps of NAGBOR or Net Adjusted Gross Box Office Receipts, defined on page 86) and ranges up to a high of 10 percent. Sometimes it is at one rate until the breakeven point has been hit and a higher rate on profits. There is sometimes a minimum amount payable regardless of how low the box office income is, so it will be an amount *versus* a percentage, whichever is higher. In circumstances where the box office revenue details are not going to be shared, it is a flat rate per performance.

- *What rights does this royalty payment cover and not cover?* It should be stipulated if this one royalty payment covers all rights to perform the work, including creative, star performer, underlying rights, etc., or if there is anything left out.

- *When is it paid?* If the royalty is a percentage of gross or adjusted gross revenue, it is reasonable to allow for the presenter to have some time—perhaps four weeks—to complete the final accounting, at which point the royalty should be paid along with the provision of a formal box office statement attesting to the tickets sold, revenue received, and adjustments made to the gross revenue that arrived at the basis for royalty calculation. If a flat rate, it should be paid with the final fee payment.

- *To whom is it paid?* In many countries, there are agencies or guilds set up specifically to collect royalties and pass the money on to their members, retaining an administrative fee. This can be confusing for internationally touring artists who are not members of the local guilds and who are more likely to actually receive money if the royalty is paid directly to the producer. If an artist tours often in a foreign country, many guilds have arrangements for registering such artists as members.

Many presenters of music in the US have annual licensing agreements with either ASCAP or BMI, which are major music licensing agencies, together representing a vast majority of composers whose work is not in the public domain. By agreement between the two agencies, an annual fee to either by the presenter covers rights to perform any of the music by any of the composers represented by either. In the event that the performance(s) is a music concert only and does not involve directorial, choreographic, scenic, lighting, costume, or other design rights, this should cover the presenter's full royalty obligations with respect to the engagement.

Note that in addition to royalties for music compositions, in the cases of performances using recorded music, such as many dance companies, the recordings themselves are generally also under copyright. It is customary in such cases for the performing entities (e.g., the dance companies) to have obtained permission for use of the recordings in advance—presumably at the time the dance was created—and to have arranged to pay appropriate royalties.

Additional creators who may receive royalties for their work include directors, choreographers, scenic and lighting designers, and occasionally sound designers. Additionally owners of underlying rights (i.e., the author of the novel from which the play was adapted or the translator of the original novel from another language) may have claims.

For theatrical productions in much of the European Union and elsewhere, unless otherwise stipulated in the presenting contract, an automatic payment based on a percentage of gross box office revenue will be paid directly by the venue—not the presenter—to the relevant guild. The oldest, in France, is SACD.[5] Local presenters are often under legal obligation to follow local procedure unless another mutually agreeable arrangement is negotiated into the contract. But unless the artist is a member of the guild, or makes a concerted effort to secure the funds from that guild as a guest artist, the guild will not seek her out and she will never see the money. So it is incumbent on the agent and artist to educate themselves to the local practices and clearly negotiate this point in the contract or the default practice will kick in—potentially at a loss of royalty to the artist.

INCLUDE IN MAIN CONTRACT BODY VERSUS ADDENDUM

As some of the items to be provided by the presenter to the producer other than fee are production specific and will vary production to production, some agents prefer to list them in an addendum that is added to a boilerplate contract. This has the advantage of being less work for the agent issuing the contract: an addendum that is standard for a particular production is simply added to a boilerplate contract generic to all productions or presentations (depending on who is issuing the contract). It has the disadvantage that if either party wants a quick overview of everything the presenter is to provide, it is not as handy if buried in an attachment as it would be if presented up front in the contract.

There is no legal difference between the information being embodied in the contract and the information in an addendum as long as the addendum is referenced above the signatures in the contract and confirmed to be integral to the contract.

Exclusivity Required by the Presenter and Agreed to by the Producer

Often this is defined by an amount of *time* before and after the engagement and a *distance* expressed as a radius in miles or kilometers from the venue within which the producer may not allow the production to appear without prior consent of the presenter. This can be important and better to get clear now as the agent is often in midbooking process at the time the deal memo is executed and will be looking for tie-in dates around this one. The agent needs to know the presenter's geographic limitations in that regard.

Note that a precise definition of what or who is excluded from performing is also important, and in what context. If our engagement is a live concert performance, presumably the starting point on exclusion is other live concert performances by this artist. What about club dates? Private corporate appearances? Media recordings? And if a production is being booked involving a number of performers, does the exclusion cover appearances by individuals in the production appearing in other productions or solo? Can it? Often there is a limit to how far the producer is able to go when contracting artists for his production in proscribing their activities outside of his production.

Live Performance Only

It is worth reiterating here that this agreement is for live, public performance only and does not permit any recording or broadcasting of any nature. If such recording or broadcast is desired by the presenter and was not specifically included in the negotiations, this needs to be addressed separately and often involves entirely separate financial consideration. This point will be restated elsewhere in the contract, but is an important point—especially related to certain countries in which national broadcasts are often expected to be allowed and related to performer union contracts, which have a lot to say on the subject.

Many presenters seek to make "archival recordings" of performances they present for which they often assume they have permission unless told otherwise (see more on this below). Some artists and producers are fine with this, and appreciate receiving an archival viewing copy, but others are opposed.

The sight of an unexpected video camera at show time can cause tremendous unwanted agitation, so be sure to work it out in advance!

EXTRA FEES FOR EXTRA SERVICES

There is often discussion about what activities beyond actual public performances should involve additional fees to be paid to the artist and what activities are reasonable to ask artists to undertake without further fee. Two guidelines we often apply to this question are: (1) Is the purpose of the activity primarily to publicize the performance to help sell more tickets (arguing that the artist should include it within promotional activity freely offered)? And (2) is admission being charged to the event (arguing that the artist should be paid extra)?

Control of Show Identity and Content

Most producers want a statement of their artistic control over their show and its image. Presenters, having previewed the show and chosen to bring it in, should have no problem. Two concerns occasionally require specific discussion in advance so there are no surprises: (a) elements of the show that may be offensive to the audience through language, nudity, etc., and (b) elements of the show that can be damaging to the physical structure of the theater or impact neighbors, notably, high sound volume.

With shows involving nudity or obscenity, it is not uncommon for a presenter to either request that the show be modified—often resented and not always agreed to by the producer and creators—or advise his audience in advance of what they will experience so they can't complain after. Likewise many venues set a maximum permissible decibel level, usually left over from a bad experience with a heavy metal band presentation or some equivalent that cracked the plaster or caused complaints from neighbors.

Star Presence and Replacement

If there is a star involved in the show whose presence is an integral part of the package the presenter is buying and who is considered essential to the show's salability, the contract will stipulate that the producer may not replace that star unless forced to by causes beyond anyone's control (*force majeure* or an "Act of God"). It will often further stipulate that the presenter has approval over the star's replacement and, if not satisfied, may consider the nonappearance of the original star to be a valid reason for cancellation.

Branded Look

If there is a precise wording or typeface the producer always wants used when the name of the show appears, she should stipulate it early on and not wait until the presenter's materials are in print.

It is not unusual for the name of a producing company to always appear with the name of the production, or the name of the director or a star to appear above or below the title.

It is also not unusual for the producer to stipulate the relative font sizes in which this information is presented using the title of the show, normally the largest font, as 100 percent and showing other lines in proportion. An ad layout requirement might look like this:

Presenter's name [40%]

Presents [10%]

XYZ Productions, LLC [25%]

Production of [10%]

Big Star Name [80%]

In [10%]

ONE HAPPY CAMPER [100%]

Directed by [10%]

Famous Director [80%]

If the precise look and format of the show title and related key credits is of importance to the producer for branding purposes, it is not uncommon for the producer to create and distribute this copy to all tour presenters pre-formatted—formerly as a hard copy and now digitally—to avoid risk that it would appear differently in different cities.

Program Content

Presenters normally specify the amount of space they can make available in their printed program and the advance time required to receive this information from producer. The producer provides program copy related to the show and normally requires that it not be edited or changed without the producer's approval. National publications such as *Playbill* are quite systematized as to the formatting and the amount of space in which they will present the show's information. Note the special issues related to crediting sponsors addressed separately below.

Producer's Approval of Layout

It is normal for the presenter to be obligated to show the producer the ad and program layouts for approval before they go to print. This is wise on the part of the presenter since once it has been signed off on by the producer, any complaints that arise when the artists get to town and see the posters or read the program become the problem of the producer and not the presenter. The challenge here is almost inevitably one of time constraint, since the presenter's marketing department is usually preparing materials at the very last minute and requires a fast approval from the producer. So whatever has been stipulated elsewhere in the contract about what constitutes formal communication between the parties (certified mail, etc.), for this purpose, it is usually specified that e-mail and/or facsimile will be acceptable and the number of hours the producer will have to approve or automatically waive the right.

Recording and Press

There are three important issues here, often grouped into the same paragraph or section of the contract:

Recording and Documentation of the Show or Rehearsals. It is normally stipulated as a starting point that neither side can undertake such recording or documentation without the express written approval of the other side. The exception is for news-related recordings (photos for the newspapers, video for TV news, audio for radio), which is normally permitted but within strict parameters. TV, which is the most contentious, is normally allowed to shoot up to fifteen minutes of the show and to broadcast up to three minutes for news purposes only.

Photographers are usually permitted to shoot if they are on specific assignment from a newspaper, intending to run a review with a photo. Presenters usually prefer to arrange for a special photo call as part of the final show preparation—often this can be for a limited period within a final dress rehearsal of the show when the lights and other scenic elements are already being operated. The photographers often prefer this as well since it allows them to set up cameras at favorable locations in the seats and to make noise instead of being confined to corners or the back of the theater when an audience is in the house and they are only allowed to shoot in the loud sections. And if the lighting of the show is particularly atmospheric, the production is occasionally willing to "cheat the lights" for this occasion to a higher level more suited to the cameras' requirements than the standard show lighting. In the case of the television and assuming the show is amplified, this is also a good opportunity for a direct sound feed to be provided into the cameras for better quality sound transmission in broadcast.

Union Restrictions. It should be noted that certain unionized venues, such as Carnegie Hall in New York City, make a distinction between press shooting for "hard news" (as in the 6 PM news or a *New York Times* review), which are permitted in photo shoots without extra charges, and what are considered "magazine" or "documentary" format shows or articles and freelance photographers and videographers not on specific assignment, which are not directly tied to promoting the sale of tickets to the show as the media often doesn't appear until the live show has closed.

It is standard in such venues for all photographers and cameramen to be required to provide letters of assignment from their media employers, and to sign statements confirming their observance of the rules of the shoot before being allowed into the venue.

Archival Videos. As mentioned above, there is often discussion of what are termed archival videos of performances. Many performing arts center presenters seek permission to film or videotape for archival purposes as part of ongoing cultural missions in their communities, and producers or artists occasionally seek to shoot their own archival videos for training purposes. It remains a somewhat grey area usually addressed on a case-by-case basis.

The requests from arts centers often guarantee that the video will never see the light of day or be released in any way commercially. Suspicious producers and artists fear that once the video is shot, no matter the formal promises in advance, there is no real control over what may happen to the video in the future and, depending on how far afield the presenter, little opportunity for the producer or artist to effectively control what happens with the video.

That being said, as noted above, producers and artists have their own reasons for desiring "viewing copies"—that is, minimally edited and not in broadcast quality format—of their shows both for internal review of their own performance and training of cast replacements, and to help present the show to prospective future presenters.

The largest concern related to any videotaping is the potential for broadcast of such recordings without the contracting parties' (and other rights-claimers') approval and receipt of appropriate payment. In the past, that issue could be reasonably addressed by shooting in a format of low enough resolution to not be "broadcast quality" for television purposes, which created a physical limitation on how the video might be used. But the newer concern is Internet dissemination where in fact the lower resolution can be preferable to accommodate download speeds, and the issue boils afresh.

PERSPECTIVES ON FILMING AND RIGHTS

I have argued all sides of this issue over the years depending on my responsibility in a particular situation. As an artist's manager, I have fiercely defended her rights to control, approve, and, if appropriate, profit from, the recording and transmission of her image and work. As a venue manager, I have been concerned that the work of our local stagehands and the venue itself is potentially being exploited without appropriate remuneration. As a presenter, I have sought some lasting benefit to my community by having an archive and have demanded to see full-length video of productions I am being asked to consider presenting (that presumably were shot in another venue). As a booking agent, I understand full well that in most cases the absence of promotional and full-length videos of a show makes booking it near impossible, and I encourage my artists to permit it for this purpose.

The advent of the Internet, with its lower image resolution requirements and ease of distribution, does give greater credence to the worry that even video that cannot be broadcast on television can nonetheless be shared with millions without stakeholder control or recompense. This is an issue in which a clear statement of best practice is hard to produce, but the bottom line as it relates to the booking process is that without being able to present good video, the show is not likely to get booked!

Press Activities

It is in the interests of both parties to cooperate fully on advance press activity to promote the sale of tickets. Even if the producer is not receiving a percentage but only a guarantee and thereby has no financial stake in whether the show sells out or not, the ongoing demand for booking the show is enhanced considerably by a reputation of strong sales. The question of how much activity is reasonable is not always easy to define in a contract—at what point does the artist's expenditure of time and energy on promotion adversely affect her performance energy and focus?

Actors' Equity has quite specific guidelines on what is and is not permissible with respect to its members cooperating with advance press requirements, two of the most important being that any activity requests must be made at least twenty-four hours in advance of the activity and must be approved by the artist.

The realities "on the ground" vary considerably according to the nature, temperament, name recognition, and availability of the artist, the quality of the artist's marketing materials, the professionalism of the presenter's publicity person, and the background of relationships already established between the presenter and the local media. For contractual purposes, we would normally include a clause to the effect that the "artist will cooperate with reasonable requests of presenter for promotional activity within the guidelines of (applicable artist's guild)."

Related Marketing Issues

Not necessarily detailed in the contract and without promising comprehensiveness on this topic, the following are some areas to consider.

Marketing materials. The quality of the production's marketing materials can be enormously important in these early days and throughout the campaign. It is not uncommon for a magazine or newspaper to select a particular event to feature based on what its editors consider a particularly attention-getting photograph, and for a television station to choose a fill item for the 6 PM news based on a compelling video clip (b-roll).

Availability for "phoners." Of equal importance is the artist's or star's availability for *phoners*—telephone interviews in advance of the show's arrival in the community.

Advance visit. Where feasible, if an artist is passing through or near a community in advance of an engagement, the agent should advise the presenter of availability for in-person advance interviews. Sometimes offering a face-to-face, in-depth interview can make the difference for the local paper in deciding to run an advance feature article, and the opportunity to take its own photo can make the difference in a decision to feature the show on the cover—press that is easily worth the presenter covering an extra night of hotel and a day of per diem.

Internet presence. Ticket buyers increasingly expect to be able to conduct online research on an artist or production before deciding to purchase, in the same way that the presenters conduct research before selecting the artist for presentation. It is expected that producers will maintain Web sites on their shows, and will provide links to presenters' Web sites for ease of research by the public. Promotional video clips are increasingly available for viewing on the artist's sites and on free-access servers such as YouTube. Webcam interviews with artists are increasingly posted on Web sites in advance of engagements.

On-site media priorities. For artists involved in fast-moving tours, the time available in the community is often limited, and the need for rest and preparation for the performance(s) can be great. Focus should be placed on the highest visibility media first and on grouping interviewers together into one interview session where possible.

Artistic ego. Artists are often highly sensitive about their work. My experience is that these individuals' relationships to self and to their work are more complex than should be easily dismissed. It is often an essential part of what drives them to their highest levels of creativity and performance. It is often tied up in a constant need to evaluate their appeal and self-worth, which many artists measure constantly in nuanced ways. The choice of venue in a given city, for instance—is it the most important theater in town or a second- or third-string venue? How large their name appears in ads and on posters and the choice of photograph. Even whether a senior person from the presenter's organization is at the airport to greet the artist or sends a hired car can be taken by the sensitive artistic ego as an indication of how appreciated their work is.

The demand for interviews by the press is a significant factor. There is a fine line for many artists between "Why do they keep demanding my time for interviews when I need to rest and prepare for the performances?!" and "Why am I not being asked for more interviews—don't they care about me and my work?!" (or "Why is this presenter not doing his job to sell my show?!") There's no simple formula, every artist is different, and of course houses full of appreciative audiences—preferably standing and cheering at the end of the performances and throwing flowers at the stage—can wash away most concerns.

Though perhaps not a contractual matter, the handling of artists on tour is subject for an entire dissertation unto itself, with some fantastic diva stories to be told. But it is important for all to recognize that the artist's sense of self and confidence in her work is tied up in nuanced indications of how the work is anticipated. A presenter's marketing intern letting slip to the artist performing that, "we've had to give away most of the tickets and this is the only media that was willing to do an interview" can do a lot to damage the mood and confidence of the artist before a performance!

Applicable Unions

It is important for both sides to state those unions that have jurisdiction with regard to the presentation, as it may impact the presenter's obligations to call union crews on her side and for the production to plan to work within certain work rules. If the actors are in the Actors' Equity Association or dancers or musicians in the American Guild of Musical Artists, there are a host of requirements about backstage conditions and rules regarding promotional activity that the venue and presenter are expected to meet. In a venue with a strict stagehands' union contract, an expectation by a touring show's crew that they will operate the light board or start and stop the sound may have to be negotiated.

Rules Notification

Either side issuing a contract that requires the other side to abide by certain rules should be prepared to provide a set of those rules in writing before contract execution, unless they are standard rules obtainable through the Internet, as are most major performers' union regulations. This applies often to presenters' contracts, which stipulate that the production will abide by the rules of the venue, which can sometimes be quite idiosyncratic. At minimum, the agent has justification in requiring that the rules by which the production is being asked to abide be a) reasonable, b) standard in the industry, c) in writing, and d) applicable to all artists performing in the venue.

Cancellation

This is an important section that should appear in all contracts. It is an area that can cause great concern and confusion.

When cancellation must take place, there are basically three conditions under which it happens:

1. Cancellation for Reasons Within Presenter's Control. While rare in a high integrity relationship among professionals, it does happen that buyers either (a) get an opportunity to book some hot show on the same night they committed to you that they think will make them much more money than your show or (b) feel at some point before the presentation is to start that their advance ticket sales are so bad they'd rather face the consequences of canceling than pay all the stage labor, remainder of the advertising, etc., if they feel that the latter will lose them more (*cut their losses*).

Normal contracts will stipulate that in this event, since the presenter is choosing to cancel, the presenter is liable for the full fee plus other expenses that may have been incurred by the producer for which the presenter is liable for reimbursement of costs (such as airfare) that are nonrefundable. Some contracts allow a sliding scale if the cancellation is far enough in advance to allow reasonable possibility of another booking by the artist, *or* they allow for a reduction in fee payment if the producer is successful in filling the date elsewhere.

If the cancellation is due to a scheduling conflict, the presenter may offer to reschedule the engagement in lieu of full cancellation, and the contract might allow for "best efforts" to reschedule as an option. If the proposed rescheduled dates are within the producer's same fiscal year and any other cost impact to the producer to such rescheduling is covered by the presenter, there would be little reason for the producer to refuse. But if the vacated dates leave a hole in the middle of a tour, even rescheduling can create havoc on the tour as salaries, per diem, and accommodations must still be covered on the newly open dates.

2. Cancellation for Reasons Within Producer's Control. The most obvious here is that the producer gets a better offer for the same date and wants to take it (and for whatever reason cannot reschedule this date). It is not unusual in such circumstances for the presenter to insist that, if this happens, the producer will reimburse the presenter for all direct, nonreimbursable expenses related to the engagement, such as the advertising money already spent, the deposit on the theater, etc., plus the costs associated with announcing the cancellation and refunding tickets. A debate point is whether the loss of anticipated profits can be considered within what the presenter is due by the producer. The producer will argue that it should not be, though, if there was a clear possibility of a profit for the presenter, there is an argument to be made. Generally producers win on this point and profits are not included in such settlements.

Needless to say, willful cancellations by either presenter or producer are to be avoided to the degree possible; word can spread quickly of such events and reputations can be damaged. The option of rescheduling should be explored if at all feasible.

ISSUES PARTICULAR TO 1 AND 2

Announcement of cancellation. Related to both of the above instances, a clause might be included in the contract about how the cancellations are announced to the public to protect the reputations of both parties.

Breach cure. It is important to note that the first two cancellation circumstances above refer to voluntary or, what might also be called, "intentional" cancellation by one or the other party. But there might also be involuntary, unintentional, or accidental breach of contract. This might be the presenter's finance office forgetting to transfer a fee payment on a certain date, or the technical director forgetting to arrange the backstage refreshments. On the assumption that the parties "of character" wish the engagement to proceed and that the breach was indeed unintentional, it is reasonable to allow a specific amount of time—usually twenty-four or forty-eight hours—from the time the offending party has been notified of the breach for the breach to be corrected or "cured."

Two exceptions to this may be:

a. The final payment of fee or any other element specifically needed to proceed with the performances where twenty-four or forty-eight hours may not be available. If under the terms of the contract the final fee payment is to be handed to the producer's on-site representative prior to the final performance and the presenter fails to do so, the producer may reasonably hold the final curtain until the presenter comes up with the funds owed.

b. The presenter fails to provide the technical resources required for the show. If the artist arrives a few hours before show time and discovers that the presenter did not prehang the stage lights or does not have stage crew available, a twenty-four-hour window to cure breach won't make the performance possible at the scheduled time.

3. Cancellation for Reasons Outside the Control of Either Party. This is commonly referred to as an "Act of God" or *force majeure* clause. It is normal to list in this clause some of the atrocities that might occur, such as fire, flood, labor strikes, and disruption to modes of transportation, etc., that would force cancellation for reasons outside of the control of either party. In this instance, it is normal that the parties are not obligated to fulfill the terms of the contract, though the presenter may still be responsible to reimburse the producer for those expenses already incurred by the producer to be reimbursed by the presenter (such as airfare) that cannot be refunded. Some producers will insist that presenters must still pay the producer's direct, nonrefundable expenses related to the cancelled engagement, including such things as salaries to performers contracted for the engagement, on the grounds that institutional presenters are in a better position to carry cancellation insurance than poor starving artists. Often fee advances to the producer must be returned in this circumstance, but occasionally presenters will agree that the producer may retain a sufficient portion of the fee to cover nonreimbursable, direct expenses incurred by producer prior to the date of cancellation.[6]

IS WEATHER A FORCE MAJEURE?

Without opening a debate about the influence of a divine being on the forces of nature, for our purposes, the question is whether or not inclement weather can be included as justification for canceling under *force majeure*. In general, it should not be included as it gives the presenter too much latitude, if she is not selling well, to say, "It's raining, so I'm canceling."

Having said that, locations and times of year in which truly severe weather can occur must be allowed for. Examples are Hong Kong when the threat of typhoons is high and where the raising of a certain color flag on the pole at the top of the mountain, signaling that a strong typhoon is likely to hit, provides a definable trigger for a *force majeure* cancellation; Alaska and Siberia where severe winter storms would make it impossible for audiences to get to the theater; and Florida and the Caribbean during hurricane season where the same is true. If a presenter insists on weather being a more generalized *force majeure* on the grounds that people cannot get to the theater, producers often counter by agreeing to this except if the artist is "ready, willing, and able to perform" on the theory that if the artist could get to the theater, the audience could too!

Special Cancellation Clauses

There are two special circumstances in which producers may reserve the right to cancel and expect no penalty.

1. Out Clause for TV, Film, or Legitimate Run. An artist anticipating the possibility of being called for a TV show, a film, or a legitimate theater run such as Broadway, is likely to insist on a clause that gives him a thirty- or sixty-day out without penalty if such comes through. Presenters, of course, hate this as such action would leave them with sold seats to a cancelled show or nonappearance of a star on which basis tickets were sold, but if the artist is strong enough in reputation, there is an accepted practice that live-performance touring engagements lose out to calls from Broadway, film, television, and other lucrative commercial opportunities for the artist.

2. "Contract Conditional" Clause. An occasional situation related to cancellation is one in which an engagement is an integral and necessary part of a regional tour, with a date and fee made possible only as part of a surrounding tour. Since in this case, cancellation and nonpayment by any one tour participant may cause the producer to face a financial loss if she delivers the rest of the tour on the contracted terms, the contract may stipulate that in the event that any other member of the tour cancels for any reason and does not pay the full fee due, the producer may cancel the entire tour or renegotiate the terms of this engagement.

Needless to say, it is often anathema to presenters to be dependent on the actions of their presenting colleagues, and can only reasonably be applied in circumstances in which the presenter has understood from the beginning that the availability of the show for his venue at the agreed upon fee is conditional on the other engagements in the tour taking place.

It can be pointed out, however, that two conditions need to apply in order for this to kick in: that another presenter cancels *and* does not pay the fee, noting that cancellation by a presenter normally does not relieve him of paying the full fee. So assuming this circumstance exists, it should only apply in the event of a *force majeure* cancellation by one of the participating presenters.

Insurance

Disclaimer: I am not an insurance expert. As with legal and accounting advice in this book, while I hope sharing of my experience and observations over the years helps the reader in thinking about the issues, a professional insurance agent should most definitely be consulted on clauses to be included or omitted, and on the types and amounts of coverage needed.

That being said, following are various insurance issues related to live-performance touring.

Minimum Coverage

Each party wants to know that the other party is reasonably insured so that the first party is not left holding the bag in the event of a suit. The primary concerns are *third party general liability*—insurance against being sued by a third party for whatever reason (the audience member who trips on the stairs of the theater and breaks a leg), *loss or damage to production's or artists' property*, and, in the case of the artist, *medical insurance including emergency care*.

In the US, the current standard minimums of general liability expected from both parties are *$1 million per occurrence* and *$2 million aggregate*, the latter meaning a total of $2 million for all claims during the policy period.

Artists' and productions' goods are generally insured for up to their full replacement value and only when in presenter's custody. Since most freight carriers independently insure goods in their custody up to the point of delivery to the stage door (going in) and storage warehouse (coming out), in practical terms this normally means while the goods are in the theater. Some presenters will request a listing of the goods and replacement values in advance, which is not an unreasonable request.

Workers' compensation[7] is generally acceptable as a minimum for US artists on tour, though specific additional travel insurance is wise.

International Insurance Issues

International touring raises complexities related to medical treatment and insurance, since it is important to know that the insurance is applicable in the country(ies) being toured. There is also often the issue of *repatriation insurance*, which is the added cost to fly the artist back to his/her home for medical care beyond what can reasonably and effectively be provided on site. For US artists touring abroad, worker's compensation is generally available with the payment of an *international premium.*

In some instances, for an artist to be covered in a country other than his own, a special medical inspection may be required and should not be taken as an offense. For artists touring from countries with lower-quality medical facilities to countries with more advanced facilities, there have been incidents of efforts to catch up on the cure of long-held medical problems at the expense of the tour insurance!

Additional Smaller but Significant Insurance Issues

Chain of Claim. Remember that the presenter and the venue may not be the same entity, but the producer's primary claim is through its contract with the presenter. The producer should reasonably insist not only that the presenter be insured but that the venue is covered as well. Proof of insurance should also apply to any subcontractors the presenter may bring in to prepare and run the artist's show, especially if they are working in comparatively dangerous areas such as electrical or rigging.

Cancellation Insurance. In the event that the artist is a single, famous, and irreplaceable name, the presenter may either carry or require the producer to carry cancellation insurance covering the eventuality of that artist not being able to appear. If it is an ensemble production, the producer is normally obligated to be ready to provide understudies.

Self-Drive Auto Insurance. If the tour will involve members of the production team driving vehicles, it is important that they be covered either by the producer's policy, extended to cover vehicle rental, or by full coverage for all drivers purchased from the rental company.

Written Proof of Insurance. Both parties will reasonably require written proof of such insurances to be provided by the other party "on demand," though, in practice, such written proof is rarely requested among professionals.

Self-Insurance. This usually applies to presenters that are large universities or municipalities in the US or those companies eligible to be self-insured through state and federal laws. This is okay for the producer and does not present a problem as long as other related issues (such as mutual indemnity—see below) are agreed to. Generally with the big universities, even the presentation of a big Broadway show is small potatoes compared to the insurance they have to carry for areas like their athletic departments.

Additional Insureds. It used to be standard practice for the producer to insist, in addition to the presenter providing proof that he is carrying X amount of insurance, that the presenter's insurance would also name the producer as an additional insured and vice versa from presenters. This can sometimes be a contentious issue in negotiations if one side insists on being covered as additional insured by the other but refuses to extend the same courtesy to the other party, quite often with excuses like "our municipal charter won't allow it." The reason given by insurance agents for "additional insured" clauses is that the insurance company assumes the defense costs of the additional insured party should a lawsuit be presented, until the negligent party is ascertained.

General advice: either both sides should name the other as an additional insured or, if objectionable to one or the other party, don't fight about it and leave out the additional insured part altogether.

Indemnity Clauses

Indemnity, or the act of indemnifying a person or organization, is to hold an entity harmless or not responsible for certain acts, or more specifically for claims resulting from certain acts. In most touring contracts, this clause can address two different circumstances, one more broad and the other narrower.

1. The *broad coverage* involves Party A promising to hold harmless, and in some cases protect (sometimes including paying reasonable legal bills), Party B against claims resulting from acts of anyone including Party B. This ends up being quite broad, since the acts could have been by any of many

other parties or anywhere in or around the facility. If this is a presentation contract between presenter and producer, the other parties may be audience members, stagehands, actors, etc., typically referred to as *third parties*. If there is no promise to actively defend (and pay legal bills for) Party B, this structure really means that if Party A is sued for something, he will not attempt to pass the suit or responsibility on to Party B even if Party B didn't do it.

2. The *narrower coverage* involves Party A promising to hold harmless, and in some cases protect, Party B only against claims resulting from negligent acts of Party A. Basically, "If I did it, I won't try to hold you responsible." The result appears the same, but if inclusion of protection and legal fees is involved, the narrower coverage opens Party A up to far less potential cost.

Additional Notes on Indemnity

While the basics of indemnity are straightforward and standard boilerplate on this topic appears in almost all contracts, there are several points within this to be noted.

Mutuality. A fair contract duplicates these clauses with the parties reversed, for what is called "mutual indemnity." Sadly, there is a trend in the US among some university and municipally controlled presenters to insist that the producers "indemnify and hold harmless" the presenters, but do not agree to the reverse. This is troubling, not only in the overall spirit of fairness in a contract, but when one considers the potential discrepancy in size and financial ability to engage lawyers and battle out issues. Imagine a string quartet of modest means battling this issue with a major municipality or university without the protection of mutual indemnity in the contract!

Subcontractors, employees, and agents. As noted above, proper wording in all clauses related to responsibility and indemnity will also encompass service providers and employees to either party. Remember that often the presenter does not own and operate the venue in which the performance is taking place and often independently contracts production services, yet the producer's only contractual access is through the presenter. Producers likewise often contract out certain aspects of the show being brought to the presenter. So, in all such areas of the contract, it is important to specify that all agents, and contractees, as well as employees, are to be held responsible.

Complexity of language. Of all clauses in standard contracts, those related to indemnity can often be the most confusing to the lay reader. It is important to wade through them, mapping out who is indemnifying who under what circumstances and whether and when you may be incurring legal expenses on behalf of another party. If you are not sure, call your attorney or insurance agent for advice!

Warranties

In this clause each side "warrants and attests" (claims and swears) that it has the legal authority to enter into this agreement, to bind its organization to the agreement, to commit what is being committed (the show, the use of the theater, etc.), and that, in signing this contract, it is not violating any other agreement it has made with anyone else.

There is often an added clause specifically stating responsibility—including in some cases paying attorney fees for the other side—for any suits or claims that are proven to have merit based on a false claim of warranty. This places the burden of responsibility on each side to be sure that it has the free and clear right to offer everything it is offering in the contract. For instance, in the case of a producer claiming to have the rights to offer the show to a presenter, if she claimed to have the performance rights to a play and really didn't and the playwright sues and wins against the presenter for presenting his play without approval, the producer will take responsibility on behalf of the presenter and pay the presenter's attorney fees plus whatever settlement is required with the playwright.

Given the potential seriousness of implications in warranties, if there are any reasons for doubt, it is not uncommon for the parties to require that written proof of the rights they claim to hold be shown—proof that the presenter really does have the theater rented for that day or that the producer really has a certain star signed up to perform or the rights from the playwright to produce the play.

Implications of Deals through Middlepersons or Brokers

The warranty issues (as well as those related to insurance) may also apply if one is working through middlemen or brokers who are not themselves either the producers, primary agents, or presenters of the artist or show. One can imagine a situation, which we have experienced in Greece, for instance, in which a local Greek agent (what we have defined as a *tour producer* in this instance) is buying an engagement of a show and reselling to a festival. And for added measure, the festival may be renting the theater for the presentation. The producer of the show is now *three* steps removed from the venue (through the tour producer and the festival), and two steps removed from the organization that is really doing the presenting. So the extension of control and compliance in the primary contract needs to be that much more thorough and the question of who is actually signing the contract becomes important.

In this example, if the Greek tour producer is "buying" the show and "reselling" it to the festival, it is important for the show's producer to remember that since the Greek tour producer is the only one signing the contract on the buying side, that organization must hold complete contractual responsibility to the producer for the acts and omissions of the festival *and* of the venue the festival will rent for the presentation. This becomes more complicated because typically, at least until the contract is fully executed, the agent will not want the producer in direct contact with the festival out of fear of being cut out of the deal, so the producer is limited in his ability to independently verify that what the agent claims on behalf of the festival is in fact the truth. *In this example, the warranty by the agent that he has the authority to enter into the agreement on behalf of the festival carries huge significance.*

Sponsorship

As financial support for at least some sectors of the performing arts shifts increasingly to corporations and market-oriented sponsors, often with a strong promotional incentive for the sponsors' products or services, the issues surrounding sponsorship and related public crediting can be quite contentious if not mapped out in the contract.

For our purposes, there are two basic types of sponsorship that vary according to which party brought in the sponsor: 1) presenting or season sponsorship brought in by the presenter and 2) tour sponsorship brought in by the producer. While few will argue the value of more money supporting the touring of artists, several issues arise with respect to control, sponsor visibility conflict, and promotional rights.

Approval of Sponsor; Limits on Implied Affiliation

Each side will want to know and approve the corporate name(s), or at least the nature of products and services, with which they are to be affiliated in relation to the engagement. Particularly sensitive are companies involved in the manufacture or distribution of alcoholic beverages and tobacco products, with which many artists and arts centers refuse to affiliate. It may not send the right message to have a family program, presumably with many child audience members, sponsored by a cigarette company or liquor distributor.

Related to this are two associated rights issues: 1) the rights of the sponsor to print ads or make announcements that imply that the artist or the arts center actively supports and encourages consumption of its product or service and 2) the rights of either the presenter or producer to presume that the other will endorse or even be willing to help promote a sponsor it secures.

Related to the first issue, it is one thing for the XYZ Bank to "proudly sponsor the ABC Ballet Company" and quite another for dancers in the Company to appear in ads in a manner that suggests that they use and personally endorse this bank. Most artists take the position that if they agree to appear actively supportive of the product or service, it must be by their own separate agreements with the sponsor and they should be independently paid for such affiliation. Likewise with ads, the bank might wish to run implying that the ballet company uses its business services.

Related to the second issue, it is wrong for the ABC Ballet Company, being presented by the DEF Arts Center to presume that it may promise to the XYZ Bank an association with the arts center without the arts center's permission to do so and vice versa. This is significant since presumably part of the bank's interest in sponsoring the tour was motivated by obtaining visible presence with the arts center's audiences; the ballet company must be careful not to promise what it can't deliver if the arts center does not agree.

The key to happiness here, as is so often true, is for the presenter and producer—in this case, the arts center and the ballet company—to discuss this issue early on, even before the bank has been identified as a potential tour sponsor. If the arts center already has a strong banking sponsor, for which a bank tour sponsor of a visiting artist would be competition, but no automobile sponsor, it would make more sense for the ballet company to go for tour sponsorship from the Ford Motor Company than from Citibank.

Category Exclusives

The bank conflict cited above arises if the producer has a national tour sponsor in the same line of product or service as, but competitive with, the presenter's season sponsor. A classic example of such a battle is the ongoing rivalry between Coca-Cola and Pepsi. If on the one hand the presenter has promised Cola-Cola visible season sponsor recognition on all events in the year, but the producer has made the same promise to Pepsi as this production's national tour sponsor, there could be a problem!

Financial Sharing—Who Benefits from Sponsorship?

Each party to a contract can lay some legitimate claim to making possible the sponsor promotion opportunity offered by the engagement covered in the contract: the presenter will claim that without her presentation of the production, the engagement would not take place, and the producer will claim that the public comes to see his show, not the curtains in the theater.

Both are correct to a degree, of course, with the balance adjustable related to the fame of the artist and the marketing strength and general appeal of the presenter or venue. It is not unreasonable that one party will lay claim to some financial benefit from the sponsorship brought in by the other.

For the producer considering sponsorship funds the presenter is receiving tied to the show, this might appear as a claim to a more aggressive percentage of back-end profits, which, presumably, are being made more likely by the presence of the sponsor's underwriting of expenses at the front end. For the presenter considering the producer's national tour sponsorship funds, this might appear as more marketing support from the presentation, which presumably aligns with the sponsor's desire for greater public visibility.

Promotional Presence

A related issue will be the presence of corporate logos and slogans in the theater, the promotion, the printed program, and even on the stage itself, the latter of which will be of special concern to the presenter, producer, *and* venue.

Additionally, certain venue contracts with printed program producers, such as *Playbill* and *Stagebill*, reserve *all* corporate visibility rights to the program publisher as one of the benefits the publisher receives in exchange for providing programs free of charge to audiences. This often includes exclusive control of corporate logos or advertising in any form within the four walls of the theater, and will affect what either the presenter or producer may deliver to a season or touring sponsor. This is sometimes negotiable if it is arranged that the sponsor buys a page of advertising in the program, which sponsors are often willing to do to extend their reach to the audience.

Resolution of Sponsorship Issues

There is no simple pattern to resolve these issues and the availability and identity of sponsors are often not known at the time the contract is executed. At best, the framework for resolution of such issues, should they arise, can be included in the contract.

The important points are for the presenter and producer to be aware of the issues early on and to establish the rights of both sides appropriately in the contract. If either party has in hand or is intending to pursue presentation, season, or touring sponsorship, he should advise the other early on so as to avoid a collision. Note again that as sponsorship agreements involve secondary contracts between one of the primary parties and his respective sponsors, each party is responsible to the other for the actions of his sponsor.

In one instance, the corporate sponsor of an American dance company's Japanese tour I had arranged took it upon itself to download a photo of one of the dancers and, without the knowledge or approval of the artist, run separate ads, using the photo in such a way as to imply that that dancer loved this product. On arriving in Japan and seeing the ads, the dancer was justifiably outraged both at the liberties taken without his approval and in not receiving due payment for use of his image. On-the-spot negotiations took place to avert cancellation and court action.

The lesson: Be up front about sponsorship between the presenter and producer, and establish mutually agreeable limits. The party negotiating for the sponsorship should insist on a solid contract with the sponsor that describes precisely what the sponsor is getting and is allowed to do in exchange for the funds being provided.

No Transfer

This clause forbids either party from transferring its rights and obligations to a third party without prior written approval from the other contracted party. This may seem obvious, but it is important to include in the contract nonetheless.

Ticketing

It is normal that the producer receive some number of *complimentary* tickets (free seats) and access to purchase additional *house* tickets (to be paid for but guaranteed to be available and usually in good locations). Additionally, if the theater is not full, the producer may have access to additional comps at the last minute on an as-available basis. The variables around this are:

- *Release Time.* By when does the artist have to notify the box office of his intention to use the tickets before unused seats are returned for public sale? The presenter will want two days' notice; the artist will want two hours. Sometimes an early, partial release offers a compromise: for instance if ten tickets are being held overall, an initial six can be released forty-eight hours before curtain time if unused, with the remaining four held until two hours before the show.

- *Transferability between Performances.* If the producer does not need all of his allocated seats for one performance but would like some extra for another, can he transfer unused tickets from one performance to another? We recommend yes, unless the desired performance is sold out at the time of the request. For a run of performances, presenters tend to be more generous with comps early in the run before word-of-mouth has spread, in the hope that there will be high purchase demand for tickets later in the run and on the weekends.

- *Director Walk-ins.* If the director of the play wants to slip in the back to see the show but does not insist on sitting down—and, in fact, he often prefers not to or, if so, in the last row by the door is fine—can he be accommodated without dipping into the comps? We recommend some flexibility in this area.

- *Discount on the House Seats.* It is not uncommon for the producer to receive the group discount price for any house seats purchased.

- *Additional Seats if Available.* If the show is not selling out, especially at the beginning of a run while waiting for the press and word-of-mouth to kick in, presenters often grant producers/artists latitude to invite more audience for free, presumably acquaintances who will be favorably disposed to the show, create an enthusiastic environment for the critics, and talk it up to their friends.

- *Shared Control if there is a Back-End Split.* If the producer is receiving a split of the box office, then the constraint on free and discounted tickets will apply not only to the producer but to the presenter as well, since they have a shared financial interest in the outcome of the engagement and a shared financial disincentive to give away more tickets than they feel absolutely compelled to.

Merchandise

Many productions carry merchandise to sell in the lobbies at their performances, often referred to colloquially as *merch*. Some larger, more commercial touring productions contract this to outside merchandisers who travel along with the show but operate independently.

Presenter's often share this issue with the venue, since quite often venues will have their own in- or out-of-house exclusive concession sales contracts. These often do not fall within the control of the presenters renting the venues and incoming shows wanting to sell merch must follow the venue's rules. It is important that if the producer or artist is considering selling caps, T-shirts, posters, and the like, that he sort this issue out early in negotiations and reflect the agreement in the contract, making sure that the presenter's side of the agreement is reflective of the presenter *and* the venue.

Who sells? A related issue is who will actually do the selling of the touring merchandise. Some venues and presenters will allow the productions to have representatives do their own selling in the lobby as an alternative to the venue selling. This normally saves the production money if someone who is already on the payroll is available. This also allows for greater profit from the merch.

Percentage to presenter and venue. It is normal in a contract that the venue and presenter combined receive a percentage of the gross sales of a production's merchandise with an added amount if the venue or presenter is providing the salesperson. An aggregate percentage to be received by the venue *and* presenter *including* sales staff rarely exceeds 35 percent, and a range of 15 to 25 percent is more normal. Note that the percentage is normally calculated net of applicable local tax. Venues/presenters often start off with a standard formula for what they expect, and producers/ artists do likewise. Experience shows that, like anything else, this is often a negotiable issue.

Count-in and -out process. Especially if the venue or presenter is doing the selling, but potentially regardless of seller, so as to verify a count of sales and confirm accuracy and no theft, it is normal procedure for a representative of the presenter to view and count the artist's items for sale both before and after sales for each performance, and to review a written documentation of sales and funds received. Once the presenter and artist's representatives have agreed on these figures for each performance, then these figures provide the basis for calculation of the presenter/venue share.

Artist/producer control of show-related merchandise. It is important for this section of the contract to stipulate that the sale of any show-related merchandise is within the ultimate control of the producer and that the presenter may not, on his own initiative, imprint products with the likeness or logo of the show or artist without negotiation and approval of the producer. So even though the act of selling merchandise within the venue cannot be done without the approval of the venue and/or presenter, the images related to the artist and show remain under the control of the producer.

Special event–related merch. For a run of a show expected to have strong attendance, it is not uncommon for the producer and presenter to agree to produce a special printing of a T-shirt, for example, that includes the dates and venue name in addition to the likeness of the artist to be specially produced for sale. Obviously this will require special negotiation between the producer and the presenter, wherein the initial costs of production will normally get paid back first before any splitting of profits.

Tax exemption does not apply. Note that as the sale of products is generally considered "unrelated business" income from the perspective of charitable status, it is often taxable even though sold by nonprofit performing companies and/or performing arts centers that otherwise would not pay tax on income.

Cross border issues. In international engagements, where carrying the goods across borders can raise issues with Customs and of importation tax, for an extended tour with revenue potential to justify the investment, it is common for the artist to license his name and image to the in-country presenter or tour producer and have the merchandise manufactured locally in the country of the tour. This may raise tax questions for the artist coming home with income that may be considered "unrelated" and therefore taxable (if the artist is a nonprofit), but that is generally easier to account for, with easier paperwork, than dealing with import taxes the other way, and in this case the tax is only calculated on the net income the artist brings home and not the gross revenue from merchandise sales.

When to decide if merch will be offered. The final decision as to whether or not the producer will offer merch, and precisely what items he will make available, does not need to have been made at the time the contract is executed. What is important is that percentages to the various parties are outlined and that the ownership and control of images by the producer of show-related merch be clearly established.

Dispute Resolution and Jurisdiction

Two issues that tend to go hand in hand in contracts are (1) what will happen in the event of a dispute and (2) where will the dispute be resolved, including both the location where arbitration would take place and the legal jurisdiction in which the sides agree the case will be tried if it ever goes to court.

Dispute Resolution

Assuming that there is a measure of good will and intention on both sides and that both sides would prefer to avoid the costs of a full-fledged trial, contracts typically include:

a) A statement to the effect that in the event of a dispute, the parties will make their best efforts to resolve it through amicable discussion.

b) If such discussion does not resolve the matter, they will take the matter to arbitration (which is not the same as taking it to a full court trial). If both parties are US entities, it is sufficient to say that the parties will agree to follow the rules and procedural guidelines of the American Arbitration Association, a nonprofit organization established for the purpose of guiding dispute resolution.[8] If the parties are not both US entities, reference may be made to UNCITRAL Arbitration Rules,[9] established by a United Nations commission in an effort to standardize international dispute resolution. In general, a standard procedure quite universally accepted is that each side will appoint one arbitrator, the two arbitrators will appoint a third, and the third will lead the procedure.

Jurisdiction

Recognizing that no amount of amicable talking or arbitrating may do the trick, contracts specify which court system the parties agree to use in filing suit or other legal action against one another. This can be a more contentious issue if the parties are from countries with substantially different underlying rules of law. It is normal that the jurisdiction will be that of the presenter.

Additional Observations on Dispute Resolution

- *Binding arbitration.* Wording will typically state that the parties will submit to binding arbitration and go further to say that they will not challenge the findings of the arbitration panel. I have seen occasions where, if one party is not 100 percent confident of a fair hearing under arbitration in the other side's territory, but the other side insists that arbitration take place there, the binding aspect is removed from the language, leaving open the theoretical possibility that the side having concerns could challenge the findings in another territory if the results do not seem fair. It does not remove the concern about unfair treatment in the other territory but at least leaves a door ajar to go elsewhere if needed.

- *Two arbitration locations.* A novel approach to location of arbitration, which would probably not be acceptable for legal jurisdiction, is to have the arbitration take place in the territory of the other party: the artist/producer claims in the presenter's territory and vice versa.

- *Who pays the legal bills?* It is not unusual to state that the side that loses pays.

Addenda or Riders Integral to the Contract

Addenda and riders, also commonly referred to outside of the US as annexes, are effectively the same thing. They are special sections added to the contract that are to be considered integral to the agreement. Depending on the form, some presenters and agents prefer contracts in which, with the exception of some basic boilerplate, most of the *meat* of the contract is in the form of riders.

One of the most important of these riders is what is called the technical rider (or technical addendum), which outlines in detail, and often in quite technical language, the precise staging requirements of manpower, lighting, and other equipment and resources needed to mount the show on tour.

If a presentation budget has been discussed and accepted by the parties as underpinning for a box office split, this can be attached as an addendum with the specific notation that "the budget appended hereto is considered an integral part of this agreement" and with space for initials of both parties on the appended budget.

We will address content details of the tech rider in a separate checklist (see appendix II), but what is important to note here is the need to specify in the main body of the contract and *above the signatures* those addenda or riders that are, by mutual agreement of the parties, integral to the contract.

Initials

Any changes made in a contract from the original printed document must have the initials of both or all signatories next to each change in order for the change to be binding.

It is also not unusual to see initials at the corners of every page of the contract confirming that that page is part of the contract and to avoid the possibility of substitution of pages. The one real effect of this is to make it impossible for anyone to fraudulently substitute a changed page prior to the final signature page after the contract has been executed (signed).

It is not uncommon for a producer to ask that the presenter's technical director initial the technical rider, not because this person has legal authority on the contract, but as a confirmation that he or she has read the rider and understands the requirements.

Signatures: The Last Item

Signatures, along with a printed version of the persons' names and titles and the signing dates are expected to be the last item in the main body of the contract. The location is critical since, by convention, the signatures apply to all that precedes. In theory at least, any item below the signatures that has not been referenced above as being incorporated is not a formal part of the contract.

Sign-by or Expiry Date. If there is any concern on either side that the other party is not entirely committed to signing, it is a good idea to include an expiry date by which the first signing party's commitment expires if the contract is not signed by the other party. This is more often an issue with deal memos that may precede contracts than with contracts since once a party *calls for a contract* and one is issued, it signals a serious intent to complete the agreement.

Not Binding Until Both Sign. An alternate method for achieving the same effect as the expiry date is to include the caveat that the contract is not binding until fully executed by both sides. Remember that in the signing process there is that fragile period following signing of the contract by the first party before the second party has signed, where the first party is potentially exposed and committed without reciprocation. This statement protects the first party if the second, for any reason, refuses or is unable at the last minute to sign.

Endnotes

1   As an agency, our general liability insurance rate each year is determined by the number of performances with which our corporate name is formally attached, and our premium is less if our name appears in fewer contracts. For this reason, unless there is a compelling reason to be mentioned, I often discourage it.

2   In a situation where you both know that a tax withhold is mandatory, such as in certain states in the US, it is better to acknowledge that specific exception here so there is no debate later.

3   A freight *forwarder* is the correct term for the company a producer is likely to engage to arrange the movement of the theatrical goods, especially if the moves are complex or international. At the US government's Web site regarding the exportation of goods (*www.export .gov/logistics/exp_whatis_freight_forwarder.asp*), a freight forwarder is defined as "an agent for the exporter in moving cargo to an overseas destination. These agents are familiar with the import rules and regulations of foreign countries, the export regulations of the US government, the methods of shipping, and the documents related to foreign trade. Export freight forwarders are licensed by the International Air Transport Association (IATA) to handle air freight and the Federal Maritime Commission to handle ocean freight. Freight forwarders assist exporters in preparing price quotations by advising on freight costs, port charges, consular fees, costs of special documentation, insurance costs, and their handling fees. They recommend the packing methods that will protect the merchandise during transit or can arrange to have the merchandise packed at the port or containerized. If the exporter prefers, freight forwarders can reserve the necessary space on a vessel, aircraft, train, or truck."

4   See *www.state.gov/m/a/als/prdm*.

5   SACD is defined in Wikipedia as "An authors' rights collective management society. Created in 1777 on an initiative taken by Beaumarchais, the SACD (Société des Auteurs et Compositeurs Dramatiques – Society of Dramatic Authors and Composers) was the very first authors' rights collective management society."

6   This comes down to which side can afford to and routinely carries *business interruption insurance*. It is not unusual for performing arts centers and presenting institutions to do so, whereas it is far rarer that artists and productions can afford it.

7   State workers' compensation statutes in the US establish a framework for employment that ensures that employees who are injured or disabled on the job are provided with fixed monetary awards, eliminating the need for litigation. US employers are required to pay for workers' compensation coverage for all employees, whether engaged on salary or contract basis, according to the laws of the state in which the employer operates. These laws also provide benefits for dependents of those workers who are killed because of work-related accidents or illnesses. Each state administers its own programs. In New York State, for instance, workers' compensation is supervised by the Workers' Compensation Board (*www.wcb.state.ny.us/index.htm*). There are also federal workers' compensation laws that primarily apply to federal employees.

8   See *www.adr.org/home*.

9   United Nations Commission on International Trade Law (see *www.uncitral.org/pdf/ english/texts/arbitration/arb-rules/arb-rules.pdf*).

Technical Rider Checklist

As with the previous Contract Checklist, provided here is a detailed listing of various elements to be considered for inclusion in a show's technical rider. Every tech rider is different and particular to an individual production, though certain core elements are common. Obviously, productions range considerably in scale, so tech riders can go from a simple paragraph or two up to a document of many pages.

Tech Rider Starting Assumptions

- *The tech rider should be prepared as a stand-alone document* that may well be read outside of the context of the contract. The rider is often sent in advance of any contract to the presenter who will pass it directly to her technical director (TD) for review and budgeting.

- *Assume that the reader of the tech rider has not seen the show,* has not been party to the agent and presenter's discussions, and may not have even seen a full-length video of the production, so it is important to open with some general description of the show, such as how many people are in the show, the length of the show and the number of intermissions, how many trucks are necessary, what technical supervisory personnel are traveling with the show, etc.

- *Describe the ideal technical conditions in the ideal venue—both size and configuration.* Not all theaters are the same and one rider may not address all particularities of each presenter's theater. But as a starting point for discussion, and assuming the initial rider is generic, this is the best place to start.

- *Clearly state those items that are absolute requirements in order for the show to go in* (minimum stage width, for instance, less than which the set will not fit), so the reader can quickly raise the alarm if the presenter is going to be physically unable to meet the minimums in that venue.

- *Separate the rider by departments.* Depending on the size and configuration of technical staff on the presenter's side, the TD will often hand off appropriate sections of the rider to the head carpenter, head electrician, sound engineer, costume department, etc., and it helps if the rider is organized to allow that to happen efficiently.

- *Write simply and clearly, and do not assume that the presenter's TD is an expert on the latest technology.* The goal of the tech rider is not to show off the issuer's expertise but to communicate clearly what the show needs! Remember that as a rule, presenters' TDs are overworked and are asked to read through and budget a large number of tech riders. A clear, well-formatted presentation helps.

- *Think ahead.* Due to the length of the booking process, tech riders issued today may govern performances that will take place over a year into the future. So the production's technical representative writing the rider must be as visionary as possible in anticipating what may be needed as the show evolves. If the show is new and still evolving at the time the rider is being issued, with a high probability of change before it gets to this venue, say so, and reserve the option for such change. The presenter may not welcome the uncertainty, but it is still better to know now and allow for contingency.

- *Identify each version of the rider.* Anticipating that revised versions of the tech rider will be issued during the lifetime of a show, each version must be clearly labeled with a version number and a date of issuance shown (many TD's use the pattern of denoting generations of computer software—i.e., Version 2.1).

- *Plan a domestic and an international version,* if the show is to tour abroad. If it will be touring a lot in one language region, arrange for a translation of the rider. Clearly identify the domestic and international versions in the titles.

Greeting and Show Outline

This opening section should describe the basics of the show on the assumption that the TD in the theater has no real idea what it is. For example:

> *The show (name) is a dramatic play running two hours and ten minutes including one twenty minute intermission. There are ten actors on stage, and a total of sixteen people traveling with the show. The additional six include the director, stage*

manager, technical director, lighting supervisor, wardrobe supervisor, and company manager. The set moves in one forty-five-foot semitruck and normally can load into a theater on the day of the first show, with presenter-provided lights and stage dressings hung in advance of setup start, and assuming an 8 AM setup start and an 8 PM show start. There are prerecorded sound effects, generated from an MP3 player provided by the show, and there is one live violin played by one of the actors on stage. The show has a unit standing set, requiring tie off above but not a full fly system. The show is nonunion. Optimal venues are proscenium theaters with seating capacities in the range of 700 to 1000. An orchestra pit is not required.

Request for Venue Information

This section should request that full venue information—both schematics or plans, and equipment inventories—be sent to the show's production manager as early as possible, and specify the preferred digital formats (e.g., MCD Vectorworks, DXF AutoCAD).

This would be a place for the show's production manager to show sensitivity by saying that best efforts will be made to work within the venue's available equipment inventory balanced by firmness in saying that any deviancy from the rider requirements not agreed to in advance by the show's production manager may be considered breach of contract.

Note that many theaters now place their technical specifications on their Web sites and it would behoove the show's production manager to take a look at the site to determine if sufficient information is available before asking for more.

Venue, Stage, and Rigging Requirements

Stage configuration and size. State clearly what stage configurations are workable for this show. Is it vital that the audience be in front of the action as in a traditional proscenium theater, or can the audience be around to the sides (thrust) or all the way around (arena)? If in front, does it require a formal proscenium, or can it be set up in a black box? Can the show work on a stage that is raked or angled? If not, say so (this is generally more of an issue outside of the US since in the US most stages are not raked). And be clear as to the minimum width, depth, and height requirements for the show to fit on the stage.

Audience size and configuration. Is there an optimal seating capacity or range, or maximum depth from the stage front to back wall that should be mentioned? State special seating issues or preferences, such as a steep audience rake to optimize sightlines to the stage floor.

Fly system, orchestra pit, and traps. State clearly what of these are required, if any. If the show does not require an orchestra pit but there is a preference as to how the pit space will be used in theaters which have elevator pits (generally either at auditorium floor level for additional seating or at stage level for more stage depth), specify. If the show does not require full fly but at minimum a grid system for tying off or rigging dead hung scenery, say so.

Floor Structure and Surface

Specify if a *sprung* floor is important, especially for dancers who can be at risk of physical harm if asked to dance on floors installed directly onto cement. Regarding color, most shows prefer matte black floors to soak up and not reflect light. Is a *Marley* or similar floor covering required to be provided, keeping in mind, for instance, that the sliding characteristics of a floor for modern dance are often opposite those required by classical ballet (which is why many dance companies prefer to carry their own floor surfaces with them)? If a show will require *lagging* or screwing into the stage floor to secure a set piece, say so here as this is often a point of discussion with theaters that do not want holes drilled into their stage floors.

Location of Soundboard

Productions often require that the soundboards be amid the audience in order for the sound operator to be able to hear what the audience is hearing and adjust volumes as needed during the show. This can be a sensitive point with presenters if it requires them to give up seats that could otherwise be sold and, in some cases, block the view to the stage from seats behind the soundboard. A presenter's rider[1] might specify that the soundboard must be at the back of the theater or in the control booth. This is one of those areas where advance awareness of the issue hopefully results in good-faith negotiation and resolution. And for obvious reasons, it should be resolved before the box office starts selling tickets to the public!

Stage Dressing

How will the stage be *dressed* and what *soft goods* are required to be provided locally? This will generally include a number of *legs* of specific color, tension, and fullness ("hard" or "soft," "pleated" or "nonpleated"?); borders or *teasers* with the same details that mask overhead lights from audience view; and one or more backgrounds such as a white cyclorama, a filled scrim, an unfilled scrim, a black traveler, etc. For dance setups in which both side lighting and entrances/exits can be particularly important, this is often described in part by describing the number of *lit* and *unlit wings*, meaning the number of up/downstage spaces between legs, which will have side lights in them, often with one upstage near the backdrop that will have no lights in order to set off projections on the backdrop. Including a diagram is a good idea.

Are moveable items such as prop tables and quick-change dressing rooms required backstage?

Is the stage manager's call desk required to be on stage, does she prefer to call from the control booth, or is she okay with either?

Production Schedule/Crew

This is an outline from the producer of the *normal* crew sizes, work hours (*calls*), and functions needed to a) unload the show's truck(s) or containers onto the stage, b) set up the show (including focusing lights, preparation of cues in dimmer boards, and running sound checks), c) run the show (including rehearsals and performances), and d) strike and load out the show.

The presenter should be reminded that this is the generic rider issued for a production with requirements based on optimal conditions and that some variation may be possible or required depending on local circumstances. Examples of variations include: a) venues with strict stagehand union contracts that do not permit crew members to cross departmental lines between electrics, carpentry, etc., may require a larger stage crew, b) academic venues with less experienced student crews whose work is often interrupted by the requirement to attend classes may also require more crew and/or more hours to set up, or c) a venue that is larger than optimal may require an expansion of the light plot, which will take more time to hang and focus.

Additional items that would be covered in this part of the rider include:

- *Prehanging requirement.* It is not uncommon to require that the presenter arrange *prehanging* before the arrival of the show crew, which at minimum, often means hanging and circuiting the presenter-provided lights, precutting gel color for the lights, and dressing the stage, all according to the light plot and stage plans advanced by show to the presenter.

It is recommended to require this as a prehang without specifying when the work is done as long as it is completed prior to the start time of work with the show's crew and the load-in of the show scenery. This allows the presenter the flexibility to prehang the day before (if the day is available in the theater), prehang during the previous show and its load-out, prehang overnight after the previous show is being loaded out, or prehang even prior to the previous show if that is possible. The touring production doesn't care when the prehang takes place as long as all is in readiness at the hour the show's load-in is to start.

- *Same crew members.* Shows will often stipulate that the same personnel must be on call for the rehearsals and the performances so the crew members working the performances are familiar with the show—especially performance sensitive roles such as lighting and soundboard, and follow spot operators. This may be important in the cases of student crews whose schedules include conflicting obligations, and union crews, where the presenter may seek to minimize overtime pay by rotating crews.

- *Prerecorded light cues.* If the show is carrying prerecorded light cues in a certain format that will work on certain light boards but not others, and if the light board being provided by the presenter does not accept the format being carried, lack of compatibility can incur tremendous time and labor costs to have the presenter's board cued up manually. This point needs to be discussed well in advance as it may be cheaper for the presenter to rent a board that is compatible with the show's cue format than to pay the staff hours necessary for the manual programming of her own board. Fortunately, the trend in the industry is toward greater cross-platform applicability and standardization.

- *Crew visible to audience.* In some shows, crew members are occasionally visible to the audience, such as in a scene change without curtain in. They should be notified of this with the requirement to wear *stage black* outfits for the performances.

- *Departmental lines.* A note about *crossing departmental lines* (typically electrics, carpentry, props) might be made, noting whether the assumption that crew members may cross departmental lines is assumed in the projected manpower schedule.

- *Staggered sound call.* Quite often, unless forbidden by a local union agreement, the sound engineer on the setup day will be scheduled with a lunch break an hour later than the rest of the crew so that he can be doing sound testing and level setting while the rest of the crew is on break and the theater is quiet (this will often apply to a piano tuner as well). This occasionally contradicts local practice in the venue and if expected by the show should be noted in the rider.

- *Crew professionalism.* Stipulate that the manpower schedule is based on the expectation of professional crew members being provided. This would apply in particular on a college or university campus where student crews may be involved who are less experienced and who often must run to class in the middle of a setup or rehearsal. If student labor is going to be involved, this must be identified up front and the implications and adjustments to the schedule talked through.

- *Responsibility for crew cost overages.* Presenters will sometimes stipulate that the cost of any crew hours over the schedule included in the rider will be borne by the producer in order to communicate that they have a cap on expenses. Producers, of course, are disinclined to agree to this since they don't know the quality and pace of the crew, and, in most cases, the local crews work under the direct supervision of the local technical director and only indirectly at the behest of the touring production manager. In most cases, the caps don't end up in the contracts. This is once again an area in which a share of back-end profits (if not based on a fixed breakeven point) provides the producer financial incentive to be sure that his tech team is moving the setup along as efficiently as possible.

Lighting/Electrical Power Requirements

Many shows require the presenters to provide the basic lights, dimmer controls, and gel coloring, with the show carrying *specials* (uncommon lighting instruments not often found in venues on tour) and/or *practicals* (lights that the audience can see in the show such as a chandelier or desk lamp). A precise listing of the instrumentation required from the presenter needs to be in or attached to the tech rider, along with a circuiting or plugging chart (that specifies which instruments through which circuits into which dimmer numbers) and color chart showing the color filter required for each instrument (normally designating standardized Rosco[2] or Lee[3] color filter numbers).

Unless the lighting requirements are very simple and a light plot can be hung based on the generic plot and some discussion with the show's techs, shows prepare a venue-specific light plot once the engagement is confirmed and the venue's scaled technical plans have been provided to the show. It is common courtesy for the show to adjust its final instrument requirements as much as possible to the inventory available to presenter, limiting the extent to which the presenter must incur the added cost of renting outside equipment.

Large productions carrying lights. Larger touring productions such as Broadway and large pop music shows often tour with their own leased lights, prehung and circuited on giant trusses that load in from semitrucks right onto the stage, requiring only electrical power and, in some cases, counterweighted overhead pipes or battens from the venue. In this case, the important requirement of the presenter is the raw electrical power needed. Most larger venues used to such touring productions have *touring disconnects*, large power boxes adjacent to the stage for the touring lights to be *tied into*, though renting electrical power generators for a production is not uncommon.

Provide complete information. Stage lighting and the electrical power to operate it are key ingredients to almost all technical riders. One cannot be too thorough in giving the presenter a complete picture of the lighting for the show, delineating that equipment that is being asked of the presenter and that which is being carried with the show but requires electrical power.

Sound Requirements

The basics for sound are much the same as for lighting, with the rider specifying in detail what equipment the presenter is being asked to provide and what the show carries.

A major difference is in the variety of manufacturers and types of equipment. If a sound designer has a preferred microphone or speaker manufacturer, for instance, he will often stipulate both manufacturer and model. This may serve as a basis for discussion of substitution if the venue does not have access to that brand but one similar. While often incomprehensible to the layman, between sound professionals a listing of detailed equipment specifications and specific brands and models conveys the quality and characteristics required.

Identify sound sources. It is a good idea to open the section on sound requirements with a basic statement of the sound sources in the show, even if they have already been mentioned in the opening general paragraph (e.g., live violin on stage, recorded sound, spoken word, etc.)

Beyond the Audience. Within the sound requirements section, it is not only what is heard from the stage by the audience that matters but backstage monitors (for the cast and crew to hear the show backstage), announcement capability from the stage manager's desk to the dressing rooms and to the audience, and crew communications.

If an audio or video recording of the show has been authorized, the sound department may be required to provide a discrete sound feed to the recording equipment.

Additionally, many theaters are equipped with hearing reinforcement systems for audience members who are hearing impaired, which transmit the sound over an infrared signal throughout the auditorium. This system also requires a sound feed from the show.

Duplicate Recorded Sound Sources. Given the occasional frailties of even the most advanced sound equipment, professional sound engineers will always have duplicate (*redundant*) sound equipment standing by for instant substitution in the event of failure.

Duplicate touring sound-source data units—most commonly disks—should be carried and often by two different people traveling with the production to provide added insurance against loss or theft.

Pretested backup microphones are often standing by back stage to be rushed out to an actor or singer on stage in the event of failure of the mike in use.

Two Sound Items Productions Often Carry:

1. *Wireless microphones.* These are delicate, expensive, and often finicky items. Most productions will choose to carry them, often bringing them onto airplanes as hand luggage rather than risk damage or loss in the hold. They are often also collected from each of the performers immediately after the performance and safely secured so as to avoid having them disappear—accidentally or otherwise.

2. *Sound sources such as MP3 players.* These are so small and so essential to the success of the performances that shows will often choose to carry their own, perhaps asking the presenter to provide a second machine as a backup.

Secure electrical source and voltage differentials. If the show is carrying any sound equipment requiring electrical power from the venue, many riders will remind and specify that this electrical power source must be separate and shielded from the power sources for other purposes such as lighting and HVAC, since these other systems can create undesirable hum or distortion in the sound output if the power sources are shared. And of course different voltage needs should be taken into account for international engagements with appropriate transformers planned in advance.

Dressing Rooms/Production Rooms

Be as specific as needed, without going overboard.

Dressing rooms. How many chorus, single, and star rooms are required? Mention the need for private toilets and showers. Mention the need for privacy and security, noting that these rooms are not to be shared with artists from other productions. If the artists always arrive in the venue a specific number of hours before show time, it is a good idea to state this so the venue management knows by what time the dressing rooms need to be cleaned, heated/cooled, and ready for use.

Production rooms. Does the production require a separate wardrobe room, props or instrument storage rooms, etc.? Often a lockable production office is required for the show's production team, preferably with telephone and Internet access.

Artist Union Affiliations

Noting that various artists' unions have quite specific requirements related to backstage needs for their members—notably the American Guild of Musical Artists (AGMA) for dancers and musicians and the Actors' Equity Association (AEA) for American actors, the rider will normally restate the applicability of such requirements.

As most of these requirements are known by most presenters, or are easily obtainable off the Internet, the rider may not repeat them in their entirety but simply state that all touring conditions required under [name of applicable union] will apply. This covers a number of the items already separately listed here, from the availability of water backstage to the requirement of private dressing rooms, acceptable temperature range (for dancers), and even the width of backstage hallways for period costumes in a dramatic production.

Hospitality

This varies according to both union requirements and the artist's needs. Diva backstage requirements are the stuff of legend in the industry. It can get extremely specific or remain general.

This section nearly always addresses food and beverage requirements. Water is a universal requirement, available on both sides of the stage. For a hard working crew starting at 8 AM and working all day, the ongoing provision of coffee, tea, pastry, and fruit is normal. Lunch for the crew on the setup days is not out of the ordinary, as they are often working through the lunch break to be prepared for the afternoon's work. This is in fact a standard requirement in the US stagehands' union rules if the crew is not given the full, normal lunch break.

For a cast being asked to perform twice in a day, often preferring not to have to remove costumes and makeup between shows, a catered backstage meal requirement between performances is common.

Specify if a hot or cold meal, vegetarian, etc., is desired or list a menu if the artists have specific wishes or needs. A happy actor or dancer with good energy equals a better performance and general good vibes backstage!

Most US venues now forbid alcohol on the premises.

Wardrobe

Beyond the wardrobe personnel specified in the stage labor section (above), be specific as to what is required in the way of racks, hangers, side-stage quick-change rooms, washers and dryers in the venue, and access to dry cleaning. Specify how often washing is required: after every performance, once a week, etc.

Other Resources to be Provided by the Presenter

Beyond the basics of lights, sound, and stage dressings, added needs vary considerably according to the nature of the show and the needs of individual artists. This might involve risers for a band or chorus, an acoustic shell, podium, chairs, and music stands for an orchestra, a piano or back line of drums and amps for a music ensemble, a local choir or added musicians or actors to participate in the performances, a runway into the audience, seats reserved for audience *plants* who are involved in the show, a stretch limousine always at the artist's disposal, apples to be juggled in the show, helium balloons, flowers, or just about anything else that the show requests that the presenter agrees to provide.

Some miscellaneous items, either stuck into appropriate sections or on their own, if important enough, include:

- *Security and venue access.* This can involve both backstage access, which both parties generally want limited anyway, and access into the auditorium during the period of setup and rehearsal. Most artists don't want extraneous people in the auditorium, both for security and concentration reasons, without prior discussion and approval, and most venues don't want people potentially getting hurt in a dark auditorium during lighting sessions. This can sometimes be a concern with historic venues, which offer tours to the public during the day. With advance coordination, these can often be limited to times when the stage work is paused for break or during less sensitive periods in the setup process and when the visitors can be kept well away from the work in progress.

- *Vehicle parking at the venue.* Depending both on how the show's theatrical goods will arrive and how the touring cast and crew will be transported to the theater daily during the engagement, parking for trucks and/or passenger vehicles may be required. At some venues parking can be quite restricted and it is important for the show to outline its expected needs early on in the technical rider.

- *Storage of road cases.* Often related to parking is the question of where the show's cases that carried the set, props, and costumes will be stored during the show. If a truck is safely parked behind or nearby the theater throughout the engagement, they will often be loaded back into the truck. Otherwise backstage space must be provided.

- *Temperature.* The American Guild of Musical Artists sets a minimum and maximum temperature within which American dancers will perform, and, whether dancers or other performers, a range should be established in the rider. Temperature—and dramatic changes thereof—can affect musical instruments, notably the tuning of pianos. It is rare in modern theaters that this becomes a problem, but you want it specified nonetheless.

- *Late seating.* The artist should specify the late seating policy that he feels will minimally disrupt the early part of the show. Most artists will plan a late seating moment within the first ten minutes of the show if possible.

- *Announcements before the show and at intermission.* Most venues have a minimum requirement to point out the auditorium exits to their audiences, as well as to admonish them to turn off cell phones and pagers and not take photographs or recordings. The cell phone/pager part sometimes needs to be announced again at the end of intermission. Many presenters also routinely thank the sponsors from the stage and announce upcoming events to which they hope the audience members will return. If the artist has a strong feeling about such announcements before the audience experiences her work, it should be stipulated here, though recognizing that in some states and countries the notice of exit signs is a legal requirement and of course the injunction to silence communication devices is in the best interests of the artist as well as audience members.

- *Oxygen.* If performing at high altitudes, it is normal to ask for oxygen to be provided on both sides of the stage.

- *Pyrotechnics, smoke, nudity, foul language, and strobe lights in the show.* Either in the tech rider or elsewhere, the producer should notify the presenter in writing if any of these are normal parts of the show. In the case of smoke and strobes, most theaters prepare a notice in the lobby for people who may have adverse reactions to these effects. In the case of pyrotechnics, it may require an on-site inspection by the local fire marshal who has the authority to override the contract and deny the use of flames.

- *Flameproofing.* Producers should expect to flameproof their theatrical goods and to carry written proof of the type and level of flameproofing applied. Presenters are within their rights to require such proof in writing. Note, however, that flameproofing requirements in one city, state, province, or country may be different than those in others, so the producer is wise to flameproof to as high a standard as possible to allow for all eventualities. Also, no amount of flameproofing and proof thereof—and no engagement contract—replaces the authority of the local fire marshal to arrive at any time prior to or during a show and apply a "match test" to the goods. If the goods fail the test and the flame lives longer than the maximum allowed, the fire marshal can stop the show from proceeding until the goods have been removed or until new flameproofing has been applied and the goods have passed the match test.

This list is by no means complete, but is provided as a checklist and to illustrate the scope of items, services, and issues that may be addressed within the framework of technical requirements for touring productions going into various venues.

Contacts

It is important to provide contact information here for the show's technical representative and to provide lines to be filled in for provision of the presenter's technical representative's contact information. This should include as much round-the-clock access information as the parties are willing to share, including cell phones and e-mail addresses, noting that the show's tech rep may well be on tour elsewhere with the show even as he or she is communicating about and planning for this future engagement.

Signatures

It is normal to include a line for that signature or at least initials of the presenter and/or his tech rep acknowledging that they have read through and agree to the terms of the tech rider. This is partly legal—recall that this document, amended as appropriate to suit the particular presenter's venue, will become part of the final engagement contract—and partly for confirmation that the technical authority on the other side has indeed read through the rider and understands and accepts the show's requirements.

Endnotes

1 Note that it is not unusual for presenters to issue their own technical riders for contracts, generally specifying the house rules, listing technical equipment and resources available in the venue, and advising of applicable union agreements.

2 Gel coloring manufactured by Rosco Laboratories in Connecticut. See *www.rosco.com/us/technotes/filters/perma_rlux_crc.asp*.

3 Gel coloring manufactured by Lee Filters, in more common usage outside of the US. See *www.leefilters.com*.

Sample Agreement for Booking Agency/ Producer Representation

Booking Agency Agreement

The following agreement, dated _____, 20__, is by and between _____ _____, having offices at _____ ("Producer"), and _____, having offices at _____ ("Agency").

Producer wishes to engage the services of Agency as booking agency for certain of its live theatrical productions mutually agreed between the parties to be appropriate for touring, and in particular the productions titled _____, hereinafter referred to as the "Productions," and Agency agrees to be so engaged, as follows:

I.   PRODUCTIONS.[1] The productions to be offered for tour will be as proposed by Producer and agreed by Agency to be suitable for touring in each performance season covered by this Agreement, with such productions added or dropped as mutually agreed during the life of the Agreement. Producer hereby grants to Agency the first option for touring representation for any and all new productions that may be created by Producer during the term of this Agreement, and Producer may not offer them to another agency unless Agency has specifically declined the option of representation. Agency will not unreasonably decline such representation.

II.   AGENCY WILL make its best efforts to secure engagements for the Productions commencing immediately upon execution of this Agreement including negotiating terms with presenters on behalf of Producer, drafting a contract form acceptable to Producer, and supervising execution of contracts and financial deposits if any. Agency will not be involved in servicing the engagements past contract execution except as may be separately agreed between the parties. Agency may at its discretion announce such representation within the industry by e-mail, Web site, mail, and/or any other form it deems most effective in securing engagements. Agency will consult Producer on issues associated with preparing the Productions for touring, including logistics and budgeting.

III.   PRODUCER WILL provide all information and marketing materials on each of the Productions and the history of the Productions' touring, production, and performance activity to Agency as Agency requires to provide the services described; will turn over any direct booking contacts it may receive to Agency in a timely manner; will list Agency as its exclusive booking representative in all reasonable locations, including but not limited to performance programs, Producer's Web site (with hyperlink to Agency), and in its printed and video materials; and will implement and service the engagements negotiated by Agency in a professional manner. In particular, Producer will arrange to produce promotional-length and full-length video in international DVD format of each of the Productions at the highest quality possible, with Agency identified as the booking contact for Agency's use in promoting engagements of the Productions, and will provide high-quality color photographs in digital format with rights for publicity use, press, and complete technical information (tech riders) for both domestic US and international touring.

Guidelines to Agency listing:

Worldwide touring representation: [agency credit line with basic contact information]

IV. TERM OF AGREEMENT. This Agreement covers all live public performances of the Productions taking place from the time of execution of this Agreement through August 31, 20YY *(two complete years plus partial year from the date of execution)* and for any engagements that have been agreed to or are in a state of serious negotiation at the time of Agreement termination scheduled or planned to take place beyond August 31, 20YY. This Agreement may be extended by mutual agreement of the parties, which will be decided by May 1, 20XX *(next year)* for the 20YY–ZZ performance season *(three seasons ahead)*, and for each season thereafter by May 15 of the year prior to the performance season to be booked.

The intention is to have the agreement cover two full seasons ahead, plus the remainder of the season current at the time the contract is signed, with both a cancellation option and a renewal for a third full season with a deadline one year from this date. These dates can get confusing, so be sure to map them out.

V. EXCLUSIVITIY. Agency will be the exclusive booking agent for the Production worldwide for the term described above, except for performances in the five boroughs of New York City in which Agency will have a nonexclusive relationship and expect commission only from those engagements in which Agency is involved in negotiating on behalf of Producer.

VI. FINANCIAL TERMS.

- Commission. For all engagements other than the following exclusion list, Agency will receive from Producer or directly from presenters a commission based on _____% of the engagement fees payable to Producer, both of guaranteed fees and box office percentages. If commission is being paid by Producer to Agency, such payments will be made within five business days after receipt by Producer of fees for engagements, including any deposits in cases of multiple-payment engagement agreements.

- Exclusion list. *[List engagements already in negotiation in which the parties agree this agent will not participate, if any.]*

- Annual contribution toward booking expenses. Producer will pay to Agency the sum of $_____ as a contribution toward expenses for Agency's booking expenses for efforts related to the 20VV–WW *[current season]* and 20XX–YY *[next season]* Seasons, payable _____. Future annual fees can be expected to be at least $ ____ covering the season ahead and payable by May 1 in each of the years prior to the seasons being booked. The foregoing expense money shall be utilized solely in connection with Producer and Artist, though Artist acknowledges that much of this cost is part of Agency expenses related to all artists on its roster, such as conference attendance, and brochure publication and distribution, and is therefore not directly accountable to any individual artist. Any amounts not so expended shall be accounted for and refundable no later than June 1 of each year.

- Other expenses. Producer will provide Agency with a FedEx account number suitable for ground and international air shipping, to be paid by Producer and which Agency may use as needed to ship Producer's materials as part of the booking process. Producer will additionally reimburse Agency for direct costs of duplicating Producer's materials (except for minor in-office duplications such as photocopy and DVD). Producer guarantees that all rights and permissions for duplication and use of the materials provided for publicity purposes have been secured, unless Producer otherwise informs Agency. Artist understands that from time to time FedEx shipments will include materials for more than one artist and trusts Agency to be fair in rotational allocation of such group shipments between its artists.

- Opt-in promotional expenses. Agency from time to time will propose cooperative advertising in trade publications, allowing special visual emphasis to artists represented by Agency who elect to contribute to the costs. In the event that Producer elects to participate in such advertising, a pro rata share of advertising costs related to Producer's productions will be paid by Producer. Likewise, Producer will be responsible for all costs associated with any showcasing or special entertainment expenses at booking conferences.

VII. RENEWAL. The parties will decide and agree by May 1, 20XX, whether or not to continue the relationship for the 20YY–ZZ Season. In the event that it is renewed, a written agreement of extension will be signed by both parties. In the event that the agreement is not renewed, Producer will nonetheless pay to Agency all commissions and other expense reimbursements on future performances that have been booked or are in negotiation at the time of cancellation.

VIII. DISPUTE RESOLUTION. In the event of a dispute between the parties, every effort will be made to resolve the dispute amicably between themselves or with the assistance of a mutually agreed upon dispute mediator. In the event that legal action is needed, the parties agree to operate under the laws of the State of _____.

IX. NONASSIGNMENT. This contract may not be assigned by either party without the consent of the other. The Agency may be transferred to another agency provided that _____ retains controlling interest over the affairs of Producer in the new agency.

X. CANCELLATION. In the event that the relationship is extremely unsatisfactory to one or the other or both parties, either party may terminate this agreement midterm. Such termination can only take place in the spring of 20XX *(next year)* affecting the 20YY–ZZ Season *(following full performance season)*. Notice must be given in writing forty-five days in advance of termination, and termination will be completed by July 15, 20XX *(next year)*. Unless such notice is provided by either party, the full term of this Agreement will automatically apply. In the event of such cancellation, Producer will nonetheless be responsible to Agency for full commissions on all engagements and activities booked or in an advance state of negotiation at the time of termination regardless of when the activities are to take place.

XI. WARRANTS AND MUTUAL INDEMNITY. Except as otherwise set forth herein, the parties each warrant that they have full authority to enter into this Agreement, and none of the terms of this Agreement conflict in any way with any other contracts to which either party is a part. Except as otherwise set forth herein, Producer specifically warrants that it exclusively represents the professional activities of Artist and that Artist has no other representation agreements outside of that with Producer. Producer also specifically warrants that it has no other agency agreements or other agreements that would conflict with this Agreement, and that it exclusively represents the Artist for the activities described in this contract. Producer agrees to indemnify and hold harmless the Agency, its employees, and agents, from any loss suffered or incurred by Agency due to misrepresentations of the Producer's authority and from any third-party claims, costs or expenses suffered or incurred by Agency arising from the production and presentation of any of the productions, other than any such claims for which Agency's indemnification would apply or that were caused by Agency's negligence or tortious acts. Agency agrees to indemnify and hold harmless the Producer, its employees, and agents, from any loss suffered or incurred by Producer or Artist due to misrepresentations of the Agency's authority, from the breach of any Agency representations hereunder and from any third-party claims, costs or expenses suffered or incurred by Producer or Artist arising from Agency's business activities, other than any such claims for which Producer's indemnification would apply.

This will constitute the entire agreement between the parties related to the subject matter herein contained and may not be changed without the written agreement of both parties.

Accepted and agreed:

[Agreement signature line]

For [*Producer*]: _____ Date: _____

By (print): _____

For [*Agency*]:_____ Date: _____

By (print): _____

Endnotes

1   Note that this format allows for multiple productions from one producer. This could be reworded in the event that there is only one production involved.

Sample Deal Memo

DEAL MEMO

DATE:

PRESENTER: *[Full corporate name]*
                 [Street address]
                 [City, state, zip]

PRODUCER: *[Full corporate name]*
                 [Street address]
                 [City, state, zip]

AGENT: *[Full corporate name]*
                 [Street address]
                 [City, state, zip]

PRODUCTION: *[Name of artist or production]*

ENGAGEMENT: Two (2) performances at the *[name of venue]*
                 (*Capacity:___*) in May of 20XX per following
                 schedule:

                 Sunday, April 29: Company (11) arrives

                 Monday, April 30: Rehearsal

                 Tuesday, May 1: Load-in/Tech

                 Wednesday, May 2: Tech Rehearsal/Performance 8pm

                 Thursday, May 3: Performance 8pm

                 Friday, May 4: Load-out/All depart

PRODUCER PROVIDES

Cast, supervisory support personnel, scenery, costumes, and special technical
equipment (except as noted to be provided by Presenter in the *[show name]* technical
rider) as Producer deems necessary for presentation of the Production, rights and royalties, per diems, salaries and benefits for its cast and support personnel as required by

law and union agreements, promotional materials as available, and reasonable access to cast for advance publicity purposes.

PRESENTER PROVIDES

- Fee of $_____ payable by corporate check or bank transfers, net of all taxes or other withholds; payable as follows:
- $_____ on contract execution (payable to Agent)
- $_____ by Monday, January 15, 20XX (payable to Producer)
- Balance by start of first public performance (payable to Producer)

ADDITIONAL CONSIDERATIONS

- Presenter will provide accommodations for eleven (11; *5 singles and 3 doubles*) the nights of 4/29 through 5/3 in a good-quality hotel.
- Presenter will reimburse Producer up to a maximum of $_____ for freight costs.
- Presenter will provide local transportation between hotel, airport, theater and residency sites as needed. It is acceptable for Presenter to rent cars for Producer provided full liability and damage insurance is included.
- Presenter will provide all resources listed in the [*show name*] technical rider, to be provided by Producer on or before [*date*] and as may be modified to suit the space by approval of Producer's technical director.

A complete contract will be issued by Agent, but this Deal Memo when signed by both parties will constitute a commitment by both parties to this engagement, permitting the parties to publicly announce the Engagement and make third-party commitments as needed for the Engagement.

Agent is authorized by Producer to sign on behalf of Producer for the purposes of this Deal Memo.

This Deal Memo will be void if not signed and returned by Presenter to Agent by _____.

Accepted and agreed:

For [*Producer*]: _____   Date: _____

By (print): _____

For [*Producer*]: _____   Date: _____

By (print): _____
Authorized Agent

Sample US Domestic Engagement Contract (As might be issued by an agent)

ARTIST ENGAGEMENT CONTRACT

The following engagement contract, dated _____, is by and between:

PRESENTER: *[Full corporate name]*
                         [Street address]
                         [City, state, zip]
                         [Contact name, telephone, and e-mail]

PRODUCER: *[Full corporate name]*
                         [Street address]
                         [City, state, zip]
                         [Contact name, telephone, and e-mail]
                         Represented for this engagement by

AGENT: *[Full corporate name]*
                         [Street address]
                         [City, state, zip]
                         [Contact name, telephone, and e-mail]

Presenter wishes to engage the services of Producer to offer public performances of *[show title]* ("Production") and related activities at the [*Venue*] (*Capacity:* _____) and Producer wishes to be so engaged. The parties hereto agree to a performance and activity schedule as follows:

I. ENGAGEMENT

Description	Date	Time	Location

II. TERMS

Fee: [*Dollar amount spelled out*] US Dollars ($[*Dollar amount numerically*]), without deduction or offset whatsoever. Fee payable by check as follows:

- $_____ on contract execution (to Agent TIN# _____)
- $_____ on or before [*date*] (to Producer TIN#_____)
- Balance by start of performance (to Producer)

Percentage: [*Describe percentage agreement here if there is one*]

Accommodations: Presenter will provide accommodations for [*number of persons*] for the nights of _____ through _____ (*X* singles and *Y* doubles) in a good quality hotel [*specify minimum number of stars if important*].

Travel:

> Intercity: [*Describe if Presenter is responsible*]

> Local: Presenter will provide transportation for Producer's staff and personal baggage to and from airport, bus/train station, hotel, press interviews, residency and lecture sites, and venue as needed. In the event that Producer's accommodations are not within reasonable (five minutes/half mile) walking distance from place of performance, or during inclement weather, Presenter will provide transportation to and from Producer's hotel and place of performance.

Freight:

> Intercity: [*Describe if Presenter is responsible*]

> Local: If needed, Producer will deliver theatrical goods to and pick them up from the theater upon arrival and departure.

Rider Considerations: Presenter will provide the agreed upon resources listed in [*show title's*] technical rider, attached and previously reviewed by Presenter and as may be modified to suit the spaces by approval of [*show title's*] technical director.

III. PRODUCER PROVIDES

Producer will provide the services of such performers and supervisory technical personnel, scenery, costumes, and special technical equipment (except as noted to be provided by Presenter in the attached technical rider) as Producer deems necessary for presentation of the Production, as well as rights and royalties, per diems, salaries and benefits for its cast and support personnel as required by law and performer agreements, promotional materials as available, and reasonable access to cast for advance publicity purposes.

Producer agrees to supply such printing and advertising material as Producer has available, and will also furnish program copy, including Production biographies, program listing and other such information, which Presenter agrees to print and distribute at its sole expense. Presenter may not amend, change, or edit Producer's photos, program copy, or other materials without express written approval of Producer. Presenter agrees to use only photographs, advertising, and promotional materials furnished by Producer and only for the purpose of promoting the Engagement. Appropriate photo credits and copyright notices must be given.

IV.   PRESENTER PROVIDES

In addition to the terms in Paragraph II above, Presenter hereby agrees to the following:

IV.1.   Presenter agrees to furnish at his sole cost and expense: said place(s) of performance on the date(s) and at the time(s) above mentioned and as may be required for advance stage preparation, properly heated, ventilated, lighted, cleaned, and in good order, with clean, comfortable dressing rooms near the stage for the Production; all other items (except those items which Producer herein specifically agrees to furnish), including but not limited to all lights, microphones, props, curtains, drapes, and tickets; personnel including but not limited to electricians, sound technicians, stagehands, riggers, carpenters, follow spot operators, truck loaders and unloaders, ushers, ticket sellers and any other box office employees required for advance and single ticket sales, ticket takers, security guards; all licenses and permissions, all fees therefore, and fire permits for use of fire on stage (if required for the Production); and any and all equipment, facilities, and other materials and services not herein listed that may reasonably be required for the proper presentation of the activities.

IV.2.   Presenter warrants and represents that it is at the present time, or will be, the owner or operator of, or has or will have a valid lease upon the place(s) of performance covering the date or date(s) of this Contract, proof of which will be given to Producer or his designee upon request. Presenter further warrants that he/she has full authority to enter into this Contract and to bind the presenting organization, and that this Contract does not interfere with or violate any copyright or proprietary right of any third party.

IV.3.   Presenter agrees that starting at 8 AM on the first day of activity listed in Engagement above, or at other setup start time as may be mutually agreed upon, the place of performance will be available exclusively for the preparation of the stage for Producer's performance, and will remain exclusively available through the strike following the final performance, for technical setup, rehearsal, performances, and strike of the Production. Presenter further agrees that at no cost to Producer the necessary stage personnel will be made available for such setup, rehearsal, performances, and strike (See TECHNICAL RIDER attached).

IV.4.   Presenter will provide advertising and performance programs, featuring billing for the Production as shall be determined by Producer. Advertising shall include, at Presenter's discretion, bill posting, mailing and distribution of circulars, daily newspaper advertising in principal newspapers in the area, radio and television advertising, and publicity services of every type.

IV.5.   Presenter agrees that no radio apparatus or transmitting or recording device, specifically including but not limited to still photographs, motion pictures, video, and television, shall be used nor permitted by Presenter during rehearsal or the performance(s) in any manner or form to reproduce the Production hereunder, and Presenter will make every effort to enforce this regulation in the theater.

IV.6.   Presenter will provide Producer with ten (10) complimentary tickets in the fifth to tenth rows of the center orchestra section for each performance.

IV.7.   Presenter shall have, secure, and maintain for the performance(s), public liability insurance covering loss from any accident resulting in bodily injury or death in the amount of not less than $1 million per occurrence and $2 million aggregate, and for complete damage to or loss of Producer's property while on Presenter's premises. If the venue in which the performances are to take place is not operated and insured by Presenter, Presenter will require that the venue owner/operator be similarly insured. Presenter agrees to provide Producer with certificates evidencing such insurance upon Producer's or his representative's request. Presenter's insurance, for the purposes of this Engagement, shall name Producer as an additional insured thereon.

V.   ADDITIONAL CONDITIONS

V.1.   In the event Presenter refuses or fails to provide any of the items herein stated, or refuses or fails to make any of the payments as provided herein or to proceed with the performance(s), Producer shall have no obligation to perform this Contract and shall retain any amounts therefore paid to Producer or on his behalf by Presenter, and Presenter shall remain liable to Producer for the Contract price and terms herein set forth.

V.2.   If legal action shall be brought by Producer or his representative to recover any sums due to Producer under this Contract, or for breach of any other covenant or condition contained in this Contract, in the event that Producer or his representative prevails in such action, Presenter shall pay to Producer or his representative, all expenses, costs, and actual attorney's fees incurred in the aforesaid action.

V.3.   If, on or before the date of any scheduled performance, Presenter has failed, neglected, or refused to perform any contract with any other performer for any earlier performance, or if the financial standing or credit of Presenter has been impaired or is unsatisfactory, Producer shall have the right to demand the payment of the full guaranteed compensation forthwith. If Presenter fails or refuses to make such payment forthwith, Producer shall have the right to cancel this performance by notice to Presenter to that effect, and in such event, Producer shall retain any amounts theretofore paid to Producer by Presenter, in addition to initiating action for any other damages that may be due Producer thereby. Paragraph VI notwithstanding, in the event such cancellation becomes necessary on the day of performance, or if there is insufficient time for certified mail to be delivered to Presenter, verbal presentation by Producer or Producer's representative on site to the ranking staff member of Presenter's organization on site at the time, will be deemed sufficient notice, with certified letter to follow as quickly as is feasible.

V.4.   FORCE MAJEURE CANCELLATION. In the event of sickness or accident to one or more of Producer's performers or essential support personnel rendering performance of the Production impossible, and the injured party(s) cannot be replaced or the show restaged to Producer's satisfaction, or if a performance is prevented, rendered impossible or infeasible by any act or regulation of any public authority or bureau, civic tumult, strike, epidemic, interruption in or delay of transportation services, war conditions or emergencies, or any cause beyond the control of Producer and Presenter, it is understood and agreed that there shall be no claim for damages by either party to this Contract, and Producer's obligation as to such performance shall be waived. In the event of such nonperformance for any of the reasons stated in this paragraph, Producer will be entitled to receive a share of the total fee based on the contracted services provided prior to, and will receive additional obligations of Presenter regarding travel, freight and accommodations as may be necessary. Inclement weather shall not be deemed an emergency and payment of this agreed upon fee shall be made notwithstanding, provided, however, that Producer is ready, willing, and able to perform pursuant to the terms hereof.

CANCELLATION WITHIN PARTIES' CONTROL. Failure to abide by any of the material terms of this Contract, by either party for reasons within control of the canceling party, may be considered by the other party as voidance of the Contract. In the event of cancellation for reasons within control of Presenter, Presenter shall be liable to Producer and Agent for the full performance fee. In the event of cancellation for reasons within control of Producer and/or Agent, Producer and Agent will forfeit the performance fee, and be liable to Presenter for reimbursement of documentable direct expenses incurred and paid by Presenter as a result of cancellation and not reimbursable from any other source. Presenter's ticket revenue shall not be considered direct expense. In the event of an unintentional nonmaterial breach, the erring party will be given twenty-four (24) hours to correct the breach.

V.5.   CONTROL OF PRODUCTION. Producer shall have the sole and exclusive control over the production, presentation, and performance, hereunder, including, but not limited to the details, means, and methods of the performance and the performances of each participant therein, and the persons to be employed by Producer in performing the provisions hereof on Producer's part to be performed. No other performer may appear at Producer's performance(s) without express prior approval of Producer. No announcements may be made from the stage prior, during, or following Producer's performance without prior approval from Producer.

V.6.   MERCHANDISE. Producer shall have the sole and exclusive right to sell souvenir programs, photographs, videos, and other Production-related merchandise on the premises of the place of performance. Presenter will provide sellers. Presenter and seller combined may not claim more than 15 percent of gross revenue from merchandise sales calculated net of any and all applicable local city/state taxes.

V.7.   It is agreed that Producer signs this Contract as an independent contractor and not as an employee, and he shall have exclusive control over the means and methods employed in fulfilling his obligations hereunder in all respects and in all details. This is a service agreement only and nothing herein contained shall be deemed to create or constitute a joint venture, partnership, or trust relationship between the parties. Neither party shall be entitled to bind the other to a contractual or other obligation except as set forth herein or by express written approval. It is expressly agreed that this Contract is entered into by and between Presenter and Producer and that any agent or representative of Producer is not responsible for any act or commission or omission on the part of either Producer or Presenter.

V.8.   Neither Production's name nor images may be used by Presenter, nor such use authorized by Presenter, as an endorsement of any product or service nor in connection with any commercial tie-up, without Producer's prior written consent. No advertising or sponsor credits may appear on or near the stage without express advance approval of Producer.

V.9.   Producer agrees to abide by all reasonable rules and policies that may be in force at the performance venue during the time in which the Production is on the premises provided that a) the Producer has been notified in writing and provided with copies of any such rules prior to contract execution, and that b) the same rules and policies are applied to all Productions performing in the venue. In the event of conflict between venue rules and the technical requirements of the Production, the parties will negotiate in good faith to resolve the issues.

VI.   NOTIFICATION

All notices required hereunder shall be given in writing by certified mail, if to Producer, care of Agent at address above, and if to Presenter, at the address of Presenter above.

VII.   NONASSIGNMENT/CONTRACT GOVERNANCE

This Contract cannot be assigned or transferred by either party without the written consent of the other party. It contains the complete understanding of the parties hereto, and may not be amended, supplemented, varied, or discharged, except by an instrument in writing. The validity, construction, and effect of this Contract shall be governed by the laws of the State of _____, regardless of place of performance. Parties hereto agree that the courts of the State of _____ will have personal jurisdiction over them and in any legal action or proceeding relating to this Contract or the subject matter thereof. The terms "Producer," "Presenter," and "Agent" as used herein shall include and apply to the singular and the plural and to all genders.

VIII.   INDEMNITY

Presenter shall indemnify and hold harmless Producer and each member of Producer's staff and theatrical company, and Agent and each member of Agent's staff and theatrical company, from and against any loss, damage, or expense, including reasonable attorney's fees, incurred or suffered by or threatened against any of them in connection with or as a result of any claim for personal injury or property damage brought by or on behalf of any third party, person, firm, or corporation that is alleged to be as a result of or in connection with the Engagement that is the subject of this Contract, including the presentation of the Production itself, which claim does not result directly from Producer's and/or Agent's active negligence and includes access to Producer's theatrical equipment not specifically agreed to and supervised by Producer.

Producer and Agent shall both equally indemnify and hold harmless Presenter and each member of Presenter's staff and theatrical company, from and against any loss, damage or expense, including reasonable attorney's fees, incurred or suffered by or threatened against any of them in connection with or as a result of any claim for personal injury or property damage brought by or on behalf of any third party, person, firm, or corporation that is alleged to be as a result of or in connection with the Engagement that is the subject of this Contract, including the presentation of the Production itself, which claim does not result directly from Presenter's active negligence.

IX.   TECHNICAL RIDER INTEGRAL TO CONTRACT

The Technical Rider attached hereto shall be considered an integral part of this Contract. Any deviation by Presenter from the obligations to provide technical resources as specified in this Rider may be considered by Producer to be a violation of the Contract by Presenter unless Producer has expressly agreed to such deviation in advance. Paragraph VI notwithstanding, for the purpose of such agreement, faxed authorization from Producer's production manager is acceptable.

Accepted and agreed:

For [*Presenter*]: _____   For [*Producer*]: _____

By (signature): _____   By: (signature) _____

Print name: _____   Print name: _____

Title: _____   Title: _____

Date: _____   Date: _____

Sample US Domestic Technical Rider

[Production Name]

TECHNICAL RIDER

[US Domestic. Version 1.0. Issued MM/YY]

[PRODUCTION NAME] RUNS APPROXIMATELY 1 HOUR AND 45 MINUTES WITH ONE 15 MINUTE INTERMISSION. THE SHOW IS SEGMENTED, BUT RUNS CONTINUOUSLY WITH SEVEN PERFORMERS CONSTANTLY ENTERING AND EXITING. THERE IS VIDEO (FRONT) PROJECTION OF MOTION PICTURE IN DVD FORMAT, WITH ALL VIDEO EQUIPMENT PROVIDED BY THE COMPANY. THERE IS NO ACT CURTAIN. FOR AN OPENING EVENING PERFORMANCE THE SHOW CAN LOAD-IN AND REHEARSE ON THE DAY OF THE FIRST PERFORMANCE GIVEN A PROFESSIONAL, WELL-PLANNED SITUATION WITH REQUISITE LIGHTING PREHANG BY HOUSE CREW. LATE SEATING IS ACCEPTABLE AND SHOULD BE COORDINATED WITH VENUE HOUSE MANAGEMENT AND THE SHOW'S PRODUCTION STAGE MANAGER. THE SHOW CAN BE MOUNTED ON ANY STAGE WITH THE MINIMUM REQUIREMENTS OF AN UNOBSTRUCTED 36' DEEP BY 36' WIDE (PROSCENIUM) SQUARE. ALTHOUGH FLYING OR WEIGHT-BEARING GRIDS ARE PREFERRED, WITH ADVANCE PLANNING, THE SHOW CAN BE MOUNTED IN AN OUTDOOR OR OTHER ENVIRONMENT WITHOUT OVERHEAD SUPPORT.

Typically the traveling company (11 to 13 persons) includes:

- Director
- Company Manager
- Technical Director/Production Manager—Oversees Load-in, Show Run, and Load-out Crews
- Production Stage Manager—Oversees Lighting and Video as well as Show Run

- Sound Engineer—Oversees Sound Load-in and Show Run
- Performers (six to eight)

HOSPITALITY:

1. <u>The Company requests that lunch be provided for the Road Crew on first day of Load-in:</u>
   - Arranged by 12pm
   - Light sandwich tray: vegetarian and nonvegetarian (turkey, chicken, tuna)
   - Nonflavored coffee, herbal tea (milk and sugar), mineral water, and fruit juices

2. <u>The Company requests the following to be backstage before and after rehearsals and in between events on days in which more than one activity has been scheduled (times will be advanced by Production Stage Manager):</u>
   - Light sandwich tray: vegetarian and nonvegetarian (turkey, chicken, tuna)
   - Fruit and mixed nuts (e.g., figs, dates, oranges, grapes, pears, apples)
   - LOTS of mineral water (sixteen 1-Liter bottles)
   - Energy bars (e.g., Balance bars)
   - Nonflavored coffee, herbal tea (milk and sugar), fruit juices

3. <u>For performances, the Company requests:</u>
   - Coffee, tea (milk and sugar), mineral water (sixteen 1-Liter bottles), fruit juices, sports drinks

MINIMUM STAGE DIMENSIONS:

- Depth—36'0" (Back wall to lip of stage)
- Width—36'0" at proscenium, ideally 82'0" wall to wall, 60'0" is acceptable.
- Height—25'0" mandatory (Clear of batons, pipes, and obstructions)
- Stage—Load bearing capacity of 3,500 pounds (2-legged box truss)

LOAD-IN ACCESS:

The show arrives in either a 48' or a 53' trailer with semitractor depending on what is available at the time of booking. Finished rig lengths can range from 63' to 73'. Ideally parking for the truck should be arranged by the venue at the venue or within close proximity. If this is not possible, the Production Manager must be notified to make other arrangements.

Access other than a loading dock at truck height with a full-size garage door at stage level must be discussed with Production Manager and approved by the Company. If the loading dock is in excess of fifty (50) feet from the stage, more labor will be required for load-in and load-out. The Venue should provide at least four (4) carts or dollies for load-in and load-out.

PRESENTER WILL PROVIDE THE FOLLOWING EQUIPMENT FOR THE PRODUCTION:

FLOOR:

A level floor that is black and free from splinters, interruptions, and any other protrusions is the only acceptable floor. The minimum performance space is thirty-six (36) feet wide by thirty-six (36) feet deep. Proscenium openings narrower than forty (40) feet must be discussed with the Production Manager. Ideally, the Company would like to drill into the floor at 8 points; if this is impossible, the Production Manager should be notified as soon as possible. Stage weight or offstage wall attachments may also be necessary.

RIGGING:

Company would require 6,000 lbs. of counterweight for securing set or adequate ground attachments. Company will provide all guy wires and rigging.

STAGE DRESSING:

- No act curtain
- No legs or borders
- One white cyclorama or seamless muslin upstage for video projection surface

LIGHTING AND POWER:

Because venues vary in size and configuration, lighting needs may change.

POSITIONS:

Production uses FOH, 1st, 2nd, and 3rd Electrics as well as three (3) booms on both stage left and stage right

INSTRUMENTS:

Production uses   S4 10 = 3

S4 19 = 25

S4 26 = 20

S4 36 = 18

S4 50 = 2

S4 Par MFL = 9

PAR64 MFL = 8

PAR38 = 6

Light Plot and Paperwork will be sent to Venue two (2) months prior to first Performance. Light Plot is on floor plan of [*said theater space*]. It can be specialized for a specific venue in which case plans of the house and electrics must be sent no later than three (3) months prior to the first performance.

Prehang to be determined with Lighting Director.

The lighting console should be a computerized/memory board able to record and playback cues. Any substitutions must be discussed with the Lighting Director. Cues come on disks formatted for ETC Expression; if translation is not available, the cues will be written on site and run from submasters.

Light board operator needs to be available to the Lighting Supervisor at least 30 minutes prior to start of *every performance*, for lighting notes.

- The company requires access to a 30' Genie lift or adequate tall ladders for focus.
- Cable requirement will be determined per venue.
- Company will confirm equipment list when drawings are received.
- Company must approve all substitutions of requested equipment.

POWER

- 50 amp 3 Phase Power (208/240 volts) MOTOR CONTROL
- Adequate feeder and distribution panels for tie-in
- Company travels with two 1-ton CM motors, and all necessary control lines and cable. Motor control box has 60' bare-end feeder cable.
- Company requires two (2) grounded 120 volt, 20 amp circuits on stage
- Production Stage Manager requires one (1) grounded 120 volt, 20 amp circuit on stage

THE COMPANY WILL PROVIDE:

- Misc. gel and templates.
- All video equipment including projector and mounting hardware.
- Typically video is front projection with the hang position being just US of the Plaster Line.

SOUND:

Sound is an integral part of [*Production's*] performance. It consists of mike pickups onstage to amplify performers and scenery as well as CD and minidisc playback to underscore pieces as well as use for preshow, postshow, intermission, and scene changes. Presenter is expected to provide the following related to sound:

LOUDSPEAKERS

- MAINS: 4 × EAW KF850 OR 4 × Meyer MSL4 (2 per side/True Stereo)
- SUBS: 2 × EAW KF940 OR 2 × Meyer 650 (2" × 18" drivers per side)
- ORCH. FILL (where required)

- BALCONY FILL (where required)
- No stage monitors required

FOH CONTROL

- 32" × 8" × 2" CONSOLE Yamaha PM 3000 OR Soundcraft Vienna OR Crest VX (Or equivalent. Please clear substitutions with Company's Sound Engineer.)
- *IMPORTANT:* Company's equipment at FOH terminates in ten 1/4" connectors.
- Adapters or DI boxes are required if provided console does not accept 1/4" line inputs.
- 2 REVERB/EFFECTS UNITS
- 4 channels COMPRESSORS and insert cabling
- 4 SEPERATE channels GATES and insert cabling
- 32-band GRAPHIC EQ per speaker zone
- DELAY UNITS for time alignment if installed speakers are available
- 2 CD PLAYERS
- Interconnect for all above
- "WING" SPACE for Company's equipment: shock-mount racks on either side of operator
- Operator prefers mix position midhouse, off center, nonbooth.

POWER

- Tie in to dedicated sound power wherever possible.
- Company's equipment requires one (1) grounded 120 volt, 20 amp circuit on stage and one (1) grounded 120 volt, 20 amp circuit at FOH position.
- DISTRO and adequate CABLES for FOH and amplifiers, which usually end up in wings.

ADDITIONAL INTERCONNECT

- Minimum 32-channel SNAKE long enough for stage box located upstage without crossing the floor in the wings (heavy rolling set pieces)
- Snake must breakout to XLR for FOH console patch as some lines divert to sidecar mixer.
- Additional 8 channels of DRIVE LINES (crossovers at amps) or 12 channels (crossovers at FOH)
- Plenty of standard XLR mic cable (minimum 10' × 10', 10' × 25', 10' × 35', 10' × 50')

SOUND MISC.

- Two 9V alkaline BATTERIES per show for Company's radio microphones
- Assorted audio ADAPTERS for FOH patching including both sexes of XLR turnarounds

- Two AUDIO ISOLATION TRANSFORMERS (IL-19/for press feed)
- Matting and gaffer tape to cover onstage cable runs
- Adequate processing, amplification, and cabling for each above (Subs fed from aux. on own driveline)
- Flying hardware for mains wherever flying is possible (NO speakers to be flown from Company truss)
- Patch access to installed speakers (center cluster, under balcony fills, etc.) wherever possible
- Backstage microphone for emergency audience and backstage announcements (God Mic)

The above are typical sound requirements for medium size theaters. Unusual spaces should contact Company's Sound Engineer.

INTERCOM SYSTEM WITH SIX (6) WIRED STATION DROPS LOCATED:

- wings downstage left
- video table (stage right)
- mix position (handset)
- lighting board
- house lights control (when separate from show control)
- WIRELESS INTERCOMS with BASE STATION tied into hardwired system
- Sufficient BATTERIES for wireless intercoms

WARDROBE:

- The Wardrobe person will be given laundry instructions by one of the performers.
- The Company's costumes must be hand washed or machine gentle washed after every dress rehearsal or performance, hung on hangers, and allowed to air dry.
- Performance towels must be machine washed and dried after every dress rehearsal and performance.
- If the load-out immediately follows a performance, the costumes should be washed, hung up, and dried with fans.
- Production Stage Manager will collect costumes and pack them on truck.

DRESSING ROOMS:

- At least two (2) Chorus dressing rooms for Performers and one (1) single room for the Director with adequate heating, hot water showers, and toilets separate from the public must be provided.
- One additional dressing room with a telephone line and a data line should be provided for use as a production office.
- Ten (10) clean towels.

WORK SCHEDULE (NORMAL SETUP):

Production requires exclusive use of Theater for duration of load-in and performance.

- Below are typical requirements for a medium size theater. Unusual spaces should contact Company's Production Manager.
- Crew numbers listed below indicate a minimum; the actual numbers may vary based on a particular venue and its configuration.
- One-day load-in times are contingent on a lighting prehang and a first performance in the evening. If the light plot cannot be hung prior to arrival, load-in call will begin at 6:00am. If the engagement starts with a daytime performance, load-in one day in advance can be expected. Revised schedule will be provided.

DAY ONE (Load-In and Performance)

8:00am–12:00pm	Unload truck, construct SET, begin ELECTRICS setup	
	LOAD-IN CREW:	

- 10 Stagehands
- 4 Electricians
- 2 Sound Technicians
- 1 Light Board Op
- 4 Loaders (if required)

12:00pm–1:00pm	CREW LUNCH BREAK	
1:00pm–5:00pm	LIGHT focus, Rehearse SET changes with Crew	
	SHOW CREW:*	

- 4 Stagehands
- 1 Deck Sound
- 1 Deck Electrician
- 1 Light Board Op

4:00pm–5:00pm	Sound Check	2 Sound Technicians
5:00pm–6:00pm	CREW DINNER BREAK	
5:00pm–6:00pm	Performers warm up Act 2	1 Stagehand
6:00pm–6:30pm	CHANGEOVER	SHOW CREW*
6:30pm–7:15pm	Performers warm up Act 1	
7:15pm–7:30pm	Prep for Top of Show	SHOW CREW*
7:30pm	House Opens	
8:00pm–9:30pm	PERFORMANCE	SHOW CREW*
8:30pm–10:30pm	Wardrobe Laundry	1 Wardrobe

SUBSEQUENT PERFORMANCES:

5:00pm–6:00pm (or beginning three hours before first performance of the day)

	Performers warm up Act 2	1 Stagehand
6:00pm–6:30pm	CHANGEOVER	SHOW CREW*
6:30pm–7:15pm	Performers warm up Act 1	
7:15pm–7:30pm	Prep for Top of Show	SHOW CREW*
7:30pm	House Opens	
8:00pm–9:30pm	PERFORMANCE	SHOW CREW*
8:30pm–10:30pm	Wardrobe Laundry	1 Wardrobe

Load-out begins no later than a half-hour after LAST PERFORMANCE.

LOAD-OUT CREW:

- 10 Stagehands
- 4 Electricians
- 2 Sound Technicians
- 4 Loaders (if required)

*Running Crew must remain the same for every rehearsal and performance. Stage floor must be swept, mopped, and dried before each rehearsal with Performers and before 5:00pm (or three hours before the start of each performance) on the day of the performance.

CONTACT

[Production Manager/Technical Director name, telephones (office and cellular), e-mail]

[Producer's office name, address, telephone, with contact person and e-mail if available]

Sample International Technical Rider

Author's note: The following is a highly developed rider for a complex theatrical production that has toured extensively internationally. It contains more detailed data than many shows would require, and I don't encourage tech riders to be longer or more complex than is needed. Chamber music ensembles and comedians may have tech riders of only a page or two. I include this here, with the permission of its author, to serve as a checklist of sorts and to demonstrate an extreme end of the range of complexity in advance technical planning.

[Letter from Production Manager of show]

Dear Colleague,

[The show] is a touring production of [name of play]. The show lasts approximately 2 hours and 45 minutes including two (2) acts and one (1) intermission. There are up to twelve (12) members of the cast (including one musician, two child actors, and two understudies) and additional touring staff (including one parent/guardian for each child actor) of up to thirteen (13). Normally at least one child tours with the show and occasionally one is cast locally with the assistance of the Presenter. The number traveling may be also be reducible a) if, in the opinion of the show's Producer, the schedule of performances does not require the presence of understudies, or b) if, in multiple-week engagements where, also at the opinion of the show's Producer, it is possible for some of the touring production staff to be replaced by local staff trained for this purpose during the first week of the run.

The production can be mounted in a variety of theater spaces including traditional proscenium houses, large flexible "black box" or warehouse spaces, and other types of flexible spaces. Regardless of the space, the design of the set and the staging of the production call for the audience to be in front of the action, so a thrust stage is not desirable. It is vital to forward us a plan and section view of the venue as early as possible. This should be in MCD (Vectorworks) format if possible but can be in DXF (AutoCAD) if necessary.

It is normal practice for us to perform an advance site visit to the venue with the Director, Producer, and Production Manager and/or Technical Director. Such site visit is generally scheduled once the engagement has been confirmed. This visit is critical to the success of the show and answers many questions on both sides.

Load-in, setup, and rehearsal through to opening of the show takes three (3) days including lighting hang, so the first performance will be no earlier than the evening of the third day of preparation in the theater. In some cases it may be desirable to have a [show] representative present for the prehang, but it is not always necessary. A local crew of fourteen (14) technicians is required for the second day of preparation and will decrease by the third day (performance day). Performances will require a minimum local running crew of nine (9) persons. The production requires dressing rooms for three male actors, three female actors and one female musician, and one to two child actors as well as space for puppet repairs (and puppeteers), and technical supervisory personnel. In addition, a production office and a wardrobe room should be available.

The normal home of the physical production is [city in US]. It will usually need to ship from there, but in some cases will ship directly from another presenter's venue. The show is able to travel by sea in one 40 foot high cube sea container. In addition to this container there is often additional airfreight when the Production is coming directly from another venue and sea freight cannot arrive in the time available, as the larger set items have been duplicated for concurrent travel, but smaller items such as wardrobe and puppets have not. To ensure a successful presentation at your venue, any and all substitutions, amendments, revisions, compromises, and deviations from the requirements outlined in this Addendum must be discussed and approved by the Producer.

I look forward to our collaboration in bringing [play] into your community and will make every effort to help in your preparations. For more detailed specifics on each technical area—staging, rigging, lighting, audio, and stage management—please see below. Upon review, please do not hesitate to call, fax, or e-mail me with any questions you may have about the production. My contact information is listed at the end of this document.

[Name]

Production Manager

[Name of show]

Please note: this Version [#] Non-US dated [*date*] supersedes all previous versions of the Technical Addendum.

General Requirements

Production will need exclusive use of the stage for two (2) days prior to the first day of performance and throughout the day of the first performance. During this time, the lights and sound must be installed and tested, which typically takes the venue one day. This can happen immediately prior to our arrival or earlier, at the discretion of the venue—in most circumstances [*show's*] personnel are not required to be present for this work. For example, if our first performance is on a Wednesday at 8 PM (20:00), lighting work might begin on Monday at 8 AM (08:00), and show-specific work (scenery, props, costumes, etc.) with the touring crew would begin in the space no later than Tuesday at 8 AM (08:00). Before Production begins show-specific work:

1. The stage (if necessary) and pit area must be built and in the configuration agreed upon by [*show's*] Production Manager during the site survey and as drawn in the plans. Floor must be flat, smooth, and splinter free.

2. The basic grid must be in the configuration and placement agreed upon by [*show's*] Production Manager.

3. The lights are hung, cabled, and patched per plot, and cues are in board.

4. Sound system is installed and checked out.

5. All required equipment is in the theater when Production arrives.

6. The theater venue shall be swept, clean, and organized prior to Production's arrival at the space. Nothing will be stored on stage or in the wings.

Production requires a digital drawing of the venue, with plan and section views, in Vectorworks (.mcd—preferred) or AutoCAD (.dxf or .dwg). This drawing must be provided to [*show's*] Production Manager prior to signing of a letter of agreement. Digital photographs of the theater are also helpful.

Three cigars are used during the show. They are lit, briefly smoked, and extinguished by the actors using fire retardant gel in metal ashtrays.

If English is not spoken by the majority of the crew, Presenter must provide two translators who are familiar with technical theater language to be present at all times that the Production is in the venue, including load-in, rehearsal, performance, and load-out. One of these translators can be the Venue Technical Director.

Dressing Rooms and Production Office

Production requests four separate dressing areas for the following groups of performers:

- 3 Male adult actors: This room must have a shower.
- 1 Female Star dressing room: This room must have a shower.
- 2 Female adult actors, 1 puppeteer, and 1 female musician: This room must have a shower.
- 2 Child actors and their caretakers: A room far enough away from the adult actors so that the children will not disturb others is preferred.

Each room must be exclusively used by the Production during the stay; lockable; and outfitted with toilets, sinks, hot water, showers, clothes racks and hangers, mirrors, cots or couches, sufficient lighting, and a comfortable air temperature.

In addition to the dressing rooms listed above, there will be two (2) additional rooms required throughout the time the Production is in the venue:

- A Production Office for exclusive use of [*show's*] Production Manager and Stage Manager. This room should be lockable and have a desk and two (2) telephone lines with local and long distance dialing capability. High-speed Internet access is also critical.

- A Costume Work Area. Please provide a sewing machine, steamer, iron and ironing board, table, and electricity, for notes and costume repairs. In addition, Production requires secured storage for costumes between performances, preferably in this same Costume Work Area.

Site Visit

An advance site visit is a key element to the success of the production. Nevertheless, Producer reserves the right to make the final decision on whether there will be a site visit. There will normally be three (3) travelers—Director, Producer, and Production Manager (or Technical Director)—and the timing of the visit will be determined by Producer in consultation with Presenter. Certain aspects of the show, such as the rigging of the stage and audience curtains, can best be planned in detail at the time of that visit. At this time, minor adjustments in the technical needs, which will be made in consultation with Presenter, may occur.

Hospitality

Please provide thirty (30) liters of water per day (minimum) in a cooler or in individual refrigerated bottles. In addition, during load-in, please provide snacks, fruit, and sodas. On rehearsal days, please provide coffee, tea, fruit juice, fresh fruit, and other healthy snacks.

A meal must be provided backstage by Presenter for cast and crew between shows on any day that more than one performance is scheduled. The meal must have both meat and vegetarian options. No fast food please! Our office can provide a meal plan upon request. The serving time of this meal is to be decided during discussions prior to Production arrival. Catering should be available in a private area exclusive to the cast and crew with appropriate dinnerware, cutlery, and napkins.

Personnel and Staffing

In addition to performers, chaperones, and Company Manager, the Production normally carries a Director, Producer, Production Manager and Technical Director (who will both function as members of the run crew), Head Audio (who will mix the show), Lighting Supervisor, Wardrobe Supervisor, a Production Stage Manager, and two (2) assistant Stage Managers. Producer's staff will handle scenery, props, and puppets extensively during the load-in, rehearsals, and show, and also appear on stage during the show.

Presenter will provide a skilled Venue Technical Director who is authorized to make decisions on behalf of Presenter. This person will be present during the entire load-in and strike, and will be at all rehearsals and performances. This person can be one of the nine members of the running crew if desired by Presenter. The Venue Technical Director will have access and keys to all appropriate areas of the building, including loading dock, dressing rooms, and any storage areas used by the show.

The technicians called for load-in and strike must be able to help unload the truck. In venues with work rules that prevent this, the Presenter must provide an additional unloading/loading crew of six (6) persons. Also, during the load-in and strike, technicians should be able to move between departments (for instance, work as an electrician for part of the time and a carpenter part of the time). In venues with work rules that prevent this, the crew may grow (at the sole discretion of Producer's Production Manager, in consultation with Venue Technical Director). In addition, if there are any irregularities with truck access to the venue (e.g., elevators, no truck height dock, etc.), Production reserves the right to call additional personnel at Presenter's expense for load-in and -out. In the event that any of the above is necessary, it will be agreed upon well in advance, during the site survey.

All numbers listed below assume that the crew members are skilled, motivated, and take direction well. If the crew members do not meet these criteria, then the load-in can take longer and/or more personnel may be required (at Presenter's sole expense). In venues that allow it, the jobs that each stagehand performs can change through the day; that is, the same fourteen crew members can fill the three calls by shifting their focus as the day goes on.

Day 1

8 AM (08:00) to 7 PM (19:00) (or per Venue Technical Director)

Sufficient qualified technicians to completely install lighting, sound, and required prerigging. Crew numbers and hours should be set at the discretion of local Venue Technical Director, so long as the work is accomplished prior to 8 AM on Day 2. Producer's personnel may not need to be present for this work.

Day 2

8 AM (08:00) to 1 PM (13:00)

Fourteen (14) qualified technicians to unload the truck (if not completed on day one) and help in the initial assembly of the set, sound, lighting, rigging, and puppeteering. Primary duties will be:

- 2 Flymen/Riggers (will help at truck)
- 7 Carpenter/Stagehands (will help at truck)
- 2 Audio Technicians (will help at truck)
- 2 Puppet Crew/Props (will help at truck)
- 1 Wardrobe

2 PM (14:00) to 6 PM (18:00) (7 PM or 19:00 for Audio)

Fourteen (14) qualified technicians to complete the assembly of the set, sound, lighting, rigging, and puppet towers and to begin focus. Audio will split the dinner break (working from 6 to 7, breaking at 7), to allow quiet time in the theater. Primary duties will be:

- 2 Flymen/Riggers
- 2 Carpenter/Stagehands
- 5 Electricians (At least one must speak and understand English, and be proficient in the use of the house lighting control console.)
- 2 Audio Technicians
- 2 Puppet Crew/Props
- 1 Wardrobe

7 PM (19:00) to 11 PM (23:00)

Fourteen (14) qualified technicians to finish the load-in. In this block of time we will complete the focus. It is imperative to complete the lighting load-in by the end of this day. This includes having the show patched, colored, and channel checked. Primary duties will be:

- 1 Flyman/Rigger
- 2 Carpenter/Stagehands
- 6 Electricians (One must speak and understand English, and be proficient in the use of the house lighting control console.)
- 2 Audio Technicians (may reduce to 1)
- 2 Puppet Crew/Props (may be able to be released or reduce to 1)
- 1 Wardrobe (may be able to be released)

<u>Day 3</u>

8 AM (08:00) to Noon (12:00)

Ten (10) qualified technicians (the running crew + 1 audio person) for technical work during the morning. If not complete the previous night, focus will be completed this morning.

- 3 Electricians as specified below (One of these is the Master Electrician.)
  - 1 Lighting Board Operator (Must speak and understand English, and be proficient in the use of the house lighting control console.)
  - 1 Deck Electrician/Deck Sound (breaks at 11 AM to return for sound check)
  - 1 Follow Spot Operator (must understand English)
- 4 Stagehands (One of these can be the Venue Technical Director. All will be seen by the audience at top of show.)
- 1 Audio (breaks at 1 PM after sound check)

- 1 Wardrobe (breaks at 11:30 AM, returns at 12:30 PM to preset)
- 1 Puppet Crew/Props

Noon (12:00) to 1 PM (13:00)—Sound Check

- 1 Audio Technician

1 PM (13:00) to 5:30 PM (17:30)

Nine qualified technicians for rehearsal running crew

- 3 Electricians as specified below (One of these is the Master Electrician.)

  - 1 Lighting Board Operator (Must speak and understand English, and be proficient in the use of the house lighting control console.)
  - 1 Deck Electrician/Deck Sound
  - 1 Follow Spot Operator (must understand English)

- 4 Stagehands (One of these can be the Venue Technical Director. All will be seen by the audience at top of show.)
- 1 Props (will appear on stage)
- 1 Wardrobe (begins at 12:30 PM)

Crew Call for Performances

Nine qualified technicians for running crew. These must be the same as crew from rehearsal and remain the same for all performances. *NB: The show call is one hour prior to half hour, that is, 1 and ½ hours prior to the advertised curtain time.*

- 3 Electricians as specified below (One of these is the Master Electrician.)

  - 1 Lighting Board Operator (Must speak and understand English, and be proficient in the use of the house lighting control console.)
  - 1 Deck Electrician/Deck Sound
  - 1 Follow Spot Operator (must understand English)

- 4 Stagehands (One of these can be the Venue Technical Director. All will be seen by the audience at top of show.)
- 1 Props (will appear on stage)
- 1 Wardrobe

Please note that if the deck electrician cannot or will not function during the play as a deck sound man, then an additional technician may be required to perform the deck sound job, for a total of ten (10) technicians. Also, if [show's] Technical Director is not permitted (by venue regulations) to run a track, Presenter will need to provide an additional stagehand. Please note that the four (4) stagehands will be briefly visible to the audience at the top of the show as they execute their first cue. The props person will be on stage several times during the performance, dressed in show running blacks, not in costume or street clothes.

Strike: Four hours following final performance

Seventeen (17) qualified technicians to load-out the set, show sound, show lighting, rigging, and puppets. Primary duties will be as follows, but everyone is expected to cross department lines and load the truck as necessary. NB: Facility lighting and/or rigging restoration *cannot* begin until [*show's*] Production Manager agrees that load-out is complete!

- 4 Flymen/Riggers (will help at truck)
- 6 Carpenter/Stagehands (will help at truck)
- 2 Electricians (will help at truck)
- 1 Audio Technician (will help at truck)
- 3 Puppet Crew/Props (will help at truck)
- 1 Wardrobe (will be required to do laundry)

Please note that these crew numbers are subject to discussion and negotiation in advance. Based upon building access, ease of use of facility, etc., it may be possible to reduce these load-in numbers. For running crew, in some cases a technician can cover two tracks if he can cross department lines (e.g., if a deck hand can plug in lights during intermission). Conversely, if special challenges exist, additional crew may be needed. Please discuss with [*show's*] Production Manager. However, once the call is agreed upon by the Presenter and Producer, it is imperative that the contracted crew numbers be present for all agreed upon calls. If insufficient numbers are present it can severely delay or prevent the load-in and load-out. *NB: In the event that insufficient crew are present for the load-out, causing delays in the freight departure and lost revenue from subsequent performance contractual obligations, the Presenter will be liable for any losses incurred.*

Whenever possible, Production will reduce the crew earlier than 11 PM on Day 2 and reduce the call for the morning of Day 3. All decisions will be made in discussion with Venue Technical Director.

Lighting Requirements

Presenter will provide a skilled Master Electrician who is familiar with the venue and the facility lighting gear. The Master Electrician will be present during the entire load-in, and at all rehearsals and performances. This technician can be one of the nine-person running crew. All lights must be hung, patched, cabled, working, and checked out *before* the load-in. The following list is typical, but subject to change based upon venue configuration and venue inventory. Please use this list for budgeting purposes, but wait for the light plot to order equipment.

The Presenter will supply:

1. Instruments

For lighting, the show will require a minimum of:

- 117 Source 4 lekos (profiles), of varying lens type depending on Front of House throw (details in plot)
- 36 1kw fresnels

- 5 15 cm fresnels of any wattage (typically 750W)
- 10 Other units of any type (for use as backstage running light)
- 1 Followspot

Venue also provides:

- 1 Fog machine (High End Systems F-100 or similar—triggered locally)
- 3 Atomic 3000 strobe lights (also acceptable: Dataflash strobes, High End AF-1000)

Please discuss any substitutions to these instrument types. All units will be in good working condition, and be supplied with safety chain and color frame. Presenter will have spare lamps of every type on hand for all rehearsals and performances.

2. Control/Power Distribution/Dimming

- 160 DMX Addressable Dimmers
- Lighting console—ETC Expression 3
- DMX cable and feeder cable as necessary
- All other cable, hardware, and supplies deemed necessary by Venue Master Electrician in discussion with [show's] Production Manager and lighting supervisor

3. Perishables

- All color and templates per provided plot and Lightwright file
- Three rolls each black and white gaffer tape (sufficient for run)
- 250 meter spool of black 3mm black line (may also be used for rigging)
- All other material and supplies deemed necessary by Venue Master Electrician in discussion with [show's] Production Manager

Required during load-in period

From show arrival at theater until opening, the following will be required:

1. A remote monitor for the lighting console at the tech table, so the lighting supervisor can see the cues from the light board.
2. Headset communication between the light board operator, the followspot operator, the stage manager, and the lighting supervisor. This must be on a separate channel from the main stage manager channel.
3. A board operator who speaks and understands English, and who is proficient in the use of the house lighting control console.

Lighting Plot and additional paperwork will be provided once Producer receives a Ground Plan, Section Drawing, and Equipment Inventory for each individual venue and after completion of site survey by [show's] Production Manager. Production will always make its best efforts to use house inventory for all lighting needs.

The Production will travel with a show disk for the facility-provided ETC Expression 3 lighting console, and every effort must be made by Presenter to provide this model even if rental is involved. In the event that Presenter cannot provide an ETC Expression 3 lighting console, the substitute lighting control console must have a minimum of 200 control channels. *Prior* to the beginning of load-in, Presenter *must* enter all show cues into the house lighting control console. This work is considerably shortened if the Production's traveling disk can be used. If manual programming is required, the cue list will be provided to Presenter by Producer with the plot. *If the cues have not been entered into the console before Production arrival, it may cause a delay in the first performance.*

Wardrobe Requirements

Venue must provide a skilled wardrobe assistant who will work with [*show's*] Wardrobe Supervisor. On Day 2 of load-in (the day before the first performance), all clothes will be unpacked, steamed, and ironed as necessary, and hung in the appropriate dressing rooms.

Each venue will be responsible for laundry as well as dry cleaning of the costumes. In some cases, Presenter will need to dry clean the costumes at the start of the run—in some cases at the end. In venues with long runs (more than one week), there may be additional dry cleaning during the run. The cost of this dry cleaning is the responsibility of Presenter.

Laundry needs to be done daily. With smaller machines, this may require as many as four loads each day.

In addition to laundry, minor maintenance and repairs will be required.

Stage, Access, and Rigging Requirements

The size of the access to the stage is very important. Due to the size and weight of the scenery, it can be very time consuming or even impossible to load into some venues that have difficult access. The largest individual pieces are:

- Six 3.8 cm diameter curved pipes each 6.1 meters in length
- Three [*special units*] on wheels that are each 1.4 meters wide, 1.1 meters tall, and 4.5 meters long and quite heavy (approximately 300 kilos each)
- One scenic [*special unit*] that is 0.5 meters wide, 2.4 meters tall, and 5.2 meters long

The loading dock *must* be even with the floor of the truck or sea container, or additional equipment and/or personnel may be required.

The ideal clear height for the stage area is 6.4 meters. The absolute minimum clear height is 5.9 meters. A fly house with at least 12 meters clear is preferable, but the rigging can be accomplished without flies if necessary. The stage area and, when possible, the audience will be surrounded on all sides by red velour curtains (except the back of the audience), which are lowered and raised during the performance. The curtains around the stage area will be rigged to a curved pipe for this purpose. There must be numerous points above the stage and in the house to be able to rig these drapes. The rigging needs for the show will always have to be determined on a venue-by-venue basis and alternate plans may be necessary in some instances.

The ideal stage dimensions are 14.7 meters wide and 12.2 meters deep. A minimum width of 12.2 meters and a total depth (including apron) of 10.6 meters are required. *The stage must be flat and NOT RAKED!* For sightlines, a steep audience rake is preferable, but a traditional shallow orchestra seating arrangement may be acceptable. The floor of the first row of seating should be approximately 1 meter below the level of the stage. In almost every theater, the show scenery will hang over the edge of the stage into the audience and will prevent the fire (or iron) curtain from being lowered completely to the stage floor. In many spaces, a raised stage will have to be constructed (the Production travels with this stage when it is necessary). The actual playing area is rectangular and normally squared at the downstage edge and 12.2 meters wide. The upstage portion of the playing area is a semicircle with a radius of 6.1 meters. Please see the plans for more details. *NB: The distance from the facility apron edge to the first available line set must not exceed 1.2 meters.*

All additional pipes, electrics, and line sets should be installed, hung, or prepared as indicated in the final drawings prior to the beginning of the load-in.

Upon arrival the following shall be in place and available to the Production:

- The stage floor of the venue will be smooth and even. One centimeter thick, medium density fiberboard, attached with a minimum of six screws per sheet, will cover the facility floor. (*Note that we will screw into the stage floor.*) This MDF will travel with the show. If the floor of the venue is level with the first row of seating, then Production will provide a platform deck and supports to create a raised stage approximately 0.7 meters high. *Regardless of the flooring choice, it is very likely that the floor and certain props will block the ability of the fire (iron) curtain to fly to the stage floor unobstructed.* Also, depending upon the stage configuration, Presenter may be required to provide platforms to extend the stage into the audience. In some circumstances, a lighting position added above the stage apron may also be required.

- Various "backstage" elements for the top of show "look," including ladders, ropes, and, whenever possible, scenery from other productions. This will be worked out with [*show's*] Production Manager and Director during the site survey and/or during the load-in.

- An extra stock of (scaffold clamps) shackles, span sets, aircraft cable, and Crosby clips to be used for rigging purposes shall be provided by the venue.

- At least two (possibly three) 2.5–3.5 meter tall black velour or serge borders at least 12 meters wide, sewn flat with no fullness, hung per the light plot.

- Ladders: two 4–5 meter tall ladders, two 3.5 meter tall ladders, two 2 meter tall ladders, and two personnel lifts at least 7 meters high.

- A rolling scaffold 3.5 to 5 meters tall with locking wheels will be provided for the exclusive use of the Production. The footprint of this scaffolding should not exceed 1.5 × 2.1 meters. This scaffolding is only needed for the load-in and load-out.

- Air compressor for filling supplied air tank to 4 bar (80 PSI) (for silk drop mechanism).
- Tables: Four for props and equipment at approximately 1 × 2 meters.
- Two production "tech" tables with work lights for rehearsals. These tables should be in the house and will need electricity and one of the phone lines from the production office. These tables should be in place at the beginning of the load-in. Position should be discussed during the site visit.
- One "artist bench-style" piano bench—Producer can provide photo—that is black, padded, and with adjustable height.

Audio and Video Requirements

Presenter shall provide:

Power

Complete AC Power Distribution for the Performance Audio System. The AC main power supply must be on its own phase and leg of a supply transformer that is completely isolated from all lighting, HVAC, and motor systems. There must not be any taps or other equipment between the transformer and the performance audio system. *This provision is absolutely essential to avoid unwanted "noise" in the sound system.* In general it should be noted that the system needs to reinforce voices and a piano, two of the most complex and recognizable sounds. The system needs to have a very low noise floor and be capable of great delicacy as well as good power.

Control

- 1 Yamaha DM-1000 digital mixing console with Version 2 software and Meter Bridge

Mix Position

It is critical that the (small) DM-1000 mixing console be placed in the house and in a good listening position. a mixing position in a tech booth or other isolated position is not acceptable.

Control/Playback

- 2 commercial CD Players. The units must have Auto-Cue (meaning you press play and the track runs to completion, stops, and then cues up the next track) and XLR outputs. Models such as Denon, Technics, and Gemini are acceptable.

Speakers

1. A true Left-Center-Right (LCR) speaker system with two subwoofers is required. These speakers can be hung on the proscenium. The LCR speaker clusters need to cover the whole house, so upper and lower speakers may be necessary in each cluster. The speaker models can be Meyer UPA-1P self-powered, or Apogee AE-5, or comparable speakers from d&b, Heil, or Renkus-Heinz. If the house is very tall, the left and right lower speakers may

be positioned separately from the upper left and right speakers. If there are upper and lower speakers in each LCR speaker cluster, these will be driven by separate sends from the mixer (i.e., the number of sends from the mixer will be six for an upper and lower LCR system). If the speaker system is not self-powered, all necessary amplifiers, processors and interconnects will need to be provided. *It is important that all of the main speakers are of the same make and model. If the speakers are not self-powered, the amplifiers and processors should be the same make and model also.* If the house is too large to be covered only by speakers on the proscenium, a delay line will be necessary. Ideally, these should be the same model or at least the same brand speakers as the proscenium system. The delay line will be driven by one send from the mixer. An LCR-line array system such as models by Nexo, Meyer, or JBL are also very acceptable. The line array would need enough cabinets to cover the house from the first row through the last row of seating in the house. All speaker rigging needs to be provided.

2. Two subwoofers are required. These can be such models as Meyer 650 self-powered. Four smaller model subwoofers may be substituted. The subwoofers need to reproduce a thunderstorm sound effect convincingly. The subwoofers are driven by one mono feed.

3. Four front fill speakers are required. These can be Meyer UPM self-powered speakers, EAW JF80, or EAW JF60. The front fills are driven by one mono feed. They will be placed along the downstage edge of the stage.

4. Two small specialty monitor speakers are required. Examples such as Fostex model 6301BEAV, JBL Control 25 or Control One, Anchor, Mackie, Tannoy, Yamaha, and Meyer are possible. One will be used for the piano player's monitor. The other will be used as an opera monitor hung on an opera box set piece and will need to be connected and disconnected at the intermission and at the end of the show. These two speakers will be driven by two sends from the mixer. These speakers can also be the same model speakers as the front fills.

5. Two backstage monitor speakers are required. These can be driven by the theater's dressing room monitor feeds or by a send from the mixer. These can be conventional wedge monitors or stereo speakers. The speaker type and model is flexible as fidelity is not critical—these are monitors for the puppeteers and they mostly need to hear the timing.

6. If the venue has balconies, it may be necessary to have under-balcony delay speakers. These speakers will all be driven by one send from the mixer. These can be the same model speakers as the front fills.

7. No additional EQ, delay, or processing is required. All signal processing will be made from the digital mixer.

8. It is important that the interconnect cables, speaker cables, and snakes be in excellent condition. *The sound design needs consistent polarity* from all of the speakers. Whenever possible, it is ideal to make a phase-test of all the speakers before or during the load-in and setup.

Microphones

1. Ten (10) channels of RF, *Sennheiser only*. Eight (8) body pack transmitters and ten receivers are required. The body pack transmitter models may be SK50, SK250, SK1093 with Lemo 3-pin connectors, *or* Evolution series EW, 100, 300, or 500 with 3.5mm locking plugs. The RF system may be placed at the mixer position or on the stage.

2. Two (2) Sennheiser MKE-2 lavalier microphones to be used with one of venue's RF transmitters. Flesh colored is preferred. (One is used, one is backup.)

3. Two (2) RF handheld wireless to be used with Presenter's Sennheiser receivers.

4. One (1) Shure SM58 on a short (10–20 cm) stand to be used as a piano lid microphone.

Backline

1. One (1) Kurzweil PC2X electric piano with sustain pedal. If the newer model PC2X is not available, the older PC88 is acceptable. *This keyboard MUST be in excellent condition.* In some cases, the Production Manager may be able to help arrange rental.

2. Two (2) DI boxes. Active models by Countryman and BSS are acceptable. Two (2) jack cables to connect the piano with the direct boxes will need to be provided.

Miscellaneous

1. One 9-channel snake (multicore) is required from FOH to Stage area. A 12-channel snake will be necessary if the proscenium speaker system has upper and lower sends. Also, additional lines will be necessary for delay, balcony, and/or under-balcony speakers.

2. Sixteen (16) 3-meter XLR interconnects. These will be used to connect the RF receivers to the mixer and to construct an emergency wireless microphone transmitter replacement system in case there is a RF microphone malfunction during a performance.

3. A 2-channel backstage and dressing room monitoring system with enough speaker boxes so actors can hear announcements and audio in all the dressing rooms (a drawing of com locations will be provided).

4. A 10-station intercom system consisting of a *minimum* of four wireless belt packs and headsets, and six (6) wired belt packs and headsets (or fewer wired if more wireless are available). Clear-Com, Telex, or comparable. *NB: Walkie talkie com systems are not acceptable.*

5. All required batteries for rehearsals and performances (eighteen AA batteries per performance if the presenter's Sennheiser system uses 2AA per transmitter).

6. Six (6) unlubricated condoms per show for wireless microphone body pack protection.

7. Two (2) small work lights for lighting at the mixer position.

<u>Video</u>

Three video monitors—one stage left, one stage right, and one at the Stage Manager calling position—fed from a FOH, color program camera. This is a general open shot of the stage and is used to help the stagehands operate the curtains in sync.

<u>Supplied by Producer</u>

[*Show*] will travel with the following equipment:

- Four (4) Countryman E6 ear-worn microphones and interconnect cables to be used with Presenter's RF body pack transmitters.
- Four (4) DPA 4066 headset microphones and interconnect adaptors to be used with Presenter's Sennheiser RF body pack transmitters.
- One (1) LXP-15 digital FX unit.
- Wireless microphone body belt packs to secure the transmitters on the actors.

Changes and Substitutions

PLEASE NOTE! Any and all changes and/or substitutions to labor, materials, and equipment from those specified in this agreement *must* be approved in writing by [*show's*] Production Manager. Changes that are not approved in advance will not be allowed by the Production.

Contact info:

[*Production Manager/Technical Director name, telephones (office and cellular), e-mail*]

[*Producer's office name, address, telephone, with contact person and e-mail if available*]

Bibliography

Studies and Papers

Armbrust, Roger. "Equity Okays Production Pact Tiered Touring, Increase in Wages, Health." *Backstage*, September 10, 2004.

"Critical Issues Facing the Arts in California." Working paper, The James Irvine Foundation, September 2006.

Jones, Jeffrey. "How Visual Arts Audiences got Comfortable with Radical Innovation, while Theatre Audiences Didn't." *American Theatre*, October 2005.

Kreidler, John. "Leverage Lost: The Nonprofit Arts in the Post-Ford Era." *In Motion Magazine*, February 16, 1996. http://www.inmotionmagazine.com/lost.html.

The League of American Theatres and Producers, Inc. Research Department Highlights, 2007.

"Live Nation Reports Fourth Quarter and Full Year 2006 Financial Results." Press release, Los Angeles, March 1, 2007.

Manzella, Abby. "The Syndicate and the Shuberts." American Studies Department, University of Virginia, December 2000. http://xroads.virginia.edu/~hyper/INCORP/theatre/overview.html.

Micocci, Tony. "State Withholding Taxes on Artists: Who's Really Paying?" Western Arts Alliance newsletter, *Western Ways*, Spring 2005.

Nichols, Bonnie. "Consumer Spending on Performing Arts: Outlays Flat for 2005; Non-Spectator Categories Show Growth." The National Endowment for the Arts, Office of Research & Analysis, Note #91, August 2006.

Ostrower, Francie. "The Diversity of Cultural Participation: Findings from a National Survey Report." The Urban Institute, 2005.

Turney, Wayne S. "The Theatrical Syndicate." http://www.wayneturney.20m.com/syndicate.htm.

Wasser, Daniel M. "Theatrical Producers Ask: Limited Liability Company or Limited Partnership?" Franklin, Weinrib, Rudell & Vassallo newsletter, *The Report*, Winter 2005–2006.

Wolf, Dr. Thomas. "The Search for Shining Eyes: Audiences, Leadership and Change in the Symphony Orchestra Field," John S. and James L. Knight Foundation, Magic of Music Initiative Executive Summary, 2006. http://www.knightfdn.org/music/part0.asp.

Books

Bazerman, Max H., and Margaret A. Neale. *Negotiating Rationally*. New York: The Free Press, 1992.

Chait, Richard P., William P. Ryan, and Barbara E. Taylor. *Governance as Leadership*. Hoboken, New Jersey: John Wiley & Sons, 2005.

Fisher, Roger, and William Ury. *Getting to Yes: Negotiating Agreement Without Giving In*. New York: Penguin Books, 1981.

Florida, Richard. *The Rise of the Creative Class*. New York: Basic Books, 2002.

Gladwell, Malcolm. *The Tipping Point: How Little Things Can Make a Big Difference*. New York: Little, Brown and Company, 2000.

Hapgood, Norman. *The Stage in America 1897–1900*. New York: The Macmillan Company, 1901.

Harvard Business School Press. *Winning Negotiations that Preserve Relationships*. Boston: Harvard Business School Press, 2004.

Hurok, Sol. *Impresario*. In collaboration with Ruth Goode. New York: Random House, 1946.

Levinson, Jan Conrad. *Guerrilla Marketing*. 3rd ed. New York: Houghton Mifflin Company, 1998.

McCarthy, Kevin, Arthur Brooks, Julia Lowell, and Laura Zakaras. *The Performing Arts in a New Era*. Rand Corporation, 2001.

Shagan, Rena. *Booking & Tour Management for the Performing Arts*. Rev. ed. New York: Allworth Press, 2001.

Sheean, Vincent. *Oscar Hammerstein I: The Life and Exploits of an Impresario*. New York: Simon & Schuster, 1956.

Trav S. D. [D. Travis Stewart]. *No Applause Please—Just Throw Money: The Book that Made Vaudeville Famous*. Faber and Faber, 2005.

Index

Books from Allworth Press

Allworth Press is an imprint of Allworth Communications, Inc. Selected titles are listed below.

Running Theaters: Best Practices for Leaders and Managers
by Duncan M. Webb (paperback, 6 x 9, 256 pages, $19.95)

The Stage Producer's Business and Legal Guide
by Charles Grippo (paperback, 6 x 9, 256 pages, $19.95)

Business and Legal Forms for Theater
by Charles Grippo (paperback, with CD-ROM, 8 1/2 x 11, 192 pages, $29.95)

Booking and Tour Management for the Performing Arts, Third Edition
by Rena Shagan (paperback, 6 x 9, 288 pages, $19.95)

Theater Festivals: Best Worldwide Venues for New Works
by Lisa Mulcahy (paperback, 6 x 9, 256 pages, $19.95)

Managing Artists in Pop Music: What Every Artist and Mangager Must Know to Succeed
by Mitch Weiss and Perri Gaffney (paperback, 6 x 9, 240 pages, $19.95)

Building the Successful Theater Company
by Lisa Mulcahy (paperback, 6 x 9, 240 pages, $19.95)

Careers in Technical Theater
by Mike Lawler (paperback, 6 x 9, 288 pages, $19.95)

Technical Theater for Nontechnical People, Second Edition
by Drew Campbell (paperback, 6 x 9, 288 pages, $19.95)

The Perfect Stage Crew: The Complete Technical Guide for High School, College, and Community Theater
by John Kaluta (paperback, 6 x 9, 256 pages, $19.95)

The Business of Theatrical Design
by James L. Moody (paperback, 6 x 9, 288 pages, $19.95)

Career Solutions for Creative People: How to Balance Artistic Goals with Career Security
by Dr. Ronda Ormont (paperback, 6 x 9, 320 pages, $19.95)

To request a free catalog or order books by credit card, call 1-800-491-2808. To see our complete catalog on the World Wide Web, or to order online for a 20 percent discount, you can find us at **www.allworth.com**.